Language, Expressivity and Cognition

Also Available from Bloomsbury

Style and Emotion in Comic Novels and Short Stories, Agnes Marszalek
Cognitive Semiotics, Per Aage Brandt

Language, Expressivity and Cognition

Edited by
Mikołaj Deckert, Piotr Pęzik, and Raffaele Zago

BLOOMSBURY ACADEMIC
LONDON • NEW YORK • OXFORD • NEW DELHI • SYDNEY

BLOOMSBURY ACADEMIC
Bloomsbury Publishing Plc
50 Bedford Square, London, WC1B 3DP, UK
1385 Broadway, New York, NY 10018, USA
29 Earlsfort Terrace, Dublin 2, Ireland

BLOOMSBURY, BLOOMSBURY ACADEMIC and the Diana logo are trademarks of
Bloomsbury Publishing Plc

First published in Great Britain 2023
Paperback edition published 2024

Copyright © Mikołaj Deckert, Piotr Pęzik, and Raffaele Zago, 2023, 2024

Mikołaj Deckert, Piotr Pęzik, and Raffaele Zago have asserted their right under the
Copyright, Designs and Patents Act, 1988, to be identified as Editors of this work.

For legal purposes the Acknowledgements on p. xiv constitute an extension
of this copyright page.

Cover design: Jess Stevens

All rights reserved. No part of this publication may be reproduced or transmitted
in any form or by any means, electronic or mechanical, including photocopying,
recording, or any information storage or retrieval system, without prior
permission in writing from the publishers.

Bloomsbury Publishing Plc does not have any control over, or responsibility for, any
third-party websites referred to or in this book. All internet addresses given in this
book were correct at the time of going to press. The author and publisher regret any
inconvenience caused if addresses have changed or sites have ceased to exist,
but can accept no responsibility for any such changes.

A catalogue record for this book is available from the British Library.

A catalog record for this book is available from the Library of Congress.

ISBN: HB: 978-1-3503-3286-7
PB: 978-1-3503-3290-4
ePDF: 978-1-3503-3287-4
eBook: 978-1-3503-3288-1

Typeset by Deanta Global Publishing Services, Chennai, India

To find out more about our authors and books visit www.bloomsbury.com and
sign up for our newsletters.

Contents

List of Figures — vii
List of Tables — viii
List of Contributors — x
Acknowledgements — xiv

1 Constructing Emotion in Contemporary Discourses: A Taste for Expressivity *Mikołaj Deckert, Piotr Pęzik and Raffaele Zago* — 1

Part I Metaphoric Conceptualizations of Emotions

2 Emotion and Reasoning in Hungarian HEART Metaphors *Judit Baranyiné Kóczy* — 17
3 A Comparative Study of English, Italian and Polish Conceptual Metaphors of Emotion Regulation and Cognitive Inhibition *Marcin Trojszczak and Chiara Astrid Gebbia* — 37
4 Linguistic Means to Discursively Construct Dehumanization *Serena Coschignano and Chiara Zanchi* — 55

Part II Constructing Emotion in Internet Discourses

5 A Comparative Study of Donald J. Trump and Matteo Salvini's Populist Strategies in the Representation of Immigrants and Refugees on Twitter *Ester Di Silvestro* — 85
6 Collective Identities and Emotions in Online Contexts *Barbara Lewandowska-Tomaszczyk and Paul A. Wilson* — 111
7 A Phraseological Perspective on Evaluation: The Covid-19 Vaccination in Polish Web-Based News *Mikołaj Deckert, Krzysztof Hejduk and Piotr Pęzik* — 137

Part III Emotion in Multimodal Discourses

8 Arabic–English Code-Switching in Egyptian Rap Music and Social Networks *Lucia La Causa* — 163
9 Innovation and Emotion in Teen Talk in TV Series *Silvia Bruti* — 187

10 An Appraisal Approach to Emotion, Culture and Discourse in
    Audio Description: Exploring Audio Description Quality in
    Turkey *Hilal Erkazanci Durmuş and Şirin Okyayuz*   209

Conclusion *Raffaele Zago*   233

Index   235

Figures

3.1	Metaphors of inhibiting unwanted emotions and thoughts in English, Italian and Polish	46
4.1	Automatic scenario detection performed with Iramuteq	64
4.2	Arrivals of migrants vs. broadcast news coverage of migrations	67
4.3	Active and passive scenarios with orientation	70
4.4	Active and passive scenarios with proportion of reference type	71
8.1	Lyrics taken from the first verse and from the chorus of the song 'Prisoner' by Arabian Knightz	168
8.2	Lyrics taken from verse 2 of the song 'Gold' by Mr Kordy	174
8.3	Transcription of the first 1:53 of a 10-minute video containing an interview with Mr Kordy	176
9.1	Key word cloud in *Skins* (vs. the Teen Corpus)	193
9.2	Key domain cloud in *Skins* (vs. the Teen Corpus)	193
9.3	Key word cloud in *Dawson's Creek* (vs. the Teen Corpus)	194
9.4	Key domain cloud in *Dawson's Creek* (vs. the Teen Corpus)	195
9.5	Some markers of teen talk in the Teen Corpus – part II	195
9.6	Some markers of teen talk in the Teen Corpus and the Teen Corpus – part II	197

Tables

2.1	Distribution of conceptualizations of the HEART based on a small-scale sample	23
4.1	Manually identified discourse scenarios	62
4.2	Automatically and manually detected scenarios	64
4.3	Number of headlines containing *rifugiato, profugo, richiedente asilo, migrante* and *immigrato*	66
4.4	Orientation by lexeme and type of reference	68
4.5	Source domain types	74
5.1	Source domain percentages	89
5.2	*Topoi* percentages	90
5.3	Representational strategies percentages	92
5.4	Occurrences and co-occurrences of *load* in Salvini's corpora	97
5.5	Occurrences and co-occurrences of *terrorism*	98
5.6	Occurrences and co-occurrences of *terrorist*	98
5.7	Occurrences and co-occurrences of *criminal*	99
5.8	Occurrences and co-occurrences of [number]	101
5.9	Occurrences and co-occurrences of *pay*	102
5.10	Occurrences and co-occurrences of *victim*	103
5.11	Occurrences and co-occurrences of *Islamic*	103
5.12	Occurrences and co-occurrences of *Immigrant*	104
7.1	Selected polls on the reception of possible Covid-19 vaccination mandate	139
7.2	Highest-ranked right-wing adjectival collocates of *szczepienie**|szczepionka*** query	145
7.3	Selection of concordances (right-wing) for the *Przymusowy*** (adjective) query	146
7.4	A selected case of concordance (right-wing) for the *Przymusowy*** adjective query	147
7.5	Highest-ranked noun collocates (right-wing) of *Szczepienie**|Szczepionka*** query	148

7.6	Selection of concordances (right-wing) for the *Przymus*** (noun) query	149
7.7	General collocates of *Przymusowy* and *Obowiązkowy* before 31 December 2019	152
9.1	Total and normalized frequencies of some markers of teen talk in the Teen Corpus and the Teen Corpus – Part II	196

Contributors

Silvia Bruti is Full Professor of English Language and Linguistics at the Department of Philology, Literature, Linguistics of the University of Pisa, Italy. Her research interests include sociolinguistics, pragmatics and applied linguistics, with a special focus on corpus linguistics, translation (especially audiovisual) and the teaching of English. She has published widely in these areas. In particular, her book-length studies are on the translation of politeness (2013) and on interlingual subtitling (a co-authored volume, 2017).

Serena Coschignano is a PhD student in Linguistic Sciences at the University of Bergamo/University of Pavia, Italy. Her research interests focus on frame semantics, cognitive metaphor theory and critical discourse analysis. She has published on metaphorical extensions of Italian temperature terms and on the discursive construction of antagonisms in political tweets.

Mikołaj Deckert is Associate Professor in the Institute of English Studies at the University of Łódź, Poland. His research is primarily in interlingual translation, with emphasis on audiovisual translation and media accessibility, but also more broadly deals with language from a cognitive perspective. He serves as peer-review editor for the *Journal of Specialised Translation* (JoSTrans) and has recently co-edited *The Palgrave Handbook of Audiovisual Translation and Media Accessibility* (2020, with Łukasz Bogucki).

Ester Di Silvestro holds a PhD in Interpretation Sciences from the University of Catania, Italy. Her PhD dissertation focused on a comparative analysis of far-right populist discourse in Italy and in the United States. Specifically, she analysed and compared the populist discourses of Matteo Salvini and Donald J. Trump. Her research is mainly located in critical discourse analysis and in corpus linguistics. In addition to political discourse, she is also interested in the textual and visual analysis of gender representations.

Hilal Erkazanci Durmuş is Lecturer at Hacettepe University, Turkey, in the Department of Translation and Interpreting. Her research interests include sociology of translation, translational stylistics and discourse analysis. Her recent works focus on image construction through translation.

Chiara Astrid Gebbia received a PhD in Linguistics from the Universities of Palermo and Catania, Italy, and is postdoctoral researcher at the University of Agder, Norway. She conducts research on the application of conceptual metaphors to the teaching/learning of English as a Second Language. Besides applied cognitive semantics, her research interests include cognitive investigations of psychology and translation studies.

Krzysztof Hejduk has graduated from the University of Łódź, Poland, with a distinguished BA thesis in linguistics. His research interests focus on audiovisual translation and media accessibility. He is a member of the Polish Cognitive Linguistics Association (PCLA) and has worked for the Common Language Resources and Technology Infrastructure projects (CLARIN). Recently, he has delivered two international conference papers on video game localization ('Cognitive Linguistics in the Year 2021', Łódź; '12th Professional Communication and Translation Studies', Timisoara).

Judit Baranyiné Kóczy is Associate Professor of Linguistics at the Széchenyi István University, Hungary. Her research focuses on language, conceptualization and culture within the framework of cognitive semantics, conceptual metaphor theory and cultural linguistics. She studies embodiment via body parts, embodied cultural metaphors, folk cultural metaphors and corpus linguistics. She is the author of *Nature, Metaphor, Culture: Cultural Conceptualizations in Hungarian Folksongs* (2018).

Lucia La Causa holds a PhD in Interpretation Sciences from the University of Catania, Italy. Her research interests focus on English variationist sociolinguistics. In her PhD dissertation, she investigated the variety of English spoken in Egypt. Her most recent article is 'Egyptian English' as an Emerging Glocal Language (*Currents*, 2022).

Barbara Lewandowska-Tomaszczyk is Full Professor Dr Habil. in Linguistics in the Department of Language and Communication at the University of Applied Sciences in Konin, Poland. Her research focuses on cognitive semantics and pragmatics of language contrasts, corpus linguistics and their applications in translation, media studies and applied linguistics.

Şirin Okyayuz is Associate Professor at Hacettepe University, Turkey, in the Department of Translation and Interpreting. Her research interests focus on literary and audiovisual translation and media accessibility practices. She has published on didactics of audiovisual translation, SDH and interlingual subtitling and remakes. Her most recent book is *Engelsiz Erişim ve Çeviri* (Media Accessibility and Translation, 2018).

Piotr Pęzik is Associate Professor at the Institute of English, University of Łódź, Poland. He is an active member of Corpus and Computational Linguistics research groups in Poland and abroad and a member of national and international language technology research projects and initiatives (e.g. NKJP, CESAR, PLEC, BootStrep). He is also a scientific consultant in the area of language technology solutions for IT and biotechnology industrial partners. His research interests are centred around phraseology, corpus linguistics and natural language processing. He has authored publications and developed spoken and written corpora with dedicated search engines and other language processing tools and resources.

Marcin Trojszczak is Assistant Professor at the State University of Applied Sciences in Konin and Research Assistant at the University of Białystok, Poland. His research interests focus on cognitive linguistics and figurative language as well as translation studies and translation technology. He has published on metaphorical conceptualizations of mental processes and the role of translation technology in translator training. His most recent publications include the chapters 'Translator Training Meets Machine Translation – Selected Challenges' (2022), 'Metaphors for Regulating Emotions – A Cognitive Corpus-Based Study of English, Italian, and Polish' (2020), and the article 'The Socio-Economics of Translation Industry as Part of Translator Training' (2021).

Paul A. Wilson is Associate Professor in the Department of Corpus and Computational Linguistics at the University of Łódź, Poland. He completed his PhD on the interplay between cognition and emotion at Birkbeck, University of London, UK, and continues to be active in this field. His other research interests include the conceptualization and lexicalization of emotions across languages and cultures as well as the role of emotions in second language learning, social robotics and cross-cultural issues in conflict.

Raffaele Zago is Researcher in English Language and Linguistics at the University of Catania, Italy. He has conducted research in the fields of English applied linguistics, corpus linguistics and discourse/register analysis, with a special focus on the quantitative and qualitative analysis of several spoken English features (e.g. vocatives, colloquiality, declarative questions, expressivity) and with particular attention to English telecinematic dialogue. In these areas, he has published two monographs and several articles.

Chiara Zanchi is Assistant Professor in Linguistics at the Department of Humanities of the University of Pavia, Italy. Her research interests focus on ancient Indo-European languages and on the pragmatics of ancient and modern languages. She has published on the representation of migrants and gender-based violence in the Italian press from a critical cognitive linguistic perspective.

Acknowledgements

We wish to thank Barbara Lewandowska-Tomaszczyk (State University of Applied Sciences in Konin) for coming up with the idea of cyclical workshops that bring together researchers interested in the interface of language and emotion – the 'Language, Heart and Mind' series of workshops. Similarly, we wish to acknowledge the advice and support on many levels from Marco Venuti (University of Catania) and Francesca Vigo (University of Catania), who have been shaping the 'Language, Heart and Mind' project from its very beginning. With high-quality papers, methodologically and disciplinarily varied line-ups as well as remarkable thematic consistency, those meetings have been a great source of insight. Notably, some of the work discussed at the workshop held at the University of Catania in December 2020 is included in the current volume, alongside invited contributions that we were fortunate enough to be able to integrate into this book.

Thanks are also due to the anonymous reviewers for their extremely helpful observations on the book and to Krzysztof Hejduk (University of Łódź) for his invaluable assistance throughout the editorial process.

Mikołaj, Piotr, Raffaele,
Łódź and Comiso, June 2022

1

Constructing Emotion in Contemporary Discourses

A Taste for Expressivity

Mikołaj Deckert, Piotr Pęzik and Raffaele Zago

Expressivity in Contemporary Discourses[1]

When one looks at many of the contemporary discourses that surround and address us every day, the dominant impression is that, albeit in different forms and to varying extents in different cultures and situational contexts, they mainly tend towards *expressing* rather than *stating*. More than being factual, informational, propositional and expository, they are emotional, affective, highly personal, in a word, *expressive*. More than talking to people's heads, they 'speak from the heart' or, to quote a popular Italian idiom, they often 'talk to the country's belly' (meaning that they appeal to basic instincts, as happens in populist political discourse). It does not seem an exaggeration to claim that the expressive/emotive function of language (Bühler 1934; Jakobson 1960) – not the referential one – is, at present, particularly prominent in contemporary – especially Western – cultures.

The traditional territory of expressivity has always been spoken language and, more specifically, informal conversation – the presentation of expressive content is, in effect, one of the diagnostic traits of informality (cf. Biber et al. 2021: 1041–2). Other long-established loci of expressivity have been advertising discourse (e.g. cf. Bhatia 2019), popular press discourse – but see also Partington et al. (2013) on quality press discourse – and fictional telecinematic discourse (e.g. see, among many others, Bednarek 2018 and Werner 2021). Expressivity abounds in non-fictional TV programmes, too, particularly in recent ones. For instance, TV channels in various countries host singing competition shows (e.g. *The Voice*) where we repeatedly hear judges enthusiastically saying how amazing the contestants are (Zago 2021), as well as culinary programmes (e.g. *America's Test Kitchen*) where the explanation of how to cook a dish – in itself, a potentially humdrum activity – is made more engaging through the use of expressive language (Berber Sardinha and Veirano Pinto 2019, 2021), not to mention the many confessionals of contemporary TV, where, as part of interviews or realities, ordinary people disclose their emotions and feelings on ordinary topics/events using ordinary language (cf. Tolson 2006: 5). Even news presentation, the most factual activity performed by the media, is often packaged expressively nowadays, as testified by the very existence of the so-called infotainment genre.

But it is perhaps with the participatory web that the 'emotional regime' of contemporary discourses – that is, as González (2012) defines it, the amount and range of emotional expression that is considered adequate and is therefore expected in a given situation – has reached its peak. On the *participatory* web, the overt, explicit, vigorous expression of personal stance is instrumental precisely in foregrounding one's *participation* in an online discussion, in flagging one's presence among a multitude of other posts, in a constant search for the maximization of popularity and visibility, measured in terms of likes, comments, shares and so on (cf. KhosraviNik 2018). For example, YouTube is full of 'reaction videos' in which both experts and laymen react, usually in involved and emphatic ways, to films, TV programmes, songs and so on – the exercise of the expressive function is practically the only communicative move performed in this genre of videos. Similarly, it is by no means difficult to find instances of expressivity-laden language on social networks. These range from a hyperbolically positive pole (e.g. posting an emphatic comment on a friend's profile picture on Facebook with the aim of enhancing his/her positive face) to an aggressively negative pole (as in the case of hate speech against women, against members of the LGBTQ community, against immigrants, against 'pro-vaxxers', etc.). The algorithms governing the workings of social media play an important role in perpetuating, or even in boosting, expressivity in that they create 'echo chambers' and 'filter bubbles' in which the user is shown only those contents that the platform predicts to be relevant for him/her based on his/her previous online behaviour (KhosraviNik 2017). If one is systematically presented with compatible topics, news items, viewpoints, people, politicians, celebrities and musicians, and so forth, it is highly likely that he/she will be triggered to react to those contents and it is also highly likely that he/she will do so through an expressive style of language as opposed to a composed or an 'aseptic' one. At the same time, this mechanism paves the way for forms of 'radicalization *in absentia*', in the sense that one is so convinced of the goodness and even naturalness of the contents that are popular in his/her bubble that, in the remote event of coming across non-compatible contents (i.e. contents that are absent from the bubble), he/she is likely to disagree with those in sharp, uncompromising, if not aggressive, ways, as in the aforementioned case of hate speech. In this respect, as argued by KhosraviNik (2017: 64), while representing an invaluable public service tool for informing citizens and for the democratic negotiation among different viewpoints, social media communication, by its very architecture, 'tends to favour and encourages like-mindedness and intensification of feelings and beliefs with little or no critical scrutiny'.

The priority of expressivity in many contemporary discourses – and in modern sensibilities at large – is evident in the fact that the very act of expressing, in a sense, takes precedence over what triggers it. For example, it is common to read online comments (on newspaper articles, on posts by other users, etc.) that are rich in their expressive content but reveal a poor reading of what is being commented, or that are only tangentially related to what is being commented, or that are completely off-topic. Another sign that reveals the present-day preference for emotional authenticity over distant rationality (Flamarique 2012: 53) is the tendency, on TV, to use confrontation (Hutchby 2006: 65–77), and more in general emotionality, as a spectacle: judges often comment scathingly on the contestants' dishes on *Masterchef*; the camera frequently lingers on quarrels between contestants and on moments in which the contestants get emotional on *Big Brother* (and the same also routinely happens in many talk shows); TV series typically insist on emotionally loaded exchanges between the characters. In all of these cases, expressivity takes centre stage, while the substantive content that triggers it tends to slip into the background. This could be framed within what González (2012: 5) calls 'psychologization of experience', that is, a process 'whereby interest in emotional processes replaces interest in the realities that are at the origin of those very processes', a phenomenon that manifests itself 'every time private emotional reactions to any event receive more attention than the event itself and its possible relevance for public life'.

What has been argued so far can be summarized by saying that contemporary discourses and communicative behaviours reflect the existence of an 'emotional culture', that is, 'a culture marked by an increasing presence of emotions in public life' (González 2012: 3), one in which we witness the 'emotional apotheosis of the self' (González 2012: 6). It is, in Flamarique's (2012: 51–2) words, a culture characterized by 'panemotivism', 'hyper-emotionality' and 'hypertrophy of emotions', where a reserved disposition is met with suspicion – an example is the criticism Mario Draghi, as Prime Minister of Italy, attracted from part of the Italian public opinion and press due to his restrained demeanour, distant from the expressive modes and constant search for media visibility typical of 'personality politics'. Such a taste for expressivity 'has resulted in an emotional typology with its own gestural and verbal language, its personal and collective expressions, and with its own icons and shrines' (Flamarique 2012: 62).

The establishment of an emotional culture, a process in which the traditional and the new media have played a crucial role, has determined an 'emotional turn' in a variety of academic fields, both scientific and humanistic, including medicine, neurology, psychology, philosophy, sociology, ethnology, anthropology and film theory, among others. Relegated to a secondary position for a long time, partly because of the pre-eminence of a rationalist, Cartesian-type paradigm (García Martínez and González 2016: 15–16), over the last few decades expressivity has attracted increasing academic attention, giving rise to the markedly interdisciplinary area of inquiry known as 'emotionology'.[2]

Linguistics has been directly involved in this epistemological turn, on the widely held assumption that, as Alba-Juez and Mackenzie (2019: 4) put it, language is no longer viewed as 'a totally objective and valid representation of reality', but rather as 'an intersubjective expression of correlational "truth", where the expression of emotion plays a fundamental part'. The growing interest in expressivity by linguists has been motivated, on the one hand, by the aforementioned ubiquity of expressive markers in contemporary discourses and, on the other, by the fact that the presentation of expressive content is a multifarious phenomenon with manifestations at practically all linguistic levels, from phonology up to discourse and pragmatics (Ochs and Schieffelin 1989: 22; Wilce 2009: 3; Foolen 1997: 21–2; Bednarek 2008: 11; Alba-Juez and Mackenzie 2019), for example, through means such as specific intonation contours (as well as their written counterparts, marked by punctuation); affixation (diminutives/augmentatives); marked word orders; emotional/evaluative/attitudinal/affective lexis (e.g. *to love, happiness, nervous, angrily*); mood; modality; grading (e.g. intensifiers and emphatic particles); swearwords; vocatives (e.g. terms of endearment) and pronoun use; interjections; certain speech acts (e.g. warning, threatening); affective connotation; repetition; metaphor; hyperbole (e.g. emphatic adjectives such as *amazing, awesome*); figurativeness; and so on. Expressivity is multifarious also in the sense that it has a number of non-verbal and co-verbal realizations (e.g. body movements, gestures, facial expressions) – it is, in other words, multimodal. The analysis of expressivity in language has been the topic of several conferences (a recent example is the seventh edition of the *Languaging Diversity* international conference on 'The Linguistic Construction of Emotional

Challenges in a Changing Society', 13–15 October 2021, University of Lille), special issues of journals (e.g. *Text* 9:1, 1989, on affect, edited by Elinor Ochs; *Journal of Pragmatics* 22:3/4, 1994, on 'Involvement in Language', edited by Claudia Caffi and Richard W. Janney), monographs (e.g. Bednarek 2008; Wilce 2009; Wierzbicka 1999), edited volumes (e.g. Pritzker et al. 2020; Lüdtke 2015; García 2016a; Foolen et al. 2012; Weigand 2004; Mackenzie and Alba-Juez 2019; Baider and Cislaru 2014; Niemeier and Dirven 1997) and individual papers (e.g. Zago 2021). The topic has been approached from a variety of angles, namely cognitive, cross-linguistic, functional (including systemic-functional), conversation/discourse/register-analytic, pragmatic/textlinguistic, linguistic-anthropological, diachronic, stylistic/literary, psycholinguistic and acquisitional (Bednarek 2008: 7–10).

The (Cross)linguistic and Cognitive Experience of Emotion[3]

A notable hypothesis on the connection between language and emotion, voiced in the psychological constructionist approach, is that rather than merely communicating emotions (Ekman and Cordaro 2011),

> emotion words play a role in constituting emotional experiences and perceptions because they help people store and then access the conceptual knowledge about emotions used to make predictions about the meaning of external (e.g. visual) and internal (i.e. interoceptive) sensations in the moment (Brooks et al. 2017: 170).

In this sense, language may play a critical role in our acquisition and use of emotion concepts, if they are understood as abstract, in line with Hale's (1988) formulation, the underlying idea being that concepts that are not paired with concrete objects in the environment draw on being paired phonologically (Barrett and Lindquist 2008; Vigliocco et al. 2009; Borghi and Binkofski 2014). In a similar vein, being exposed to emotion utterances in infancy predicts an individual's ability to produce (e.g. Cervantes and Callanan 1998) and understand (Dunn et al. 1991) emotion language. Then, drawing on results from studies like Lindquist et al. (2006, 2014) or Gendron et al. (2012), Lindquist et al. (2015: 3) conclude that 'access to the meaning of emotion words (and the concepts that they represent) is an essential component of understanding the discrete meaning of emotional facial expressions'. Acquiring more fine-grained emotion terms enables infants to categorize emotion perceptually beyond the coarse-grained valence-based pleasant–unpleasant–neutral dimension (cf. Widen 2013). Likewise, semantic satiation (Black 2004) has been used to demonstrate that hindering an individual's access to emotion terms hinders their perception of emotion (Lindquist et al. 2006). Analogous evidence has been found with non-experimentally induced impairment of access to linguistic emotion concepts whereby patients with dementia categorized facial expression of emotions more schematically than their non-impaired counterparts (Lindquist et al. 2014).

In a cross-linguistic perspective, languages which structure emotion at a higher level of detail may be conditioning their users to be better at emotion differentiation and emotion regulation (cf. Pavlenko 2014). In turn, when it comes more precisely to L1 versus L2 use, there are significant affective-cognitive implications, as speaking in one's L2 might be resulting in what can metaphorically be construed in terms of increased distance. L1 is thus linked to higher emotionality (Pavlenko 2012), with examples ranging from advertising (Puntoni et al. 2009) to moral dilemmas which are reasoned about more utilitarianly when expressed in one's L2, likely by virtue of lowering the emotional response present in the case of L1 (Costa et al. 2014).

Overview of the Book[4]

Language, Expressivity and Cognition aspires to add to the developing field of emotionology and to the description and understanding of contemporary emotional cultures by providing a panoramic view of the workings of the expressive function in present-day communication. It sets out to do so by exploring, on the one hand, the conceptualization of emotions and, on the other, the emotional 'temperature' of a variety of contemporary discourses. The volume looks at expressivity through the essentially dual lens of language as it shapes communicative and cognitive processes but, at the same time, is also shaped by those processes.

The aim of the book is not to propose a general theory of expressivity in language. It has been designed, instead, to be at the intersection of different, but complementary, lines of research in linguistic emotionology, namely (1) the study of expressive language from a conceptual/cognitive point of view (e.g. see Kövecses 2000); (2) the study of expressivity across different languages and cultures (e.g. see Wierzbicka 1999); (3) the study of the ways in which expressivity is linguistically conveyed in specific registers and discourses (e.g. see Niemeier and Dirven 1997: 231–326), and, within this, (3.1) the more recent line of research on expressivity in online environments (e.g. see Fuoli and Bednarek 2022). By programmatically juxtaposing and bringing these lines of research together, the volume aims to foster cross-pollination; to provide a diversified picture of the relationship between words, heart and mind; and to document and reflect on the centrality of the expressive function in contemporary communication at different levels, in an era in which, as argued earlier, what is emotional, affective, highly personal, that is, expressive, tends to take precedence over what is factual, informational, propositional and expository. The rationale behind the book's design is that, being a macro-linguistic phenomenon, expressivity cannot be studied mono-dimensionally, but rather requires investigation from multiple standpoints (cf. Niemeier 1997; Alba-Juez and Mackenzie 2019: 4), an endeavour that lends itself particularly well to the edited-book format. At the same time, while, in emotionology, multiplicity of standpoints can get to the point of interdisciplinarity (e.g. combining contributions from medicine, psychology, philosophy, sociology, ethnology, anthropology), that is not the case in the present book, whose contributions are linguistic in nature.

The volume's treatment of expressivity is panoramic in that it is multi-perspective, cross-linguistic and updated. The contributions represent a number of methodological approaches from linguistics and media/communication studies, both qualitative and quantitative, encompassing insights from cognitive linguistics, (critical) discourse analysis, corpus linguistics and sociolinguistics – as well as insights resulting from the combination of these approaches. From these diverse methodological angles, a wide set of data types are examined, ranging from newspaper headlines to tweets and from TV dialogues to song lyrics, and drawing on naturally occurring language from corpora, as well as on data extracted from dictionaries, questionnaires and focus groups.

The languages and cultures covered in the volume go well beyond English and include Arabic, Polish, Italian, Hungarian and Turkish. The chapters offer both intra-lingual as well as contrastive/comparative investigations. The adoption of a cross-linguistic stance is, on the one hand, necessary, as different languages and cultures locally bend expressivity in their own ways, not to mention that the same speaker may convey expressivity differently in the various languages he/she speaks; on the other, it is instrumental in capturing cross-linguistic affinities in the workings and phenomenology of expressivity.

The analyses gathered in the book are up to date in two senses. First, they concern not only traditional media (e.g. newspapers) and genres (e.g. political speeches) but also newer, digital ones (e.g. online user comments). Second, they include examination of discourses regarding hotly debated current affairs topics (the Covid-19 pandemic; immigration). Symbolically, the chapters dealing with expressivity in internet discourses (Part II, as illustrated later) take up the central part of the book. This choice alludes to the key role of the new media/technologies in contemporary societies and communication, especially in the (post)pandemic world, and to the crucial importance of the internet in the study of expressivity, the internet being – as pointed out earlier – an emotionally loaded landscape and, as such, representing an invaluable observatory of expressivity.

The volume is divided into three thematic sections of three chapters each. Part I, the most cognitively oriented one, is devoted to 'Metaphoric conceptualizations of emotions', in line with the view that, as Foolen (1997: 15) puts it, 'the analytical tools of cognitive semantics, like metaphor, metonymy, polysemy, grammaticalization, etc., can be of use in the study of the expressive function' and vice versa. In Chapter 2 ('Emotion and Reasoning in Hungarian HEART Metaphors'), Judit Baranyiné Kóczy problematizes the dichotomy, both linguistic and cognitive, between 'head' and 'heart' in Hungarian – a dichotomy that, as the author points out, exists in several other languages, including English. Looking at data extracted from both dictionaries (phrases and proverbs) and the Hungarian National Corpus, she illustrates that while, in Hungarian, the term 'head' (*fej*) is used in the conceptualization of cognitive, rational activities and the term 'heart' (*szív*) serves primarily to conceptualize emotions and feelings, the latter body part has metaphorical extensions that also refer to intellectual processes such as decision making, opinion, thinking, advice taking and understanding. Kóczy articulates this finding as evidence of the interconnectedness – as opposed to the dualism – between the emotional and the cognitive components in language – one of the assumptions underlying the entire volume, hence the choice to use Kóczy's as the opening case study. The reflection on the conceptualization of emotions continues in Chapter 3 by Marcin Trojszczak and Chiara Astrid Gebbia ('A Comparative Study of English, Italian and Polish Conceptual Metaphors of Emotion Regulation and Cognitive Inhibition'). Drawing on data retrieved from various corpora (British National Corpus; Corpus di Italiano Scritto; Paisà; Aranea; National Corpus of Polish), the authors identify a number of similarities, as well as some differences, in the English, Italian and Polish metaphors used to refer to emotion regulation and cognitive inhibition activities, for instance, the overarching metaphor EMOTION REGULATION/COGNITIVE INHIBITION IS LIMITING PHYSICAL CONTACT and its sub-metaphors (as in the case of the English expression *to scrap the idea* or the Italian expression *non farsi prendere dalla tristezza* 'not to let oneself be taken by sadness'). Chapter 4 ('Linguistic Means to Discursively Construct Dehumanization'), by Serena Coschignano and Chiara Zanchi, completes Part I and is, at the same time, the first of a series of investigations that, in the volume, deal with specific discourse types. Coschignano and Zanchi look at an Italian corpus of newspaper headlines on migration, in which they detect what might be termed 'forms of expressivity via dehumanization', that is, a range of discursive choices whereby refugees and asylum seekers are metaphorically framed – not to say (mis)represented – for instance, as an indistinct category, as an abstract issue, as numbers, as invaders, as natural disasters and so forth.

Part II – 'Constructing Emotion in Internet Discourses' – opens with Chapter 5 by Ester Di Silvestro ('A Comparative Study of Donald J. Trump and Matteo Salvini's Populist Strategies in the Representation of Immigrants and Refugees on Twitter'). The chapter highlights macro-similarities and micro-differences in the discursive means – metaphors, *topoi* and representational strategies – used by Trump and Salvini in both tweets and traditional speeches when referring to immigrants and refugees (e.g. the *topos* of threat and danger, the insistence on oppositional rhetorical tactics). Di Silvestro shows how these discursive ploys cause a lack of empathy towards immigrants and refugees, typically by evoking negative emotions, feelings and attitudes (e.g. fear, anger) in voters – findings which mirror those obtained for newspaper discourse in Chapter 4. Chapter 6 ('Collective Identities and Emotions in Online Contexts'), by Barbara Lewandowska-Tomaszczyk and Paul A. Wilson, deals with cooperation and conflict dynamics – and with the increasing emotionality levels accompanying them – in Polish and English online comments, analysed comparatively and considering the position of the Polish and the English cultures on the collectivism–individualism axis. The authors treat cooperation and conflict as the major driving forces in online identity formation and view them as moves ultimately directed at reaching a status of well-being in online group action. Also, they discuss the understudied phenomenon of 'devirtualization', that is, the process whereby online activities (e.g. protest movements) are transferred from the virtual sphere to the real world. The investigation of Polish online language goes on in Chapter 7 ('A Phraseological Perspective on Evaluation: The Covid-19 Vaccination in Polish Web-Based News'), which focuses on prefabricated phraseological units. Here Mikołaj Deckert, Krzysztof Hejduk and Piotr Pęzik use the Monco PL corpus to examine linguistic and cognitive aspects of stance communication in political discourse on Covid-19 vaccination in Poland. They carry out a quantitative and qualitative analysis of the affective dimension emerging in their data set, drawing on the left-leaning versus right-leaning political–ideological categorization of sources.

Part III, about 'Emotion in Multimodal Discourses', begins with Lucia La Causa's study on 'Arabic–English Code-switching in Egyptian Rap Music and Social Networks' (Chapter 8). Challenging the commonly held view according to which the L1 functions as the 'language of the heart' for multilingual speakers, the author shows that English, typically used together with Egyptian Arabic as part of a code-switching praxis, serves as a powerful carrier of emotions – particularly to express strong feelings and contents that could sound disturbing in Arabic – for Egyptian rappers in their songs, video interviews and social network pages (in this last context, the use of English tends to be reciprocated by Egyptian fans in their comments). The study elaborates on the sociolinguistic reasons for the aforementioned trend through a questionnaire administered to young Egyptian fans of Egyptian rap, unearthing, among other facets, the fact that, in a 'glocal' fashion, Arabic–English code-switching simultaneously allows Egyptian rappers to be in tune with international – especially American – rap and to communicate their ethnicity. In Chapter 9 ('Innovation and Emotion in Teen Talk in TV Series'), by Silvia Bruti, the focus moves to another register where expressivity matters, namely the language of fictional TV series. The author looks at more and less recent American and British TV series from the particular viewpoint of teen talk – a variety with respect to which data are not abundant, hence the methodological importance of using TV series about teenagers as data sources. Through a corpus-based examination of the frequencies and functions of a series of markers of teen talk (the phonological reductions *gonna* and *wanna*; the lexical items *fuck*, *shit* and *dude*; the intensifier *totally*), Bruti discusses the language of teenagers as a repository of heightened emotions and as a source of innovation, highlighting, among other things, how changeable teen talk is and how TV products help linguistic habits to settle. In the closing chapter ('An Appraisal Approach to Emotion, Culture and Discourse in Audio Description: Exploring Audio Description Quality in Turkey'; Chapter 10), Hilal Erkazanci Durmuş and Şirin Okyayuz deal, from an appraisal theory perspective, with the practices followed and the challenges tackled in audio describing telecinematic language, particularly those linked to the relaying of emotions. Reporting the results of a focus-group discussion with members of SEBEDER (the Audio Description Association, a Turkish non-governmental organization), the authors address a number of issues concerning emotional accessibility in quality audio description, such as the criteria professionals follow in deciding what and how to audio describe, the importance of specific linguistic items in rendering and graduating the emotive layer of meaning (e.g. adjectives and adverbs) as well as the imperative of objectivity with its limitations.

Notes

1. This section was written by Raffaele Zago.
2. This is not to say that research on emotions and expressivity is a twenty-first century line of research, as it can be traced back to such important antecedents as Freud, Darwin and, earlier, to the Greek philosophers. Cf., also, García (2016b: 2–5), who argues that an affective *re-*turn has occurred in film theory (italics added), and Foolen (1997: 17), who claims that 'in recent years, there seems to be a *revival* of interest in the expressive function of language' (italics added).
3. This section was written by Mikołaj Deckert and Piotr Pęzik.
4. This section was written by Mikołaj Deckert, Piotr Pęzik and Raffaele Zago.

References

Alba-Juez, L., and J. L. Mackenzie (2019), 'Emotion Processes in Discourse', in J. L. Mackenzie, and L. Alba-Juez (eds), *Emotion in Discourse*, pp. 3–26, Amsterdam/Philadelphia: John Benjamins.

Baider, F., and G. Cislaru (eds) (2014), *Linguistic Approaches to Emotions in Context*, Amsterdam/Philadelphia: John Benjamins.

Barrett, L. F., and K. A. Lindquist (2008), 'The Embodiment of Emotion', in G. R. Semin, and E. R. Smith (eds), *Embodied Grounding: Social, Cognitive, Affective, and Neuroscientific Approaches*, pp. 237–62, New York: Cambridge University Press.

Bednarek, M. (2008), *Emotion Talk across Corpora*, Basingstoke: Palgrave Macmillan.

Bednarek, M. (2018), *Language and Television Series: A Linguistic Approach to TV Dialogue*, Cambridge: Cambridge University Press.

Berber Sardinha, T., and M. Veirano Pinto (2019), 'Dimensions of Variation across American Television Registers', *International Journal of Corpus Linguistics*, 24(1): 3–32.

Berber Sardinha, T., and M. Veirano Pinto (2021), 'A Linguistic Typology of American Television', *International Journal of Corpus Linguistics*, 26(1): 127–60.

Bhatia, T. K. (2019), 'Emotions and Language in Advertising', *World Englishes*, 38: 435–49.

Biber, D., S. Johansson, G. Leech, S. Conrad, and E. Finegan (2021), *Grammar of Spoken and Written English*, Amsterdam/Philadelphia: John Benjamins.

Black, S. R. (2004), 'A Review of Semantic Satiation', in S. P. Shohov (ed.), *Advances in Psychology Research*, pp. 95–106, Huntington: Nova Science.

Borghi, A. M., and F. Binkofski (2014), *Words As social Tools: An Embodied View on Abstract Concepts*, New York: Springer.

Brooks, J. A., H. Shablack, M. Gendron, A. B. Satpute, M. H. Parrish, and K. A. Lindquist (2017), 'The Role of Language in the Experience and Perception of Emotion: A Neuroimaging Meta-Analysis', *Social Cognitive and Affective Neuroscience*, 12: 169–83.

Bühler, K. (1934), *Sprachtheorie*, Stuttgart: Gustav Fischer.

Caffi, C., and R. W. Janney (eds) (1994), 'Special Issue on "Involvement in Language"', *Journal of Pragmatics*, 22(3/4).

Cervantes, C., and M. A. Callanan (1998), 'Labels and Explanations in Mother-Child Emotion Talk: Age and Gender Differentiation', *Developmental Psychology*, 34(1): 88–98.

Costa, A., A. Foucart, S. Hayakawa, M. Aparici, J. Apesteguia, J. Heafner, and B. Keysar (2014), 'Your Morals Depend on Language', *PLoS ONE*, 9(4). doi.org/10.1371/journal.pone.0094842.

Dunn, J., J. Brown, C. Slomkowski, C. Tesla, and L. Youngblade (1991), 'Young Children's Understanding of Other People's Feelings and Beliefs: Individual Differences and Their Antecedents', *Child Development*, 62(6): 1352–66.

Ekman, P., and D. Cordaro (2011), 'What is Meant by Calling Emotions Basic', *Emotion Review*, 3: 364–70.

Flamarique, L. (2012), 'From the Psychologization of Experience to the Priority of Emotions in Social Life', in A. M. González (ed.), *The Emotions and Cultural Analysis*, pp. 51–67, Surrey/Burlington: Ashgate.

Foolen, A. (1997), 'The Expressive Function of Language: Towards a Cognitive Semantic Approach', in S. Niemeier, and R. Dirven (eds), *The Language of Emotions: Conceptualization, Expression and Theoretical Foundation*, pp. 15–31, Amsterdam/Philadelphia: John Benjamins.

Foolen, A., U. M. Lüdtke, T. P. Racine, and J. Zlatev (eds) (2012), *Moving Ourselves, Moving Others: Motion and Emotion in Intersubjectivity, Consciousness and Language*, Amsterdam/Philadelphia: John Benjamins.

Fuoli, M., and M. Bednarek (2022), 'Emotional Labor in Webcare and Beyond: A Linguistic Framework and Case Study', *Journal of Pragmatics*, 191: 256–70.

García, A. N. (ed.) (2016a), *Emotions in Contemporary TV Series*, London: Palgrave Macmillan.

García, A. N. (2016b), 'Introduction ', in A. N. García (ed.), *Emotions in Contemporary TV Series*, pp. 1–10, London: Palgrave Macmillan.

García Martínez, A., and A. M. González (2016), 'Emotional Culture and TV Narratives', in A. N. García (ed.), *Emotions in Contemporary TV Series*, pp. 13–25, London: Palgrave Macmillan.

Gendron, M., K. A. Lindquist, L. W. Barsalou, and L. F. Barrett (2012), 'Emotion Words Shape Emotion Percepts', *Emotion*, 12(2): 314–25.

González, A. M. (2012), 'Introduction. Emotional Culture and the Role of Emotions in Cultural Analysis', in A. M. González (ed.), *The Emotions and Cultural Analysis*, pp. 1–15, Surrey/Burlington: Ashgate.

Hale, S. C. (1988), 'Spacetime and the Abstract/Concrete Distinction', *Philosophical Studies*, 53: 85–102.

Hutchby, I. (2006), *Media Talk: Conversation Analysis and the Study of Broadcasting*, Maidenhead: Open University Press.

Jakobson, R. (1960), 'Closing Statement: Linguistics and Poetics', in T. A. Sebeok (ed.), *Style in Language*, pp. 350–77, Cambridge, MA: MIT Press.

KhosraviNik, M. (2017), 'Right Wing Populism in the West: Social Media Discourse and Echo Chambers', *Insight Turkey*, 19(3): 53–68.

KhosraviNik, M. (2018), 'Social Media Techno-Discursive Design, Affective Communication and Contemporary Politics', *Fudan Journal of the Humanities and Social Sciences*, 11(4): 427–42.

Kövecses, Z. (2000), *Metaphor and Emotion: Language, Culture, and Body in Human Feeling*. Cambridge: Cambridge University Press.

Lindquist, K. A., L. F. Barrett, E. Bliss-Moreau, and J. A. Russell (2006), 'Language and the Perception of Emotion', *Emotion*, 6(1): 125–38.

Lindquist, K. A., M. Gendron, L. F. Barrett, and B. C. Dickerson (2014), 'Emotion, but Not Affect Perception, is Impaired with Semantic Memory Loss', *Emotion*, 14(2): 375–87.

Lindquist, K.A., J. K. MacCormack, and H. Shablack (2015), 'The Role of Language in Emotion: Predictions from Psychological Constructionism', *Frontiers in Psychology*, 6(444): 1–17.

Lüdtke, U. (ed.) (2015), *Emotion in Language: Theory-Research-Application*, Amsterdam/Philadelphia: John Benjamins.

Mackenzie, J. L., and L. Alba-Juez (eds) (2019), *Emotion in Discourse*, Amsterdam/Philadelphia: John Benjamins.

Niemeier, S. (1997), 'Introduction ', in S. Niemeier, and R. Dirven (eds), *The Language of Emotions: Conceptualization, Expression and Theoretical Foundation*, pp. VII–XVIII, Amsterdam/Philadelphia: John Benjamins.

Niemeier, S., and R. Dirven (eds) (1997), *The Language of Emotions: Conceptualization, Expression and Theoretical Foundation*, Amsterdam/Philadelphia: John Benjamins.

Ochs, E. (ed.) (1989), 'Special Issue on "Affect"', *Text*, 9(1).

Ochs, E., and B. Schieffelin (1989), 'Language has a Heart', *Text*, 9(1): 7–25.

Partington, A., A. Duguid, and C. Taylor (2013), *Patterns and Meanings in Discourse: Theory and Practice in Corpus-Assisted Discourse Studies (CADS)*, Amsterdam/Philadelphia: John Benjamins.

Pavlenko, A. (2012), 'Affective Processing in Bilingual Speakers: Disembodied Cognition? ', *International Journal of Psychology*, 47(6): 405–28.

Pavlenko, A. (2014), *The Bilingual Mind and What It Tells Us About Language and Thought*, New York: Cambridge University Press.

Pritzker, S. E., J. Fenigsen, and J. M. Wilce (2020), *The Routledge Handbook of Language and Emotion*, London/New York: Routledge.

Puntoni, S., B. De Langhe, and S. M. J. Van Osselaer (2009), 'Bilingualism and the Emotional Intensity of Advertising Language', *Journal of Consumer Research*, 35(6): 1012–25.

Tolson, A. (2006), *Media Talk: Spoken Discourse on TV and Radio*, Edinburgh: Edinburgh University Press.
Vigliocco, G., L. Meteyard, M. Andrews, and S. Kousta (2009), 'Toward a Theory of Semantic Representation', *Language and Cognition*, 1(2): 219–47.
Weigand, E. (ed.) (2004), *Emotion in Dialogic Interaction*, Amsterdam/Philadelphia: John Benjamins.
Werner, V. (2021), 'A Diachronic Perspective on Telecinematic Language', *International Journal of Corpus Linguistics*, 26(1): 38–70.
Widen, S. C. (2013), 'Children's Interpretation of Facial Expressions: The Long Path from Valence-Based to Specific Discrete Categories', *Emotion Review*, 5: 72–7.
Wierzbicka, A. (1999), *Emotions across Languages and Cultures: Diversity and Universals*, Cambridge: Cambridge University Press.
Wilce, J. M. (2009), *Language and Emotion*, Cambridge: Cambridge University Press.
Zago, R. (2021), 'Televisual Expressivity: Emphasis and Emotionality in American and British Singing Competition Shows', *Expressio*, 5: 209–28.

Part I

Metaphoric Conceptualizations of Emotions

2

Emotion and Reasoning in Hungarian HEART Metaphors

Judit Baranyiné Kóczy

Introduction

In the cultures dominated by the 'Western' tradition and thought, the concept of HEART is generally associated with emotions, especially the romantic concept of LOVE. This view has a strong bodily basis, namely, that the physiological, expressive and behavioural responses of love are often linked to the heart. The metaphorical extensions of the heart have been observed from the perspective of numerous languages, including English (Niemeier 2000, 2008), Chinese (Yu 2007, 2008), Japanese (Ikegami 2008; Occhi 2008), Korean (Yoon 2008), Swahili, (Kraska-Szlenk 2005), Turkish (Baş 2015) and others. These studies have shown that the 'heart', of the most frequently utilized organ for figurative extensions, is not universally the locus of certain psychological faculties, but certain cultures attribute specific and altering meanings to it. The study of the metaphoric meanings of the HEART is fruitful for the theory of the 'embodiment via body parts' (Yu 2007, 2008), which explores how the human body is exploited for the conceptualization of abstract concepts and how the figurative usage of body part terms unveils cross-cultural specificities in the way they are applied to various aspects of life (e.g. Sharifian et al. 2008, Maalej and Yu 2011). This observation is reflected in the notion 'cultural embodiment' (Maalej 2004), which emphasizes the fact that the conceptualizations of body parts are grounded in cultural models (Quinn and Holland 1987) and they often contradict scientific knowledge. The metaphoric meanings of body parts can be regarded as cultural conceptualizations because they incorporate and transmit the beliefs and ideas of the members of a cultural community about various aspects of their life, environment, religion and many other themes. In general, different cultures apply the body parts to human activities and values (psychological, intellectual and other person-bound concepts in different ways).

Head–Heart Dichotomy in Language

In relation to human faculties, emotions and intellect are considered as core human abilities, although it has not always been so from a cross-cultural and historical perspective. The classification of human faculties and their respective dominance or marginal state to a group's cultural cognition have always been dependant on the cultural models which structure a community's comprehensive ideas about human nature and psyche. Taking the example of heart in English, one can follow the process by which the meaning extension of the HEART changed in relation to the various dimensions of personality – emotions, mind or soul. Geeraerts and Gevaert (2008) show that in Old English-language use, the HEART referred to the mind and soul, and the MOOD alluded to cognition, emotion and will. Later on, due to the introduction of certain cultural ideologies, mainly humanism, a novel model was gradually developed, the so-called cardiocentric model, which became widespread in the Middle English (Geeraerts and Gevaert 2008: 342). This model relied on the historical belief that the heart controls sensation, thought and body movement. Another turn of the model of the HEART took place in the seventeenth century when, upon the influence of the Cartesian dualism, the dichotomic model of 'emotion versus thinking' became prevalent in English, which separated rational thinking from irrational feelings (Niemeier 2008). Foolen also adds that under the pressure of Cartesian philosophy in Descartes, in order to be separated from the rational faculty, the 'heart' has become the seat of religious faith in Catholic culture, thus becoming the symbolic 'physical' residence of God (Foolen 2008: 388). In today's English-language use, the secular and Christian (primarily Catholic) HEART metaphors are different: in Christian lyrics they are mainly associated with positive emotions (as opposed to secular language), and the metonymy HEART FOR DESIRE is common, where the heart is an entity that hungers, thirsts, sings or praises God. In addition to locating EMOTION, the HEART is also the SEAT OF MORALITY and HOLINESS (Pattilo, in press).

The act of conceptually linking the HEART to different human faculties, especially in terms of emotion and intellect, serves as a ground for the classification of languages. There are basically two models apparent in various cultures, the 'dualistic' and the 'holistic' ones; however, an intermediate cluster with certain flexibility can also be observed which can be regarded as 'continuum' types Kraska-Szlenk 2014). Languages with a holistic model are the ones which feature a conceptualization system where one body part serves as the holistic centre of emotional and rational human faculties. For example, in Tsou (an Austronesian language), *koyu* 'ear' functions as the locus of emotion and cognition (Huang 2002), or in the Ifaluk (a Micronesian language) it is the GUT (a body part which comprises the stomach and the abdominal region) which anchors both faculties (D'Andrade 1987). In some languages, like Indonesian (Siahaan 2008) or Malay (Goddard 2001), the centre of emotions and intellectual abilities is *hati* 'liver', which may be explained by the old ritual of liver divination where the liver was perceived as the central inner organ by means of which spiritual beings communicate with human beings. In other languages like Chinese, *xin* 'heart' is conceptualized as the ruler of the body (Yu 2007, 2008), similarly to Thai *jai* 'heart' (Berendt and Tanita 2011).

Languages which retain a 'dualistic' model are the ones where the irrational emotions and the cognitive processes are clearly divided, and two body parts serve as distinct loci of emotional and rational human faculties. A well-known example is English, where the HEART stands for EMOTIONS and the HEAD for INTELLECT (Niemeier 2000, 2008). The rare exception *learn by* heart, which connects memory to the heart, may be 'a remnant of earlier cultural models of the heart from Old or Middle English, where the heart was still conceptualized as not only being the locus of emotions but also of rational thought' (Niemeier 2008: 355–6). Unrelated to English, Japanese features the same 'head–heart' model as observed by Ikegami (2008). There are also cultures where the two faculties are allocated to two distinct body parts but not the head and the heart: in Marind (Papua New Guinea), *kambét* 'ear' stands for thinking, knowledge and remembering, while *békai* 'heart and lungs' stands for emotions (De Witte 1948); on the other hand, in Kuuk Thaayorre, it is again *kaal* 'ear' used for the intellectual faculty but *ngeengk* 'belly' for emotion, spirit and life force (Gaby 2008).

Apart from the two basic clusters, a third one, the 'continuum' languages can be identified where there is a division between body parts which serve as centres of emotional and rational human faculties, but some flexibility can be observed (Kraska-Szlenk 2014). This flexibility manifests in denoting certain processes of cognition to the heart. To name some of these languages, in Persian, *del* 'heart, stomach, abdomen, belly, guts' is the centre of EMOTIONS but also as the centre of THOUGHTS and MEMORIES (Sharifian 2008); in Kazakh, *júrek* 'heart' hosts secret thoughts in that 'the heart feels, guesses, and gives its final decision' (Abdramanova, in press). The Kurdish *dil* 'heart' (Nosrati, in press) and Buryat (a Finno-Ugric language) *zürxen* 'heart' (Khabtagaeva and Szeverényi, in press), apart from being the seat of EMOTIONS, are also responsible for DECISION MAKING. Further examples include Swahili where *moyo* 'heart' hosts THOUGHTS, DOUBTS, QUESTIONS, FAITH, MEMORY and WORDS (Kraska-Szlenk 2005), Fulfulde (Peul) where *ɓernde* 'heart' locates NEGATIVE THOUGHTS and WORRIES, INFORMATION, REMEMBRANCE/MEMORY, INTENTIONS, DOUBTS and, in general, the HEART serves as COMMANDER OF THE BODY (Shehu, in press), or Tunisian Arabic where the HEART is conceptualized as a RATIONAL AND FORESEEING GUIDE (Maalej, in press). As we can see, MEMORY and DECISION are often associated with the heart, and other cognitive faculties identified in these languages are NEGATIVE THOUGHTS and DOUBTS. These categories suggest that it is well worth raising the question whether these faculties are purely rational ones. Can 'doubts' or 'negative thoughts' be conceived without emotional experience? Or can all kinds of memories be evoked without emotional involvement? The findings from these languages indicate that the interconnectedness of body parts/organs and human faculties, and the reconstruction of the cultural model of the HEART based on linguistic evidence, are rather complex issues and they need thorough consideration regarding the actual meanings of the different human abilities.

Before turning to the analysis of Hungarian data, some of the basic tenets of the 'head versus heart' dichotomy needs to be clarified first. As noted, it generally refers to the ideology prevalent in Western culture, which resides in a dichotomic view of human psyche, namely, a clear distinction between irrational emotions and rational thinking as exemplified by English (Niemeier 2008). Accordingly, the heart is responsible for hosting emotions whereas the head locates, controls and represents intellectual capacities. The Head–Heart dichotomy relates to traditional cultural and ethnomedical beliefs in a specific period in language and thought development, the seventeenth century, when Descartes and his successors propagated the latent dualism between emotions and reason. Its preceding philosophical doctrine, 'The four humours theory', was an ethnomedical belief in the sixteenth and seventeenth centuries, which viewed the heart as the locus of EMOTIONS, TEMPERAMENT and also RATIONALITY. The Humoral doctrine was overtaken in the seventeenth century by Descartes' mathematically based rationalism and his belief in the dualism of mind and body, inherited from the Judeo-Christian traditions and Greek philosophy (Niemeier 2008: 366). It emphasized the superiority of the head, that is, intellect and thinking, and ideal thinking was logical thinking without emotional intervention. Thus, the Cartesian philosophy did not only separate the emotional self from the intellectual one, but it also advocated the power of the mind over feelings.

Research Questions and Methodology

This chapter aims at examining which cluster (dualistic or continuum) of the cultural models the Hungarian language belongs to. Accordingly, it focuses on the following research questions:

1. To what degree is the dualistic view of head versus heart manifested in Hungarian as evidenced by language data?
2. What is the metaphorical role of the HEART in reasoning?

The study employs the framework of conceptual metaphor theory (e.g. Kövecses 2015, Lakoff and Johnson 1980) and the analyses assert essentially a qualitative method where data (phrases and proverbs) are extracted from various dictionaries (Bárczi and Országh 1959–62; Bárdosi 2013; Szemerkényi 2009) and the *Hungarian National Corpus* (HNC). This approach is complemented by a small-scale analysis of a random sample of 100 expressions containing the lemma *szív* 'heart' (HNC), but both scientific and literary texts were excluded from the corpus.

Cultural Conceptualizations of *Szív* 'Heart'

HEAD as the Seat of INTELLECT

Considering the head–heart dichotomy in Hungarian, it has been shown that thinking and intellectual processes are extensively linked to the head. Baranyiné Kóczy (2019), based on data extracted from the *Hungarian National Corpus*, identifies various conceptualizations of THINKING in relation to the HEAD, and identifies the head as the SEAT OF INTELLECT/THINKING. She argues that, in Hungarian, the HEAD-AS-CONTAINER metaphor is prevalent in as much as thoughts, ideas, data and memories are imagined as animate or inanimate entities that exist in the head. The most frequent conceptualizations of THOUGHT and THINKING in the Hungarian language are the following (Baranyiné Kóczy 2019):

- THOUGHTS AS ENTITIES IN A DRUG STORE
- THOUGHTS AS THREADS
- THOUGHTS AS MOVING ENTITIES
- THOUGHTS AS NOISE/MUSIC
- THOUGHTS AS HUMANS
- THOUGHTS AS ANIMALS

- THOUGHTS AS PLANTS
- THINKING AS CRACKING ONE'S HEAD
- THINKING AS A WORKING MACHINE
- THINKING AS MARKING A WOODEN BOARD
- THINKING AS LIGHT

As the conceptualizations indicate, both the ontological metaphors of THOUGHT and THINKING locate these entities and processes inside the head. These metaphors represent various aspects of reasoning, for example, representing THOUGHTS as tiny objects which need to be organized and ordered by sorting, filtering, unbinding, putting them to their places, and which can move about in one's head or produce pleasant or unpleasant sounds. In other cases, thoughts are also conceptualized as animate entities which settle, live, grow, develop or perform different activities within the container of the head. In terms of THINKING, it is commonly mapped onto human physical work and machinery in work, both of which reflect the hardships of mental activity. The head is also conceptualized as a dark room where THINKING may generate LIGHT (cf. UNDERSTANDING IS A LIGHT metaphor).

Conceptualizations of the HEART

Having seen that the head can be regarded as the SEAT OF INTELLECT in Hungarian, let us move on to the figurative extensions of the heart, namely, to observe which human faculties are closely connected to it. According to Baranyiné Kóczy (in press), various conceptualizations can be expressed via using the *szív* 'heart':

- EMOTIONS
- CHARACTER TRAITS (BENEVOLENCE, MEANNESS, CARING, HOSPITALITY, HONESTY)
- MORALITY/CONSCIENCE (CULTURAL VALUES)
- RELIGIOUS FAITH
- REASONING

One important question about unfolding the conceptualizations of the heart is which target domain is utilized most often in the metaphors and metonymies based on the heart (Table 2.1).

Table 2.1 shows that *szív* 'heart' is referenced in a figurative sense in the vast majority (86 per cent) of the cases, and within the metaphoric/metonymic cluster, it is the domain of EMOTION to which the HEART is mostly extended (56 per cent, which is more than half of the figurative usage). What is interesting about the results is that CHARACTER TRAITS, which ranks third in frequency (8 per cent) is

Table 2.1 Distribution of conceptualizations of the HEART based on a small-scale sample

Conceptualization	Percentage of frequency (%)
HUMAN ORGAN (NON-FIGURATIVE)	14
EMOTION	56
CHARACTER TRAIT	8
REASONING	7
PERSONALITY, SELF	5
RELIGIOUS FAITH	4
MORALITY (CONSCIENCE)	2
LIFE FORCE	2
GEOGRAPHICAL CENTRE	1
ANIMAL ORGAN (FOOD)	1

closely followed by REASONING (7 per cent). Further conceptualizations include PERSONALITY/SELF, RELIGIOUS FAITH and MORALITY.

The overwhelming superiority of the conceptualization of HEART in relation to EMOTION is displayed in a variety of emotion metaphors which deploy *szív* 'heart'. As in many other languages related to the Western tradition cultures, the heart is primarily connected to romantic and non-romantic LOVE, but other emotions are also associated with it, such as COURAGE, HAPPINESS, SADNESS, EXCITEMENT/SURPRISE, ANXIETY, RELIEF and ENTHUSIASM. The different conceptualizations (metaphors and metonymies) of the HEART identified in the expression of emotions are detailed in Baranyiné Kóczy (in press):

LOVE:	PHYSICAL CLOSENESS TO THE HEART
	PART OF THE HEART
	A HEART FACING SB.
	POSSESSING ONE'S HEART
	HAVING A MAGNETIC HEART
	HAVING SB. IN THE HEART
	EATING SB.'S HEART
	HAVING A BURNING HEART
COURAGE:	HAVING ONE'S HEART AT ITS NORMAL PLACE
	LIFTING ONE'S HEART UP
	PHYSICALLY STRENGTHENING THE HEART
HAPPINESS:	INTENSIVE HEART BEATING
	SPATIAL EXPANSION OF THE HEART
	FLYING HEART
	LIGHTENED (CLOUDLESS) HEART

SADNESS:	PHYSICAL PAIN IN THE HEART
	HEART WOUNDED BY A KNIFE, A DAGGER OR AN ARROW
	HEART WRUNG, FRACTURED, TORN OR BROKEN
	THE HEART UNDER HEAVY BURDEN
EXCITEMENT/SURPRISE:	
	FAST/STRONG FLUTTERING OF THE HEART
	JUMPING HEART
	UNEXPECTED SEIZURE/ATTACK ON THE HEART
ANXIETY:	THE HEART UNDER HEAVY BURDEN
	PRESSURE ON THE HEART, GRABBING THE HEART
RELIEF:	LIGHT HEART
	SPATIAL EXPANSION OF THE HEART
ENTHUSIASM:	HAVING A BIG HEART
	RELOCATING THE HEART

It can be observed that the emotions are described via a range of qualities of the heart, spatial properties such as orientation, location, size and so on; physical qualities such as weight. In other cases, the physical manipulation of the heart is profiled, such as grabbing, pressing, wounding an so on. Finally, different actions of the heart are also represented in the form of unusual beating or the figurative 'burning'.

Although the quantitative analysis does underlie the importance of the target domain MORALITY on the basis of frequency, from the point of the present research, it is worth taking a look at this domain. Various expressions can be clustered under the label of MORALITY, especially representing CONSCIENCE and HONESTY/STRAIGHTFORWARDNESS. The examples (1–5) attribute honesty and conscience to the heart.

(1) *szívből jön* 'honest, true' (it comes from the heart).
(2) *nyelvén a szíve* 'honest, s/he is telling the truth' (his/her heart is on his/her tongue).
(3) *nincs szíve ezt tenni* 'he/she can't bear to do this' (he/she has no heart to do this).
(4) *nyomja a szívét* 'something is in his/her heart, on his/her mind, on his/her conscience' (sg. presses his/her heart).
(5) *tiszta szívű* 'honesthearted, pure hearted' (clean/clear/pure hearted).

Example (1) conveys the idea that the inner part of the heart-container is a locus of true feelings and honesty. Various types of things and actions may come from the heart, such as gifts or good wishes – in the case of the former one, it is rather the emotions evoked, but in the latter case, good wishes, the heart represents honesty. However, the heart as a whole is also utilized as a source domain for honesty in example (2). Example (3) may refer to benevolence as well as conscience: having no heart to do something means one is prevented from completing an action by their conscience. A burden on one's heart is conceptualized not only as sadness (Baranyiné Kóczy, in press) but also as having something on one's conscience. Having a pure/clear/clean heart (example 5) means being free from immorality.

HEART in Relation to REASONING

From the findings delineated in the previous sections, we may well agree that there is plenty of evidence that in the Hungarian language, the head is viewed as the body part which hosts intellectual abilities, and the heart is perceived as the organ of various emotional processes. In this regard, the cultural model of the body seems to represent the HEAD–HEART dichotomy as evidenced in English and other languages. However, the bulk of expressions and corpus data, including *szív* 'heart', include numerous examples where the heart is referenced in connection with faculties which are believed to belong to reasoning.

First, the heart is often linked to MEMORY, as in examples (6–9).

(6) *emléke örökké szívünkben él* 'his/her memory will live in our heart forever'.
(7) *az emlék belevésődött a szívébe* 'the memory was engraved into his/her heart'.
(8) *emlékét a szívébe zárta* 'he/she closed his/her memory into his/her heart'.
(9) *ki akarta tépni a szívéből az utolsó emléket is* 'she wanted to tear even the last memory out of her heart'.

Accordingly, memories are located inside the heart: long-lasting memories 'live' in the heart (6) or they are engraved into the heart (7); note that MEMORY is also conceptualized via engraving something into the head. Pleasant memories are closed into the heart (8) and may become part of the heart (9), so when they turn to be bad ones, they need to be torn out of one's heart (9). In the case of memory, one may argue whether this faculty is purely intellectual, as remembering data may well differ from remembering someone or an event. The metaphorical examples of (6–9) are more similar to emotion metaphors than intellectual ones, for example, closing somebody into one's heart alludes to a love bond, hence closing memories of somebody into one's heart is understood in the same vein.

There are also several expressions where the heart is represented as part of thinking. The idea of having a burden on one's heart in example (4), *nyomja a szívét* 'sg. is in his/her heart, on his/her mind, on his/her conscience' (sg. presses his/her heart), may as well be used to refer to having a bad thought. Observe the following examples:

(10) *a szíve mélyén tudta* 'he knew deep in his heart'.
(11) *Az áttekintés alapján ugyanis nyugodt szívvel állíthatom, hogy. . .* 'Based on the review, I can say that' (Based on the review I can say with a calm heart that).
(12) *mindenki úgy gondolkodhat, ahogy a szíve diktálja* 'everybody can think as they like' (everybody can think as their heart dictates).

It can be observed that the heart can be linked to thinking in many ways. Example (10) relates to the issue of honesty in that truth is located deep inside the heart. Furthermore, reasonable thinking is ensured by having a 'calm heart', which may be based on the experience that the heart can disturb or influence thinking. However, it can also imply honesty and clear conscience: making a statement with a 'calm heart', that is, clear conscience, seems to be analogous to other usages of 'calm heart': *nyugodt szívvel elveheted* 'you may freely take it' (you may take it with a calm heart). In example (12), the heart is conceptualized as a commander of thinking, which guides the direction of thoughts.

Similar to THINKING, the process of UNDERSTANDING is captured in the following data (13-15):

(13) *Járjunk nyitott szemmel és nyitott szívvel, hogy felismerhessük és befogadhassuk ezeket a dolgokat.*
'Let's walk with open eyes and an open heart so that we can recognize and embrace these things.'
(14) *Olvass nyitott szívvel!* 'Read in an open-minded manner!' (Read with an open heart!)
(15) *A Biblia [. . .] helyes megértéséhez csak úgy lehet eljutni, ha minden más iratot és tudományt is az ember nyitott szívvel tanulmányoz.*
'A proper understanding of the Bible can only be achieved by studying all other writings and sciences with an open heart.'

As these usages show, performing an intellectual process with an open heart provides the ability to embrace experiences and impressions in a proper way. As in (13), while open eyes enable us to perceive external stimuli, in the next step, an open heart helps us implement these impressions into our reasoning. Reading in examples (14–15) is also an intellectual activity which is based on comprehension. Taking a look at these examples raises the question of what precisely is the meaning of 'open heart' in the context of understanding. In Hungarian, when talking about close reading, it is also possible to refer to it as reading with open ears (*nyitott füllel. olvas* 'he/she is reading with open ears'). The difference between reading with open ears or open heart emphasizes different aspects of understanding: in these contrastive examples, it is the EAR which indicates the logical part in cognition, for example, it indicates that one pays attention to every detail and he is able to capture the overall meaning of the message. On the other hand, comprehension with an 'open heart' conveys the idea that one is open to embracing novel and often unusual ideas, which may even have an impact on his whole personality. Thus, the HEART maps onto one's full involvement into mental processes and represents the SELF, or the whole personality.

Language expressing OPINION may also entail figurative reference to the HEART.

(16) *Én szívem szerint ingyenessé tettem volna a karácsony előtti tömegközlekedést.* 'I would have made public transport in the period prior to Christmas free of charge.' (According to my heart, I would have made public transport in the period prior to Christmas free of charge.)
(17) *Ki mit szól hozzá, az a szíve joga.* 'what anyone thinks about it is up to them' (what anyone says to it is the right of their heart).
(18) *szívéből szól/beszél* 'he/she means it' (he/she speaks form his/her heart).

All the examples in (16–18) evidence that opinion is guided by the heart, moreover, according to (17), judgement is the 'right of the heart', which attests that decision making is primarily the responsibility of the heart. Speaking 'form the heart' (18) refers to the act of expressing one's point of view firmly. Again, similar to several earlier examples, the inner part of the heart is associated with truth and honesty, whatever a person thinks, feels or morally perceives. Related to opinion, the heart is also involved in giving ADVICE.

(19) *Kinek-kinek szive tanácsadó.* 'Our acts are driven by our heart' (everyone's heart is their advisor).
(20) *szívére kötötte* 'he/she persuaded him/her' (he/she tided it onto his/her heart).

The common interpretation of the conceptualization HEART AS ADVISOR is that emotions have quite a responsibility in driving our actions. The expression 'to tide/knot something onto one's heart' is also related to advice but in this case, the HEART represents OPINION analogous to the former cases (16–18). In this metaphor, 'persuasion' is the physical act of tiding an entity (an ontological metaphor for THOUGHT or IDEA) onto the external surface of the heart. This conceptualization is also present in connection with the soul: *lelkére kötötte* 'he/she persuaded him/her' (he/she tided it onto his/her soul). Interestingly, the fact that the entity which stands for the convincing argument is not located inside the heart, which suggests that it is not yet entirely accepted by the owner of the heart.

Another faculty considered 'mental' is DECISION, where the semantic role of the HEART is represented by expressions as follows:

(21) *Csak akkor tudunk ennek a hitelnek a sorsáról nyugodt szívvel és felelősséggel dönteni, ha . . .*
'We can only make a decision about this loan with responsibility if . . . (We can only make a decision about this loan with a calm heart and responsibility if . . .)'

(22) *nyugodt szívvel tesz* 'he/she acts without any problem' (he/she acts with a calm heart).

(23) *Adjunk lehetőséget a minisztériumnak arra, hogy átszámolja a költségeket, és azt mi nyugodt szívvel megszavazhassuk.*
Let the ministry have the opportunity to recalculate the costs so that we can vote for it. (so that we can vote for it with a calm heart).

The recurring expression which involves the heart is *nyugodt szívvel* 'with a calm heart', whose meaning unfolds in the usage context. In example (21) 'calm heart' and 'responsibility' appear side by side, which suggests that having one's heart in a calm state is a basic condition for making well-founded and informed decisions. In reality, RESPONSIBILITY is not a concept which is linked to the intellectual self, but rather it has a moral relevance. In this respect, 'calm heart' may refer to 'clear conscience'. However, examples (22), and especially (23), seem to describe the role of the heart in reasoning as a supporter of decisions, where the quality of 'calmness' is mapped onto 'informed, reasonable decisions', contrary to a 'disturbed' state of the heart, which may mean an emotionally disturbed decision.

We have seen that in various figurative expressions in Hungarian the HEART is involved in intellectual processes such as MEMORY, THINKING, UNDERSTANDING, OPINION, ADVICE and DECISION. A closer look at these expressions, especially from a usage-based perspective, raises several questions concerning their meanings. Two of these will be discussed in the next section, namely, (1) What is/are the figurative meaning(s) of the HEART in the expressions describing intellectual processes? (2) What explains these conceptualizations of the heart?

Heart as a Verifier of Reasoning

During the analysis of expressions referring to various intellectual faculties, I indicated that in some cases the figurative meaning of the HEART seems to unfold easily while in other cases it remains rather vague. There are three clusters of meaning which emerge in the expressions.

HEART AS EMOTIONS:

(24) *jó szívvel ajánlhatom* 'I can recommend it' (I can recommend it with a good heart).
(25) *Jó szívvel támogatjuk az előterjesztést.* 'We wholeheartedly support the proposal' (We support the proposal with a good heart).
(26) *Szívből gratulálok!* 'My heartfelt congratulations!' (I congratulate from my heart).
(27) *Szívesen meghallgatlak* 'I'm ready to listen to you' (I will listen to you heartily).

In these cases, the heart embodies a positive emotional attitude towards some act, such as suggestion, support, congratulation or listening. The meaning of the heart may be described as 'benevolence' in (24) and (25), while emotional involvement (liking, favour) is clearly present in (26) and (27). It was also indicated that emotional attachment is present in examples in connection with MEMORY.

(28) *ki akarta tépni a szívéből az utolsó emléket is* 'she wanted to tear even the last memory out of her heart'.

As mentioned, the proverb (19) conveys the meaning that emotions have a dominant role in decision making. The interface between intellectual acts and emotions may have two basic interpretations. One observation is that each of these phrases exist and are often used without the heart expression, such as, *támogatjuk az előterjesztést* 'we support the proposal' or *gratulálok* 'congratulations'. By comparing *gratulálok* 'congratulations' and *szívből gratulálok* 'my heartfelt congratulations', the involvement of the heart accentuates that the acting person 'means' what he/she is doing. Consequently, the HEART AS EMOTIONS metaphor in the context of reasoning indicates that emotional support strengthens one's engagement in certain mental activities. In a slightly different interpretation, emotional underpinning does not only support intellectual activities but it is essential for responsible mental activity.

In some other instances, the HEART represents MORAL CONSCIENCE, which is a core concept of Christian religious belief.

HEART AS MORAL CONSCIENCE:

(29) *nyugodt szívvel tesz* 'he/she acts without any problem' (he/she acts with calm heart).
(30) *nyugodt szívvel fogok meghalni* 'I can die without any regrets' (I will die with a calm heart).
(31) *szívére kötötte* 'he/she persuaded him/her' (he/she tided it onto his/her heart).
(32) *tiszta szívű* 'honesthearted, pure hearted' (clean/clear/pure hearted).
(33) *nincs szíve ezt tenni* 'he/she can't bear to do this' (he/she has no heart to do this).
(34) *nyomja a szívét* 'something is in his/her heart, on his/her mind, on his/her conscience' (sg. presses his/her heart).

A 'calm heart' may have various meanings such as a positive mood not affected/disturbed by negative emotions. However, 'calmness' is commonly associated with conscience: *nyugodt lelkiismeret* 'clear conscience' (calm conscience) or *nyugodt a lelkiismerete* 'he/she has a clear conscience' (his/her conscience is calm) is the general expression for morality and virtue. The semantic component of 'tiding' which is present in the metaphorical example (31) can be also found in similar expressions, such as *lelkére kötötte* 'he/she persuaded him/her' (he/she tided it onto his/her soul). Both expressions may allude to situations where persuasion involves addressing one's conscience. In example (32), the heart connects to one's moral character, while (33-34) exhibit the heart as THE SEAT OF CONSCIOUSNESS. Thus, this conceptualization resides in the idea that reasoning and intellectual acts require moral guidance.

Finally, in the vast majority of phrases, it is honesty, truth, the 'real self', which are metaphorically represented by the heart. Speaking from the heart or knowing something deep in one's heart refers to one's real ideas, opinion or feelings, which are often kept in secret. In this respect, honesty is not always linked to one's conscience but rather to inseparable faculties of the self. Thus, in various usage instances, the heart stands for the whole personality.

HEART FOR THE WHOLE PERSON:

(35) *ki mit szól hozzá, az a szíve joga* 'what anyone thinks about it is up to them' (what anyone says to it is the right of their heart).

(36) *Bármilyen szolgálatot kész szívvel vállalnék.* 'I would take any service eagerly' (with a willing/ready heart).

If the heart has a fundamental role in judgement (35), it means that whatever one thinks or believes is up to them; therefore, the underlying metonymy for this expression is THE HEART FOR THE WHOLE PERSON. In another example (36), a 'ready' heart stands for willingness, a persons' positive and active attitude in general towards undertaking a service.

We can observe three conceptualizations of the HEART in close relation to intellectual processes: HEART AS EMOTION, HEART AS MORAL CONSCIENCE and HEART FOR THE WHOLE PERSONALITY. The question is therefore: What is the conceptual/psychological/cultural foundation for these conceptualizations? A(n at least) partial explanation can be the following. Damasio in *Descartes' Error* (1994) argues that the Cartesian dualism covers a theory which is not applicable to human psyche because mere intellectual reasoning is an impossibility: human thinking is always supported and strengthened by emotions. He asserts that emotions are created in the brain, which controls the accompanying bodily reactions and thus links physiological body changes with emotions. Intellectual processes are in this way naturally interwoven with emotional reactions. Following this view, we can also claim that at least a large part of reasoning requires moral reflection, hence reasoning is also closely connected to the concept of morality. Finally, if rational and irrational faculties are to some extent blended, it is easy to understand that HEART FOR THE WHOLE PERSON conceptualization, which implies that rational acts often entail the involvement of various faculties of a person at a time.

Conclusion

To sum up the observations, we can conclude that at first sight, the Hungarian cultural cognition primarily attests rational thinking to the HEAD and irrational (emotional) faculties to the HEART. However, our analysis and especially corpus data show that, contrary to the Cartesian dichotomic view of the emotional versus intellectual faculties, in many cases the two faculties are naturally linked. The linguistic data provides evidence that the heart functions as an advisor, supporter, intensifier or even controller of various processes of intellectual reasoning. Furthermore, these roles of the heart are related to three metaphorical meanings: HEART AS EMOTION, HEART AS MORAL CONSCIENCE and HEART FOR THE WHOLE PERSONALITY. Based on these observations, it is evidenced that the Hungarian language features basically a dualistic cultural model but it exhibits flexibility in various intellectual domains, such as MEMORY, THINKING, UNDERSTANDING, OPINION and DECISION. The present chapter also argues that, although these faculties are considered intellectual ones in theory, the language data proves well how they are naturally combined with emotional or moral reflections and considerations in practice. Sometimes the whole personality, that is, the 'self' is involved in supporting or urging rational acts.

These findings are not only relevant to a closer understanding of the cultural models present in the Hungarian language, but they also highlight the necessity of usage-based and corpus-driven research of the figurative extensions of body parts across languages. Several examples discussed in the previous sections (e.g. 'open heart', 'calm heart') highlight that figurative meaning is strongly context-dependent. As we have seen, the metaphoric and metonymic meanings of the HEART in any language and culture highlight how the human faculties are interconnected in the cognition of a cultural community.

References

Abdramanova, S. (in press), 'HEART in the Kazakh language', in J. Baranyiné Kóczy, and K. Sipőcz (eds), *Embodiment in Cross-Linguistic Studies: 'The Heart'*, Leiden: Brill.

Baranyiné Kóczy, J. (2019a), 'More than Emotions: Cultural Conceptualizations of *szív* "Heart" in Hungarian', In J. Baranyiné Kóczy, and K. Sipőcz (eds), *Embodiment in Cross-Linguistic Studies: 'The Heart'*, Leiden: Brill.

Baranyiné Kóczy, J. (2019b), '"He Cracked His Head Feverishly": Conceptualizations of Head and Thinking in Hungarian', in I. Kraska-Szlenk (ed), *Embodiment in Cross-Linguistic Studies: The 'Head'*, 219–44, Leiden: Brill.

Bárczi, G., and L. Országh (1962), *A magyar nyelv értelmező szótára VI.* [Dictionary of the Hungarian Language VI.], Budapest: Akadémiai Kiadó.

Bárdosi, V. (2013), *Lassan a testtel! Emberi testrészek a magyar szólásokban, közmondásokban [Not So Fast! Human Body Parts in Hungarian Proverbs and Sayings]*, Budapest: Tinta Kiadó.

Baş, M. (2015), 'Conceptualization of Emotion through Body Part Idioms in Turkish: A Cognitive Linguistic Study', PhD Diss., Turkey: Hacettepe University.

Berendt, E. A., and K. Tanita (2011), 'The "Heart" of Things: A Conceptual Metaphoric Analysis of Heart and Related Body Parts in Thai, Japanese and English', *Intercultural Communication Studies*, 20(1): 65–78.

Damasio, A. (1994), *Descartes' Error: Emotion, Reason and the Human Brain*. New York: Avon.

D'Andrade, R. (1987), 'A Folk Model of the Mind', in D. Holland, and N. Quinn (eds), *Cultural Models in Language and Thought*, 112–48, Cambridge: Cambridge University Press. doi:10.1017/CBO9780511607660.006

Foolen, A. (2008), 'The Heart as a Source of Semiosis: The Case of Dutch', in F. Sharifian et al. (eds), *Culture, Body, and Language: Conceptualizations of Internal Body Organs across Cultures and Languages*, 373–94, Berlin, New York: Mouton de Gruyter.

Gaby, A. (2008), 'Gut Feelings: Locating Intellect, Emotion, and Life Force in the Thaayorre Body', in F. Sharifian et al. (eds), *Culture, Body, and Language: Conceptualizations of Internal Body Organs across Cultures and Languages*, 27–44, Berlin, New York: Mouton de Gruyter.

Geeraerts, D., and C. Gevaert (2008), 'Hearts and (Angry) Minds in Old English', in F. Sharifian et al. (eds), *Culture, Body, and Language: Conceptualizations of Internal Body Organs across Cultures and Languages*, 319–48, Berlin, New York: Mouton de Gruyter.

Goddard, C. (2001), '"Hati": A Key Word in the Malay Vocabulary of Emotion', In J. Harkins, and A. Wierzbicka (eds), *Emotions in Cross-Linguistic Perspective*, 167–95, Berlin/New York.:Mouton de Gruyter.

HNC=Magyar Nemzeti Szövegtár [Hungarian National Corpus] (1998–2003), Budapest: Magyar Tudományos Akadémia Nyelvtudományi Intézete. http://corpus.nytud.hu/mnsz/

Huang, S. (2002), 'Tsou is Different: A Cognitive Perspective on Language: Emotion and Body', *Cognitive Linguistics*, 13(2): 167–86.

Ikegami, Y. (2008): 'The Heart: What it Means to the Japanese Speakers', in F. Sharifian et al. (eds), *Culture, Body, and Language: Conceptualizations of Internal Body Organs across Cultures and Languages*, 169–90, Berlin, New York: Mouton de Gruyter.

Khabtagaeva, B., and S. Szeverényi (in press), 'The HEART in Buryat', in J. Baranyiné Kóczy, and K. Sipőcz (eds), *Embodiment in Cross-Linguistic Studies: 'The Heart'*. Leiden: Brill.

Kraska-Szlenk, I. (2005), *The Semantic Network of Swahili Moyo 'Heart': A Corpus-Based Cognitive Analysis. Studies of the Department of African Languages and Cultures*, Warsaw: University of Warsaw.

Kraska-Szlenk, I. (2014), 'Semantic Extensions of Body Part Terms: Common Patterns and Their Interpretation', *Language Sciences*, 44: 15–39.

Kövecses, Z. (2015), *Where Metaphors Come From: Reconsidering Context in Metaphor*. Oxford: Oxford University Press.

Lakoff, G., and M. Johnson (1980), *Metaphors We Live By*. Chicago: University of Chicago Press.

Maalej, Z. (2004), 'Figurative Language in Anger Expressions in Tunisian Arabic: An Extended View of Embodiment', *Metaphor and Symbol*, 19(1): 51–75.

Maalej, Z. (in press), 'Culturally Embodied Conceptualizations of the *Heart*, with Special Reference to Tunisian Arabic', in J. Baranyiné Kóczy, and K. Sipőcz (eds), *Embodiment in cross-linguistic studies: 'The heart'*. Leiden: Brill.

Maalej, Z., and N. Yu (2011), *Embodiment Via Body Parts: Studies from Various Languages and Cultures*. Amsterdam: John Benjamins Publishing.

Nosrati, V. (in press) 'On the Linguistic Expressions of *dil* "Heart" in Kurdish', in J. Baranyiné Kóczy, and K. Sipőcz (eds), *Embodiment in Cross-Linguistic Studies: The Heart'*. Leiden: Brill.

Niemeier, S. (2000), 'Straight from the Heart – Metonymic and Metaphorical Explorations', In A. Barcelona (ed), *Metaphor and Metonymy at the Crossroads: A Cognitive Perspective*, 195–213, The Hague: Mouton de Gruyter.

Niemeier, S. (2008), 'To Be in Control: Kind-Hearted and Cool-Headed The Head-Heart Dichotomy in English', in F. Sharifian et al. (eds), *Culture, Body, and Language: Conceptualizations of Internal Body Organs across Cultures and Languages*, 349–72, Berlin, New York: Mouton de Gruyter.

Occhi, D. J. (2008), 'How to have a HEART in Japanese', in F. Sharifian et al. (eds), *Culture, Body, and Language: Conceptualizations of Internal Body Organs across Cultures and Languages*, 191–213, Berlin, New York: Mouton de Gruyter.

Pattilo, K. (in press), 'The Sanctity of English 'Heart'', in J. Baranyiné Kóczy, and K. Sipőcz (eds), *Embodiment in Cross-Linguistic Studies: The 'Heart'*, Leiden: Brill.

Quinn, N., and D. Holland (eds) (1987), *Cultural Models in Language and Thought*, Cambridge: Cambridge University Press.

Sharifian, F. (2008), 'Conceptualizations of Del "Heart-Stomach" in Persian', in F. Sharifian et al. (eds), *Culture, Body, and Language: Conceptualizations of Internal Body Organs across Cultures and Languages*, 247–65, Berlin, New York: Mouton de Gruyter.

Sharifian, F., R. Dirven, N. Yu, and S. Niemeier (eds) (2008), *Culture, Body, and Language: Conceptualizations of Internal Body Organs across Cultures and Languages*. Berlin, New York: Mouton de Gruyter.

Shehu, A. (in press), 'The Conceptualizations and Semantic Extensions of 'Bernde' 'Heart' in Fulfulde', in J. Baranyiné Kóczy, and K. Sipőcz (eds), *Embodiment in Cross-Linguistic Studies: The 'Heart'*, Leiden: Brill.

Siahaan, P. (2008), '"Did He Break Your Heart or Your Liver?" A Contrastive Study on Metaphorical Concepts from the Source Domain Organ in English and in Indonesian', in F. Sharifian et al. (eds), *Culture, Body, and Language: Conceptualizations of Internal Body Organs across Cultures and Languages*, 45–74, Berlin, New York: Mouton de Gruyter.

Szemerkényi, Á. (2009), *Szólások és közmondások* [Proverbs and sayings], Budapest: Osiris Kiadó.

Witte, J. J. de (1948), 'De betekeniswereld van het lichaam. Taalpsychologische, taalvergelijkende studie [The Meaning World of the Body: Language Psychological and Language Comparative Study]', PhD Diss., Nijmegen.

Yoon, K. Y. (2008), 'The Korean Conceptualisations of Heart: An Indigenous Perspective', in F. Sharifian et al. (eds), *Culture, Body, and Language:*

Conceptualizations of Internal Body Organs across Cultures and Languages, 213–47, Berlin, New York: Mouton de Gruyter.

Yu, N. (2007), 'Heart and Cognition in Ancient Chinese Philosophy', *Journal of Cognition and Culture*, 7: 27–47.

Yu, N. (2008), 'The Chinese Heart as the Central Faculty of Cognition', in F. Sharifian et al. (eds), *Culture, Body, and Language: Conceptualizations of Internal Body Organs across Cultures and Languages*, 131–68, Berlin, New York: Mouton de Gruyter.

# 3

A Comparative Study of English, Italian and Polish Conceptual Metaphors of Emotion Regulation and Cognitive Inhibition

Marcin Trojszczak and Chiara Astrid Gebbia

Introduction[1]

The role of figurative language in understanding emotion and cognition has been one of central topics in cognitive linguistics since its inception (see Lakoff and Johnson 1980). Although both of these domains have received a lot of scholarly attention (see, for instance, Kövecses 1986, 1990, 2000; Ansah 2014, for emotions; and Jäkel 1995; Lakoff and Johnson 1999; Fortescue 2001; Amberber 2007; Trojszczak 2019a for cognition), there are still some issues that deserve a more in-depth investigation. One of them is the role of metaphor in understanding and describing two closely connected yet linguistically under-researched concepts, that is, emotion regulation and cognitive inhibition.

The present chapter aims to address this issue by means of the comparative and contrastive analysis of the way we metaphorically speak about emotion regulation and cognitive inhibition in English, Italian and Polish. In order to achieve this goal, it combines empirical findings about the metaphors of emotion regulation from Trojszczak and Gebbia (2020), language data from selected corpora of English (BNC), Italian (CORIS, Paisà, Aranea) and Polish (NKJP) concerning cognitive inhibition, and theoretical insights from conceptual metaphor theory (Lakoff and Johnson 1980, 1999; Kövecses 2015, 2020) and its recent extension, that is, theory of objectification (Szwedek 2011, 2014).

Regulating Emotions and Thoughts[2]

Emotions are among the finest and most crucial means at the disposal of humans, not only for their biological adaptive role in our evolution but also for serving a wide range of interpersonal functions on a daily basis, for instance, affiliation, distancing (see Fisher and Manstead 2016; Niedenthal and Ric 2017; Dukes, Samson and Walle 2022, for more details). As regards the latter aspect, not all emotional reactions are perceived as socially functional. Human beings have, therefore, evolved to regulate, intentionally or subconsciously, an emotion which is perceived as inappropriate in a particular situation (instrumental motivation), for the self-well-being (hedonic motive), or to preserve social bonds (prosocial motive) – this ability is called *emotion regulation* (see Koole 2009; Fisher and Manstead 2016; Niedenthal and Ric 2017; Duncan Kerr 2021; Garofalo 2022; Riediger and Bellingtier 2022, for discussions approaching this issue from different angles).

We can intervene on the emotion before it is elicited (situation selection, situation modification, attentional deployment), or as it is experienced (expressive behaviour regulation, physiological arousal regulation, cognitive change) (Suri and Gross 2016; Niedenthal and Ric 2017). Emotion regulation *stricto sensu* may occur through physical changes, by controlling the intensity or the type of emotion displayed or felt (Niedenthal and Ric 2017: 197–8). We may also tend to re-evaluate our interpretation (or mentalization) of a situation or event (Greenberg et al. 2017), or we can decide to focus on certain thoughts over others in order to modify the emotions felt (attentional deployment) (MacLeod 2007: 5).

Whenever we aim to ignore an interfering stimulus, try to suppress a mental representation, or to turn off a mental process which is too costly to process in a given situation, we perform a closely connected mental activity of *cognitive inhibition* (Arbuthnott at al. 2000: 331; MacLeod 2007: 5). Sometimes referred to as cognitive repression, thought suppression or restraining, this cognitive mechanism functions as part of the more general cognitive control system and includes, among others, mental processes such as alternating attention and refreshing information in working memory (MacLeod 2007). Moreover, cognitive inhibition is inextricably linked to white bear problem (ironic rebound), which is a psychological process in which deliberate attempts to inhibit certain thoughts make them more likely to appear in the mind (see, for instance, Wegner 1994).

Metaphors, Emotions and Cognition[3]

Research on metaphor and its role in our understanding of the outside world and our experiences has a long tradition stretching back to antiquity (see Taverniers 2002; Rolf 2005). In contemporary linguistics, this phenomenon has been studied in great detail in cognitive linguistics, which emphasizes embodiment and cultural-situatedness of language as well as its multiple interconnections with psychological processes (see Dancygier 2017). In this context, conceptual metaphor theory (Lakoff and Johnson 1980, 1999; Kövecses 2015, 2020) is particularly important and influential. This approach assumes that metaphors are not mere stylistic figures of speech, but they are systematic and unidirectional (from concrete-to-abstract domains) conceptual mappings which organize to a large extent our ways of thinking (see Lakoff and Johnson 1999; Lakoff 2016). According to conceptual metaphor theory, metaphorical linguistic expressions such as *scacciare via i pensieri* 'to chase away thoughts' or *przełamać strach* 'to break through fear' are grounded in our everyday experiences including bodily reactions as well as perception of subjective similarities and repeated correlations between physical objects (Kövecses 2005).

The importance of sensory, particularly tactile, experience of physical objects in the creation of linguistic metaphors is highlighted in theory of objectification (Szwedek 2011, 2014, 2018), which is one of the most recent developments of Lakoffian and Johnsonian framework. In this approach, a metaphorical linguistic expression such as *to suppress anger* or *to reject the idea* is the final result of the process of objectification (concrete-to-abstract metaphorization) which starts with perceptual experiences of the properties of physical objects, involves the storage of this sensory data in THE PHYSICAL OBJECT schema and ends up with mapping them onto abstract and impalpable concepts such as anger or idea in order to facilitate their understanding (see Szwedek 2014, 2018, for more details).

Since concepts such as emotions and cognition are highly abstract, metaphors seem to be natural means of comprehending them, which is well attested by a plethora of linguistic research. As for emotions, based on his extended research into different types of emotion metaphors, Kövecses (2008) distinguishes the overarching metaphor EMOTIONS ARE FORCES, common conceptualizations such as EMOTION IS A FLUID IN A CONTAINER or EMOTION IS HEAT/FIRE as well as a range of emotion-specific metaphors including LOVE IS A NUTRIENT, FEAR IS AN ILLNESS and ANGER IS A CAPTIVE ANIMAL (see Kövecses 2000, for more examples). Although his findings are applicable to most surveyed languages, it is worth mentioning that especially on more fine-grained levels, both evaluative and phenomenological, we could find more culturally specific metaphors such as HAPPINESS IS ELECTRICITY in Persian (Safarnejad et al. 2014) or ANGER IS A GROWING WEED in Akan (Ansah 2014).

Cognitive processes are no different than emotions as they also require metaphorical language in order to be understood and described. Jäkel (1995) proposes the cognitive model of mental activity which is based on the overarching metaphor MENTAL ACTIVITY IS MANIPULATION and the specific conceptual metaphor THINKING IS WORKING ON THE OBJECT-PROBLEM WITH THE HELP OF THE TOOL-MIND. Other metaphors of thinking include THINKING IS MOVING, THINKING IS PERCEIVING and THINKING IS OBJECT MANIPULATION (Lakoff and Johnson 1999) as well as cross-linguistically varying metaphors THINKING IS WEIGHING and THINKING IS CALCULATING (Fortescue 2001). On the other hand, ideas are mainly conceptualized as physical and manipulable objects with various sensory qualities (see Lakoff and Johnson 1999; Szwedek 2014; Trojszczak 2019a). Research into metaphors of cognition is, however, not exhausted by insights about thinking as it also includes an array of findings concerning attention (see Fernandez-Duque and Johnson 2002; Trojszczak 2017a), memory (see Amberber 2007; Trojszczak 2019b) and mind (Koivisto-Alanko and Tissari 2006).

Methodology[4]

This chapter investigates metaphorical conceptualizations of emotion regulation and cognitive inhibition from the perspective of corpus-based cognitive linguistics (Lewandowska-Tomaszczyk 2012), in particular a corpus-illustrated approach (Tummers, Heylen and Geeraerts 2005). In this methodological perspective, language corpora are seen as reliable sources providing systematic and comprehensive insights into real language data in general and cognitive conceptualizations in particular (Stefanowitsch 2006b; Deignan 2008).

The analysed data is comprised of seventy-four metaphorical expressions for emotion regulation and thirty-four for cognitive inhibition.[5] These expressions have been retrieved from the following selection of corpora for each of the languages considered: the British National Corpus (BNC), the Corpus di Italiano Scritto (CORIS), Paisà and Aranea for Italian and the National Corpus of Polish (NKJP). While the BNC, CORIS, Paisà and NKJP are standard reference corpora, Aranea is identified as a set of comparable corpora

(Benko 2014). In this latter case, solely Italian corpus has been included in the analysis.[6]

As regards basic emotions (see Trojszczak and Gebbia 2020, for the discussion of this concept), the investigated lexemes included *anger, disgust, happiness/joy, surprise, sadness, fear(s)* (for English); *rabbia, disgusto, gioia/felicità, sorpresa, tristezza, paura* (for Italian) and *gniew, wstręt/obrzydzenie, radość/szczęście, zaskoczenie, smutek, strach/obawa* (for Polish). Conversely, in the analysis of metaphorical conceptualizations of thoughts, the lexemes analysed consisted of *thought(s)* and *idea(s)* for English, *pensiero/i* and *idea/e* for Italian, and *myśl(i), pomysł(y)* for Polish.

While extracting language data, we made use of search engines developed for the corpora as well as the approach known as *source domain vocabulary search* (Stefanowitsch 2006a). In KWIC (Key Word in Context) analysis, the entries denoting basic emotions and thoughts have been scrutinized by typing in the selected lexical item and checking up its verb + noun concordances (see also Trojszczak and Gebbia 2020, for a similar methodology). The verb was marked as metaphorical if it satisfied the criteria of metaphorical identification procedure (Pragglejaz Group 2007), according to which a lexical item is metaphorical if there is a substantial difference, yet some degree of similarity, between its most basic sense or etymological sense and its contextual one (see Trim 2011, for the role of etymology in metaphor studies).

Lastly, it is important to underline that the present analysis does not tackle the differences among six basic emotions or among three languages taken into account, as these aspects were extensively analysed in our former study (Trojszczak and Gebbia 2020). On the contrary, this research focuses on identifying possible overarching metaphors (see Kövecses 2010) for the control of emotions and thoughts, and the underlying ones which are more specific for each of the concepts investigated. In so doing, only expressions found in at least two languages will be scrutinized.

Inhibiting Emotions and Thoughts is Limiting Physical Contact with Them[7]

The analysis of corpus data from English, Polish and Italian indicates that as far as similarities between metaphorical conceptualizations of regulating unwanted emotions and inhibiting intrusive thoughts are concerned, they can be grouped under the overarching conceptual metaphor EMOTION REGULATION/COGNITIVE

INHIBITION IS LIMITING PHYSICAL CONTACT. This general metaphor can be seen as the objectification which consists of three specific mappings. First, both emotions and thoughts are metaphorically perceived as physical objects possessing various default sensory properties such as weight, size, self-propelled movement or manipulability (see Szwedek 2011, 2014, 2018; Lakoff and Johnson 1999). Second, regulating or inhibiting emotions and thoughts is conceptualized in terms of the human agent attempting to limit or reduce the physical contact with these physical objects either completely or to a certain degree. This is achieved by means of various manipulations and interactions (see Jäkel 1995, for OBJECT MANIPULATION metaphor). Third, if the human agent manages to limit the physical contact, he or she regains control over unwanted emotions or thoughts and does not suffer from their negative impact (see Kövecses 2000: 83, for the metaphor EMOTIONAL EFFECT IS PHYSICAL CONTACT). Overall, the essence of this overarching metaphor could be described in the following way: the less intense the physical contact with unwanted emotions and thoughts, the better their inhibition/regulation.

Major Similarities: Pushing Away and Moving Away

Within this general metaphor, we can distinguish five more specific metaphorical images that differ in terms of (1) physical activities by means of which the limitation of contact can be achieved; (2) their language distribution; and (3) their distribution across six basic emotions. Among these metaphorical images, the most important are INHIBITING UNWANTED EMOTIONS AND THOUGHTS IS PUSHING THEM AWAY and INHIBITING UNWANTED EMOTIONS AND THOUGHTS IS MOVING THEM AWAY as they are found not only in the corpus data from three analysed languages, but also in the majority of basic emotions plus thoughts.

The metaphor INHIBITING UNWANTED EMOTIONS AND THOUGHTS IS PUSHING THEM AWAY is the most widespread one as it is used in three analysed languages to describe and comprehend the activities of inhibiting unwanted thoughts, for example, *sopprimere i pensieri* 'to suppress thoughts', *stłumić myśli* 'to suppress thoughts',[8] *wyprzeć myśli* 'to displace, to crowd out ideas', *to suppress the idea*,[9] *push the thought away, force the thought away*, and regulating five basic emotions with the exception of surprise, for example, *to suppress anger, to eliminate fears*,[10] *tłumić gniew* 'to suppress anger', *confinare la rabbia* 'to intern, retain anger within limits'. This metaphor consists of three mappings: (1) unwanted emotions and thoughts are perceived as physical objects that are in physical contact with the human agent and exert some kind of pressure on him or her, for example, because they are too heavy or they press forward; (2) the human agent perceives the intensity of this physical contact as no longer acceptable – the pressure or physical force is too high to bear (see Kövecses 2010: 63, for the emotion metaphors of pressure and physical force); (3) the human agent attempts to reduce it by pressing or pushing unwanted emotions and thoughts back/away from himself or herself. If he or she is successful in this attempt, the physical object-emotion/thought which was pressing forward does not do it anymore, ergo the physical contact has been limited.

The second most widespread metaphor, which can be found in all analysed languages and in four basic emotions except for joy and surprise, is INHIBITING UNWANTED EMOTIONS AND THOUGHTS IS MOVING THEM AWAY. In this metaphor, unwanted emotions and thoughts are conceptualized as purportedly immobile physical objects which are placed in the vicinity of the human agent. Although this physical closeness does not necessarily entail physical contact or pressure from emotions or thoughts as in the previously described metaphor, the human agent finds their presence unbearable. In an attempt to deal with this displeasing situation, he or she decides to metaphorically widen the distance. The first way of doing this is putting thoughts or emotions away as manifested in metaphorical linguistic expressions such as *spazzare i pensieri* 'to sweep thoughts away', *allontanare i pensieri* 'to take away thoughts', *odsuwać myśli* 'to put thoughts away', *pozbyć się myśli* 'to get rid of thoughts', *to get the thought out, to remove fear, to extinguish fear*,[11] *allontanare la tristezza* 'to take away sadness', *allontanare la paura* 'to take away fear', *pozbyć się strachu* 'to get rid of fear'. The second type of action is throwing them away, for example, *to reject the thought, to scrap the idea, wyrzucić myśli* 'to throw away thoughts', *to ease sadness*,[12] *odrzucić obawy* 'to throw away fears'. Here, unwanted emotions and thoughts are metaphorically objectified as small physical objects that could be easily picked up and thrown away by means of hands. All in all, in both sub-images, the success of the activity of moving unwanted emotions or thoughts away is measured by a lack of physical contact or closeness between them and the human agent.

A Minor Similarity: Stopping the Movement

The metaphor INHIBITING UNWANTED ANGER AND THOUGHTS IS STOPPING THEIR MOVEMENT is the example of a shared, specific conceptualization whose distribution across languages and emotions is very limited. It can be only found in the corpus data from Polish and Italian where it is employed to metaphorically describe thoughts and only one emotion, that is, anger. In this metaphor, which is manifested in the expressions such as *arrestare i pensieri* 'to block thoughts', *zahamować myśli* 'to stop thoughts', *bloccare la rabbia* 'to stop, block anger', *zahamować gniew* 'to stop anger', dealing with unwanted emotions and thoughts is conceptualized as the physical activity in which a human being attempts to slow down, reduce or entirely halt the movement of intrusive ideas or feelings. This metaphor consists of three specific mappings. First, emotions and thoughts are objectified as physical objects which can move of their own accord with a certain speed and in a particular direction – towards the human agent, closer to him or her. Second, the human agent perceives this movement as dangerous because it might result in too much physical contact, for instance, running over or breaking him or her apart. Third, in order to avoid this scenario, the agent exerts a counterforce aiming at stopping, blocking or slowing down the incoming emotions or thoughts. If he or she manages to do so, the intensity of the movement is reduced and, as a result, the actual or potential physical contact is limited and no longer threatening.

Major Differences: Chasing and Running Away

Major differences within this overarching metaphor, which indicate two alternative ways of limiting contact with unwanted emotions and thoughts, include INHIBITING UNWANTED THOUGHTS IS CHASING THEM AWAY and INHIBITING SADNESS IS RUNNING AWAY FROM IT.

As far as the first metaphor is concerned, it is thought-specific and could be found in three analysed languages. This metaphor is manifested in the expressions such as *to drive the thought from, scacciare via i pensieri* 'to chase away thoughts', *przepędzić myśli* 'to chase thoughts off', *odganiać myśli* 'to chase thoughts away from', *nie dopuszczać myśli* 'not to let thoughts in', or *tenere lontano i pensieri* 'to keep thoughts away'. In this metaphor, unwanted and intrusive thoughts are perceived as self-propelled objects which move in groups similar to swarms of bees or herds of animals (see Lakoff and Johnson 1999, for the metaphor THINKING IS MOVING; see also Kövecses 2000: 69, for the metaphor EMOTION IS A WILD ANIMAL). These dynamic and actively moving objects attempt to be in physical contact with the human agent who in order to avoid or limit it performs an equally dynamic counteraction, that is, running after them and, by doing so, trying to force them away and scare them off from his or her surroundings.

The second difference that pertains to the analysed overarching metaphor refers to sadness and is found only in Polish and Italian data. In the specific metaphor INHIBITING SADNESS IS RUNNING AWAY FROM IT, attempting to regulate or control sadness is conceptualized in terms of escaping from a moving and self-propelled physical object which tries to touch us or get hold of us. This metaphorical image is indicated by the expressions *uciec od smutku* 'to run away from sadness', *sfuggire dalla tristezza* 'to escape from sadness', and *non farsi prendere dalla tristezza* 'not to let yourself be taken by sadness'. Here, the successful escape is equated to a lack of physical contact which metaphorically stands for the control over sadness.

Other Metaphorical Images and Differences[13]

Besides the overarching metaphor, we also distinguished two other, emotion-specific images that deserve to be mentioned since they concern fear, which not only plays a key role in protecting us from life-threatening situations (see Scarantino 2016) but also, as shown in our data, is characterized by the highest number of metaphors and metaphorical linguistic expressions. The regulation of fear is conceptualized by means of two additional metaphors: INHIBITING FEAR IS GOING OVER IT and INHIBITING FEAR IS FIGHTING IT. As regards the first metaphor, it motivates the English expression *to overcome fears*[14] and the Italian *superare la paura* 'to go beyond, to get over'. Here, fear is conceptualized in terms of a physical obstacle similar to a hill, wall or a mountain and regulating it is metaphorically perceived as moving over this obstacle.

As regards the second metaphorical image, it has been found in language data from three analysed languages, for example, *combattere la paura* 'to fight fear', *affrontare la paura* 'to face, to confront fear'[15] and *vincere la paura* 'to win, to defeat fear' for Italian; *to conquer fear*[16] for English, and *przezwyciężać strach* 'to vanquish fear', for Polish. The metaphor INHIBITING FEAR IS FIGHTING IT is the example of personification, which is a common figurative means of understanding abstract entities that makes use of 'one of the best source domains we have – ourselves' (Kövecses 2010: 39). In this metaphor, trying to regulate fear is metaphorically conceptualized in terms of physically fighting with an opponent and the success in this struggle metaphorically stands for no longer feeling this negative emotion (see Kövecses 2000: 68, for the metaphor EMOTION IS AN OPPONENT).

Personification seems to motivate yet another metaphor which was found, however, only in thought-related lexemes: INHIBITING THOUGHTS IS MAKING THEM INAUDIBLE. This metaphorical image is attested by Italian and Polish linguistic expressions such as *mettere a tacere i pensieri* 'to make thoughts silent, quiet', *wyciszyć myśli* 'to hush up thoughts', *uciszyć myśli* 'to make thoughts quiet' and *zagłuszyć myśli* 'to make thoughts inaudible, to deafen, stifle them'. In this personification, we can distinguish three specific underlying mappings: (1) unwanted thoughts and emotions are human beings that emit intrusive sounds; (2) the human being is the agent who tries to eliminate these sounds perceived as unbearable; (3) controlling intrusive thoughts and emotions is physically eliminating such sounds. It is believed that the experiential motivation of this specific personification is the fact that our thoughts often materialize in our minds in the form of inner speech, also known as 'verbal thinking' (see Alderson-Day and Fernyhough 2015, for more details).

Results Summary[17]

The analysis of metaphorical expressions from Italian, Polish and English has shown that when we try to regulate unwanted emotions or inhibit intrusive thoughts, we mostly turn to the concrete experiential basis of physical contact. More specifically, we objectify these abstract concepts as independent, discrete and tangible entities with whom we can actively interact in order to get them under control.

As shown in **Figure 3.1**, the overarching conceptual metaphor EMOTION REGULATION/COGNITIVE INHIBITION IS LIMITING PHYSICAL CONTACT comes in five more specific subtypes, which are differently distributed according

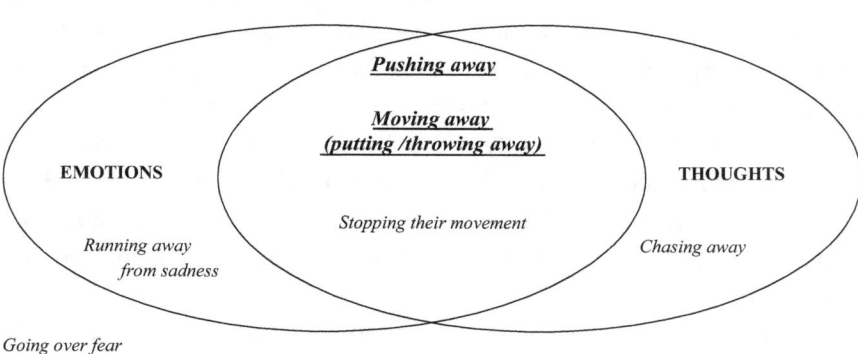

Figure 3.1 Metaphors of inhibiting unwanted emotions and thoughts in English, Italian and Polish.

to their degree of incidence in the data (as per languages, emotions and thoughts). At the heart of the diagram, where thoughts and emotions overlap, we find two most important conceptualizations: (1) INHIBITING UNWANTED EMOTIONS AND THOUGHTS IS PUSHING THEM AWAY and (2) INHIBITING UNWANTED EMOTIONS AND THOUGHTS IS MOVING THEM AWAY. Next, still in the overlapping section, there is another shared metaphor which is, however, far less prevalent, that is, INHIBITING UNWANTED ANGER AND THOUGHTS IS STOPPING THEIR MOVEMENT.

When it comes to metaphorical differences within the overarching metaphor, we have observed two sub-metaphors: (1) thought-specific: INHIBITING UNWANTED THOUGHTS IS CHASING THEM AWAY and (2) sadness-specific: INHIBITING SADNESS IS RUNNING AWAY FROM IT.

Lastly, below the diagram lie three metaphors which are not shared and represent different underlying mappings. More specifically, these are fear-specific metaphorical images of going over an obstacle and fighting it as well as the metaphor INHIBITING UNWANTED THOUGHTS IS MAKING THEM INAUDIBLE. Despite the basic difference concerning their target domain, what connects the last two is the fact that they are both examples of personification.

Conclusions[18]

The findings presented in this chapter fit into a wide array of patterns involving the objectification of abstract mental phenomena which have been unearthed in metaphor research (Jäkel 1995; Lakoff and Johnson 1999; Kövecses 2000; Szwedek 2014). The presence of various metaphorical linguistic expressions indicating the overarching and shared metaphor EMOTION REGULATION/ COGNITIVE INHIBITION IS LIMITING PHYSICAL CONTACT not only confirms the underlying image of emotions and thoughts as physical objects that could be manipulated and interacted with but also highlights the importance of the idea of physical contact in metaphorically describing our inner life (see Kövecses 2000: 83, for EMOTIONAL EFFECT IS PHYSICAL CONTACT). This, in turn, provides some further linguistic evidence for the role of sensory perception in metaphor creation (see Speed et al. 2019). Moreover, the chapter confirms that, despite the key role of objectification, some other related images are also metaphorically used, especially personification (see Kövecses 2000; cf. Szwedek 2014, for personification as type of objectification).

Despite its conformity with previous research, the chapter also shows that the metaphorical image of emotion regulation and cognitive inhibition is much more nuanced. Above all else, the data shows that only two images, that is, pushing away and moving away, are widely shared between emotions and thoughts as they are found in three languages and in 5/4 basic emotions, respectively (cf. Kövecses 2000, for other metaphorical ways of emotion control which were not found in our data). Because of their prevalence in the analysed data, these two specific metaphors could be seen as candidates for default and prototypical means of describing and understanding inhibiting unwanted thoughts and emotions.

Other sub-metaphors based on the idea of limiting physical contact are more idiosyncratic. The metaphor INHIBITING UNWANTED THOUGHTS IS CHASING THEM AWAY is particularly important here as it suggests that intrusive thoughts could be perceived on a phenomenological level as more dynamic and active entities than emotions. As for different metaphors, the presence of INHIBITING FEAR IS GOING OVER IT points out that emotions could also be conceived of as physical obstacles, which expands the scope of use of this metaphor (cf. Trojszczak 2017b for problems as obstacles). At the same time, it is crucial to remember that the conclusions about these differences are necessarily qualified by the limited character and quantity of the analysed corpus data. Another factor that could motivate these discrepancies is the phenomenon of highlighting and hiding, that is, the fact that metaphors usually emphasize some aspects of the target domain and simultaneously conceal the others (see Kövecses 2010).

Besides expanding on previous findings in conceptual metaphor theory, the present chapter could also be seen as providing some inspiration for future psychological research (see Gibbs 2007) into emotion/cognition interactions (see Pessoa 2013; Keltner and Holberg 2015; Greenberg et al. 2017). By showing that the phenomena of emotion regulation and cognitive inhibition overlap to a large extent on the linguistic and figurative levels and, at the same time, indicating some interesting paths of divergence, for example, concerning personification or a more dynamic character of thoughts, it points out two opposing directions for experimental research that could shed even more light on these key mental processes.

Notes

1 This section was written by Chiara Astrid Gebbia.
2 This section was written by Chiara Astrid Gebbia.

3 This section was written by Chiara Astrid Gebbia.
4 This section was written by Marcin Trojszczak.
5 In this chapter, we do not discuss all emotion-related and thought-related expressions that were found in the analysed corpora as our main goal is to present key overarching similarities and differences instead of taking stock of all extracted data.
6 The BNC includes circa 100 million words (Aston and Burnard 1998); the NJKP contains 240 million words (Przepiórkowski et al. 2012); the CORIS consists of entries 130 million words from different text categories (Xiao 2008) and the Paisà, a large collection of Italian web texts, comprises about 250 million words (see corpusitaliano.it).
7 This section was written by Marcin Trojszczak, with the exception of subsection 5.3 which was written by Chiara Astrid Gebbia.
8 The verb *tłumić* originates from Proto-Slavic *tlmit* 'to calm down by means of pushing, pressing'.
9 The verbs *sopprimere* and *suppress* come from Latin *supprimere* which means 'to press down'.
10 The verb *eliminate* originates from Latin *eliminare* 'to thrust out of doors'.
11 The verb *extinguish* comes from Latin *extinguere* 'to put out (what is burning)' which apparently evolved from Proto-Indo-European root *steig- 'to prick, stick, pierce'.
12 The verb *ease* stems from Latin *iacere* 'to throw'.
13 This section was written by Marcin Trojszczak.
14 The verb *overcome* has its roots in Old English *ofercuman* 'to reach, to prevail over' and ultimately derives from the Old English preposition *ofer* 'beyond, above, past' and verb *cuman* 'to come, to reach some point'.
15 The verb *affrontare* comes from Late Latin *affrontare* 'to strike against'.
16 The verb *conquer* originates from Old French *conquerre* 'conquer, defeat, vanquish' but ultimately stems from Latin *conquirere* 'to search for, win'.
17 This section was written by Chiara Astrid Gebbia.
18 This section was written by Marcin Trojszczak.

Bibliography

Alderson-Day, B., and C. Fernyhough (2015), 'Inner Speech: Development, Cognitive Functions, Phenomenology, and Neurobiology', *Psychological Bulletin*, 141 (5): 931–65.

Amberber, M. (ed.) (2007), *The Language of Memory in a Crosslinguistic Perspective*, Amsterdam: John Benjamins.

Ansah, G. N. (2014), 'Cognitive Models of Anger in Akan: A Conceptual Metaphor Analysis', *Cognitive Linguistics Studies*, 1 (1): 131–46.

Arbuthnott, K., and J. I. D. Campbell (2000), 'Cognitive Inhibition in Selection and Sequential retrieval', *Memory & Cognition*, 28: 331–40.

Aston, G., and L. Burnard (1998), *The BNC Handbook: Exploring the British National Corpus with SARA*, Edinburgh: Edinburgh University Press.

Benko, V. (2014), 'Aranea: Yet Another Family of (Comparable) Web Corpora', in P. Sojka, A. Horák, I. Kopeček, and K. Pala (eds), *Text, Speech and Dialogue. TSD 2014. Lecture Notes in Computer Science*, Vol. 8655, 247–56, Cham: Springer.

Dancygier, B. (ed.) (2017), *The Cambridge Handbook of Cognitive Linguistics*, Cambridge: Cambridge University Press.

Deignan, A. (2008), 'Corpus Linguistics and Metaphor', in R. W. Gibbs (ed.), *The Cambridge Handbook of Metaphor and Thought*, 280–94, Cambridge: Cambridge University Press.

Dukes, D., A. C. Samson, and E. A. Walle, eds (2022), *The Oxford Handbook of Emotional Development*, Oxford: Oxford University Press.

Duncan Kerr, A. (2021), 'On the Rationality of Emotion Regulation', *Philosophical Psychology*, 34 (4): 453–73.

Fernandez-Duque, D., and M. Johnson (2002), 'Cause and Effect Theories of Attention: The Role of Conceptual Metaphors', *Review of General Psychology*, 6 (2): 153–65.

Fisher, A., and A. S. R. Manstead (2016), 'Social Functions of Emotion and Emotion Regulation', in L. Feldman Barrett, M. Lewis, and J. M. Haviland-Jones (eds), *The Handbook of Emotions*, 4th edn, 424–39, New York: The Guilford Press.

Fortescue, M. (2001), 'Thoughts About Thought', *Cognitive Linguistics*, 12 (1): 15–39.

Garofalo C. (2022), 'Emotion and Emotion Regulation', in C. Garofalo, and J. J. Sijtsema, (eds), *Clinical Forensic Psychology*, 87–107, London: Palgrave Macmillan.

Gibbs, R. W. (2007), 'Why Cognitive Linguists Should Care More About Empirical Methods', in M. Gonzalez-Marquez, I. Mittelberg, S. Coulson, and M. J. Spivey (eds), *Methods in Cognitive Linguistics*, 2–18, Amsterdam: John Benjamins.

Greenberg, D. M., J. Kolasi, C. P. Hegsted, Y. Berkowitz, and E. L. Jurist (2017), 'Mentalized Affectivity: A New Model and Assessment of Emotion Regulation', *PLoS ONE*, 12 (10): e0185264.

Jäkel, O. (1995), 'The Metaphorical Conception of Mind: "Mental Activity is Manipulation"', in J. R. Taylor, and R. E. MacLaury (eds), *Language and the Cognitive Construal of The World*, 197–229, Berlin: Mouton de Gruyter.

Keltner, D., and E. J. Horberg (2015), 'Emotion-Cognition Interactions', in M. Mikulincer, P. R. Shaver, E. Borgida, and J. A. Bargh (eds), *APA Handbook of Personality and Social psychology*, Vol. 1. *Attitudes and Social Cognition*, 623–64, Washington, DC: American Psychological Association.

Koole, S. L. (2009), 'The Psychology of Emotion Regulation: An Integrative Review', *Cognition and Emotion*, 23 (1): 4–41.

Koivisto-Alanko, P., and H. Tissari (2006), 'Sense and Sensibility: Rational Thought Versus Emotion in Metaphorical Language', in A. Stefanowitsch, and T. S. Gries (eds), *Corpus-based Approaches to Metaphor and Metonymy*, 191–213, Berlin and New York: Mouton de Gruyter.

Kövecses, Z. (1986), *Metaphors of Anger, Pride, and Love: A Lexical Approach to the Study of Concepts*, Amsterdam: John Benjamins.

Kövecses, Z. (1990), *Emotion Concepts*, Berlin and New York: Springer.

Kövecses, Z. (2000), *Metaphor and Emotion: Language, Culture, and Body in Human Feeling*, Cambridge: Cambridge University Press.

Kövecses, Z. (2005), *Metaphor in Culture: Universality and Variation*, Cambridge: Cambridge University Press.

Kövecses, Z. (2008), 'Metaphor and Emotion', in R. W. Gibbs (ed.), *The Cambridge Handbook of Metaphor and Thought*, 380–96, Cambridge: Cambridge University Press.

Kövecses, Z. (2010), *Metaphor: A Practical Introduction*, 2nd edn, New York: Oxford University Press.

Kövecses, Z. (2015), *Where Metaphors Come From*, Oxford: Oxford University Press

Kövecses, Z. (2020), *Extended Conceptual Metaphor Theory*, Cambridge: Cambridge University Press.

Lakoff, G. (2016), *Moral Politics: How Liberals and Conservatives Think*, 3rd edn, Chicago: University of Chicago Press.

Lakoff, G., and M. Johnson (1980), *Metaphors We Live By*, 1st edn, Chicago: University of Chicago Press.

Lakoff, G., and M. Johnson (1999), *Philosophy in the Flesh: The Embodied Mind and Its Challenge to Western Thought*, New York: Basic Books.

Lewandowska-Tomaszczyk, B. (2012), 'Cognitive Corpus Studies: A New Qualitative & Quantitative Agenda for Contrasting Languages', *MFU Connexion. A Journal of Humanities and Social Sciences*, 1 (1): 29–63.

MacLeod, C. M. (2007), The Concept of Inhibition in Cognition, in D. S. Gorfein, and C. M. MacLeod (eds), *Inhibition in Cognition*, 3–23, Washington, DC: American Psychological Association.

Niedenthal, P. M., and F. Ric (2017), *Psychology of Emotion*, London: Psychology Press.

Pessoa, L. (2013), *The Cognitive-Emotional Brain. From Interactions to Integration*, Cambridge, MA: The MIT Press.

Pragglejaz Group. (2007), 'MIP: A Method for Identifying Metaphorically Used Words in Discourse' *Metaphor and Symbol*, 1: 1–39.

Przepiórkowski, A., M. Bańko, R. L. Górski, and B. Lewandowska-Tomaszczyk, eds (2012), *Narodowy Korpus Języka Polskiego [National Corpus of Polish]*, Warsaw: PWN.

Riediger, M., and J. A. Bellingtier (2022), 'Emotion Regulation Across the Life Span', in D. Dukes, A. C. Samson, and E. A. Walle (eds), *The Oxford Handbook of Emotional Development*, 93–109, Oxford: Oxford University Press.

Rolf, E. (2005), *Metaphertheorien: Typologie: Darstellung. Bibliographie*, Berlin: Walter De Gruyter.

Safarnejad, F., I. Ho Abdullah, and N. Mat Awal (2014), 'A Cognitive Study of Happiness Metaphors in Persian and English'. *Procedia - Social and Behavioral Sciences*, 118: 110–17.

Scarantino, A. (2016), The Philosophy of Emotions and Its Impact on Affective Sciences, in L. Feldman Barrett, M. Lewis, and J. M. Haviland-Jones (eds), *The Handbook of Emotions*, 4th edn, 3–48, New York: The Guilford Press.

Speed, L. J., C. O'Meara, L. San Roque, and A. Majid, eds (2019), *Perception Metaphors*, Amsterdam: John Benjamins.

Stefanowitsch, A. (2006a), 'Corpus-Based Approaches to Metaphor and Metonymy'. In A. Stefanowitsch, and T. S. Gries (eds), *Corpus-Based Approaches to Metaphor and Metonymy*, 1–17, Berlin and New York: Mouton de Gruyter.

Stefanowitsch, A. (2006b), 'Words and Their Metaphors: A Corpus-Based Approach'. In A. Stefanowitsch, and T. S. Gries (eds), *Corpus-Based Approaches to Metaphor and Metonymy*, 63–105, Berlin and New York: Mouton de Gruyter.

Suri, G., and J. J. Gross (2016), 'Emotion Regulation: A Valuation Perspective', in L. Feldman Barrett, M. Lewis, and J. M. Haviland-Jones (eds), *The Handbook of Emotions*, 4th edn, 453–66, New York: The Guilford Press.

Szwedek, A. (2011), 'The Ultimate Source Domain', *Review of Cognitive Linguistics*, 9 (2): 341–66.

Szwedek, A. (2014), 'The Nature of Domains and the Relationships Between Them in Metaphorization', *Review of Cognitive Linguistics*, 12 (2): 342–74.

Szwedek, A. (2018), The Object Image Schema, in P. Zywiczynski, M. Sibierska, and W. Skrzypczak (eds), *Beyond Diversity: The Past and the Future of English Studies*, 57–89, Berlin: Peter Lang.

Taverniers, M. (2002), *Metaphor and Metaphorology. A Selective Genealogy of Philosophical and Linguistic Conceptions of Metaphor from Aristotle to the 1990s*, Gent: Academia Press.

Trim, R. (2011), *Metaphor and the Historical Evolution of Conceptual Mapping*, Basingstoke: Palgrave Macmillan.

Trojszczak, M., and C. A. Gebbia (2020), 'Metaphors for Regulating Emotions – A Cognitive Corpus-Based Study of English, Italian, and Polish', in B. Lewandowska-Tomaszczyk, M. Venuti, and V. Monello (eds), *Language, Heart, and Mind*, 255–78, Frankfurt am Main: Peter Lang.

Trojszczak, M. (2017a), 'On 'Paying Attention' – Metaphorical Objectification of "Attention" in English and Polish', in W. Wachowski, Z. Kövecses, and M. Borodo (eds), *Zooming In: Micro-Scale Perspectives on Cognition, Translation, and Cross-Cultural Communication*, 81–100, Frankfurt am Main: Peter Lang.

Trojszczak, M. (2017b), 'Problem Solving in English and Polish – A Cognitive Study of Selected Metaphorical Conceptualizations', in P. Pęzik, and J. T. Waliński (eds), *Language, Corpora, and Cognition*, 201–20, Frankfurt am Main: Peter Lang.

Trojszczak, M. (2019a), 'Grounding Mental Metaphors in Touch: A Corpus-Based Study of English and Polish', in L. J. Speed, C. O'Meara, L. San Roque, and A. Majid (eds), *Perception Metaphors*, 209–30, Amsterdam: John Benjamins.

Trojszczak, M. (2019b), 'Similarities and Contrasts in Multisensory Conceptualisations of Memories in Polish and English', in B. Lewandowska-Tomaszczyk (ed.), *Contacts and Contrasts in Cultures and Languages*, 85–101, Cham: Springer.

Tummers, J., K. Heylen, and D. Geeraerts (2005). 'Usage-Based Approaches in Cognitive Linguistics: A Technical State of the Art', *Corpus Linguistics and Linguistic Theory*, 1 (2): 225–61.

Wegner, D. M. (1994), 'Ironic Processes of Mental Control', *Psychological Review*, 101 (1): 34–52.

Xiao, R. (2008), 'Well-Known and Influential Corpora', in A. Lüdeling, and M. Kytö (eds), *Corpus Linguistics: An International Handbook*, 383–457, Berlin: de Gruyter.

4

Linguistic Means to Discursively Construct Dehumanization[1]

Serena Coschignano and Chiara Zanchi

Introduction

Misrepresentation in *discourse*, that is, language in its relations with other elements involved in the social process (Fairclough 2015: 8), is an ever-present feature of asymmetrical power relationships (Scott 1990). In fact, the more forceful the abuse of power, the more effectively such abuse has to be justified and/or concealed through discourse by its perpetrators and their supporters (Coates and Wade 2007: 512). Media often act as conscious smugglers or unconscious sounding boards of these asymmetrical power relationships, by repetitively 'marginalizing, trivializing and constructing as deviant or dangerous any challenge' to the dominant ideology (Meyers 1997: 22; see also Fairclough 1989). Importantly, not necessarily is this behaviour a by-product of media's conspiracy against weaker social groups, but it may well be due to institutionalized professional imperatives, commercial interests or unconscious stereotypes. Media discursive representation is paramount due to the pervasive power of repetition (e.g. Fairclough 1989; van Dijk 2005): an isolated newspaper article has no power per se, but the repetition of storytelling patterns gives media a pervasive influence on our conceptualization of events and/or social groups.

Within the framework of critical discourse analysis (CDA) – a broad approach to discourse studies investigating how discursive practices represent, reproduce, legitimize and, occasionally, fight systems of social inequality (see e.g. Weiss and Wodak 2003) – racism is defined as a system of social inequality based on ethnicity, in which an opposition is perceived between the in-group, that is, 'white folks', and the out-group, that is, migrants and other ethnic minorities (e.g. van Dijk 1998, 2004). A number of studies highlight how forms of racism emerge in public discourse all over the world (see, among many others, van Dijk 1984 on Netherlands; van Dijk 1999; KhosraviNik 2009; Musolff 2015 on UK; van Leeuwen and Wodak 1999; Reisigl and Wodak 2001 on Austria; Santa Ana 1999 on the United States; Teo 2000; Clynes 2005 on Australia; van der Valk 2000 on France; Blommaert 2001 on Belgium; Flowerdew et al. 2002 on Hong Kong; Pietikainen 2003 on Finland; van Dijk 2005 on Spain and Latin America; Tileaga 2005 on Romania; Colombo 2013; Orrù 2017 on Italy; Mollica and Wilke 2017 on Italy and Germany). Migrants are frequently depicted as an issue, which causes administrative and social criticalities for the hosting country (ter Wal 2002; KhosraviNik 2009), and/ or as rivals or even parasites of the citizens of the hosting country, with whom migrants share physical space and socio-economic resources (van Dijk 1991; ter Wal 2002; Rydgren 2008; Musolff 2015; see also Wodak 2015 on the use of fear in right-winged political discourse against migrants). Moreover, the extent of the migratory phenomenon is often dramatized through the so-called number-game strategy, providing statistics and numbers to lend greater credibility to arguments (van Dijk 1998; KhosraviNik 2009). In addition, media use a routinized set of metaphors to stress the problematic nature of the migratory process (Reisigl and Wodak 2001): reference is often made to WAR (e.g. 'invasions' or 'arms'), WATER (e.g. 'waves', 'flows', 'tides') or ANIMALS ('parasites'). In particular, ANIMAL metaphors are frequent in migration discourse, as a part of the discursive process through which migrants are dehumanized (e.g. Santa Ana 1999; Hart 2011; KhosravNik 2010; Musolff 2015; Hart 2021).

Although most CDA research is primarily qualitative in nature, recent studies have proven that integrating both quantitative and qualitative approaches can carry interesting results (e.g. Taylor and Marchi 2018; Baker et al. 2008). In this chapter, we fit into this line of research, by offering a corpus-assisted study that quantitatively and qualitatively investigates the discursive usages of the terms *rifugiato*, *profugo* and *richiedente asilo* in a corpus of headlines from Italian written daily newspapers. Our goal is to understand if these lexemes lose part of their meaning, and in particular their [+HUMAN] trait, and, if so, through what discursive devices.

Before summarizing the contents of this chapter, we outline the technical meanings of the Italian terms under investigation. Although both *rifugiato* and *profugo* are translated with the English term 'refugee', only *rifugiato* carries a precise legal connotation, defined by the UN 1951 *Refugee Convention* as follows:

any person who 'owing to well-founded fear of being persecuted for reasons of race, religion, nationality, membership of a particular social group or political opinion, is outside the country of their nationality and is unable or, owing to such fear, is unwilling to avail themselves of the protection of that country; or who, not having a nationality and being outside the country of their former habitual residence as a result of such events, is unable or, owing to such fear, is unwilling to return to it.'

The meaning of *profugo,* similarly, includes the reasons for which a person has been forced to leave their country of origin but lacks any juridic nuances. *Richiedente asilo* (asylum seeker) also carries a legal connotation, as reported by the UN *Refugee Agency*: specifically, 'an asylum-seeker is someone whose request for sanctuary has yet to be processed'. It is worth emphasizing that, from 2015 onwards, the English term 'refugee' has been used in international media discourse as a catch-all term substituting 'migrant', since the latter 'has evolved . . . into a tool that dehumanizes and distances, a blunt pejorative' (in the words of an online al-Jazeera editor).[2] Up to now, *migrante* (migrant) holds the status of umbrella term in an Italian context. However, this usage raises some issues, as *migrant* carries no internationally agreed definition. In the rest of the chapter, we will use English 'refugee(s)' to generically refer to the participants in the migratory process.

This chapter is organized as follows. In the next section, we discuss our theoretical assumptions and the ratio behind our corpus and study design. The following sections contain our quantitative and qualitative analyses: the latter unfolds in three subsections, each one devoted to a different parameter. Finally, we summarize our findings and draw future lines of research.

Theory and Methods

Background Theoretical Assumptions

As research in CDA has emphasized (van Dijk 2003, 2005), media can play a paramount role not only in spreading racist ideologies but also in (re)creating and (re)sounding prejudiced attitudes and biased conceptualization of events. Our conceptualization of events is driven by various conceptual operations (cf. Hart 2015 with references), including *framing,* that is, building mental structures that make up a coherent view of reality. The same (set of) events can be represented from different viewpoints, choosing to foreground or background certain participants and aspects of them, and to relate or not to relate them with varied, supposedly linked, events. The essential idea of framing is that such representational options are not free of ideological charge: much to the contrary, they shape the conceptual schemata we use to interpret the world (Lakoff 2004: xv).

One of the most powerful means of framing is *metaphor* (Chilton and Lakoff 1995: 56; Charteris-Black 2004: 28). In line with cognitive linguistics, we do not understand metaphor as a mere figure of speech, but as a pervasive means humans employ to think and linguistically describe complex, abstract and/or unusual sets of concepts, that is, conceptual domains, in terms of simpler, more concrete, and/or more familiar conceptual domains (Lakoff and Johnson 1980). For example, TIME is often thought of and described in terms of SPACE: in the sentence *Winter is coming*, the season is conceptualized as an entity moving towards the speaker. The simpler conceptual domain (e.g. SPACE) is named 'source domain', while the 'target domain' is the more complex one (e.g. TIME). In the literature on immigration discourse, the two notions of metaphor and *framing* have been integrated through the analytical construction of *scenario* (Musolff 2015: 44), which is used to capture recurrent clusters of conceptually related metaphoric formulations.

Since in this work we aim to uncover scenarios that contribute to building and spreading a dehumanized representation of refugees, we summarize the main semantic traits associated with human beings:

(a) individuation, that is, the propensity of an entity to be conceptualized as a single individual (e.g. Grimm 2018);
(b) animacy, that is, the degree to which an entity is conceptualized as living or sentient (note that, in linguistic typology, the so-called animacy hierarchies feature two distinct positions for humans and other animate entities, such as animals; e.g. Vihman and Nelson 2019);
(c) agentivity and volitionality, that is, the ability to trigger events as principal initiators and with specific intentions (e.g. Verhoeven 2017).

These features have been proven by typologists to prominently affect the way the systems of the world's languages are shaped. Owing to their observed relevance for natural languages and to the assumed link between our concepts and our linguistic expressions, these typically human characteristics are very likely to be prominent for our cognition as well – that is, to suggest that we conceptualize an entity as [+/− HUMAN].

Corpus and Study Design

For our analysis, we used a digitalized corpus of 93,934 headlines of Italian printed newspaper articles on migratory precesses, chronologically ranging from January 2013 to December 2019 (included). The corpus includes local and national newspapers known for being ideologically closer to the left- and to the right-winged parties. We opted to focus on headlines owing to their pivotal role in directing the conceptualization of the events narrated in news reports (Teo 2000: 13–14; cf. also Van Dijk 1991).

In the quantitative study, we wished to focus on the relationship between the discursive usages of *refugees* and of *migrants*: these two categories, which are in principle distinct owing to the presence or lack of legal connotations, have been observed to merge in the British media (Baker et al. 2008). This merge led to paradoxical new designations such as 'illegal refugees'. As we aimed to investigate whether the same merge is occurring in the Italian printed media as well, in the quantitative section of this study we took into consideration the frequencies of all mentioned migration lexemes in the whole corpus. In particular, we compared the usage over a seven-year time span of *rifugiato, profugo, richiedente asilo, migrante* and *immigrato*.

For the qualitative analysis, we extracted all headlines containing the lexemes *rifugiato, profugo* and/or *richiedente asilo* in all their inflected forms. We decided not to include headlines containing the terms *migrante* and *immigrato* for both practical and theoretical reasons. First, we aimed to conduct a corpus-assisted fine-grained corpus-based analysis and, therefore, had to carve up our data set in some ways. Eventually, we did so on a semasiological basis. Second, we wanted to focus on the misuse of the most connoted terms among those that can identify the participants in migratory processes.

Then, we manually cleared the data from irrelevant and/or unclear headings: in particular, we excluded headlines concerning famous refugees, and headlines that were not straightforward to interpret.[3] We thus obtained 2,294 headlines containing *rifugiato*, 8,386 headlines containing *profugo* and 526 headlines containing *richiedente asilo*.[4] With the aim, on the one hand, to take into account the highest number of relevant headlines, and the necessity, on the other, to work with a manually manageable amount of data, we included 5,114 headlines: all 526 headlines with *richiedente asilo*, all 2,294 headlines containing *rifugiato*, and a random sample, though balanced per year, of 2,294 headlines featuring *profugo*.[5] This way, we obtained three subcorpora, one for each investigated lexeme, on which we carried out a manual analysis according to the parameters presented in the next section.

Parameters of the Manual Annotation

To answer our research questions, we operationalized our background theoretical assumptions in the following parameters.

Orientation

Orientation concerns the general attitude expressed towards refugees (values: positive ~ negative), as shown in (1)a–b:

(1) a. *Più solidarietà verso i rifugiati africani*   [positive]
     'More solidarity toward African refugees' (L'Osservatore Romano, 2014)
     b. *Senegalese richiedente asilo preso con droga*   [negative]
     'Senegalese asylum seeker caught with drugs' (Giornale di Sicilia, 2015)

As mentioned earlier, our corpus includes headlines from newspapers having more or less explicit political tendencies, which can be mirrored in their general orientation towards migrations. For this reason, in order to avoid our awareness of such tendencies to influence the annotation, we obscured the news provider of the headlines during the annotation.

Type of Referent the Lexemes Point At

This parameter aims to operationalize individuation and animacy, by tagging whether refugees are depicted as single entities, as a collective mass or as abstract entities (values: individuals ~ category ~ topic/issue), as exemplified in (2)a–c:

(2) a. *Richiedente asilo denunciato per molestie sessuali*   [individuals]
     'Asylum seeker charged with sexual harassment' (Il Piccolo, 2016)
     b. *Accoglienza ai rifugiati anche in Costa Smeralda*   [category]
     'Hospitality for refugees also in Costa Smeralda' (L'Unione Sarda, 2015)
     c. *«Qui c'è chi specula sui profughi»*   [topic/issue]
     '«There is someone who speculates on refugees»' (Il Gazzettino, 2014)

Discourse Scenarios

In order to identify relevant scenarios, we annotated a small sample of headlines conjunctively, defining scenarios in an open-coding fashion. While tagging the remaining data, we adjusted the boundaries of the previously identified scenarios and defined new ones when necessary, also re-annotating the already classified headlines according to the new tagset. Finally, we tested the output of our open-coding manual annotation against the automatic thematic clustering of the textual analysis tool Iramuteq, performed on the pre-sampled corpus (for information on how Iramuteq works, visit http://www.iramuteq.org). Table 4.1 provides a list of discourse scenarios as identified through manual annotation, together with an explanatory gloss and an example for each of them (scenarios are ordered by decreasing frequency).

The second column of Table 4.1 indicates whether refugees, in each scenario, are depicted as active or passive participants, that is, if they possess agentivity and intentionality. For instance, *scappa* (runs away) in (3)a indicates an action voluntarily performed by refugees, whereas in (3)b refugees are *investiti* (run over) and thus undergo an action performed by someone else.

(3)   a. «*Scappa un rifugiato su due*»   [Escape: active]
       '«Every other refugee runs away»' (Libero, 2016)
      b. *Investiti 2 richiedenti asilo: nessun soccorso*   [Death: passive]
       '2 asylum seekers run over: no emergency aid' (Il Fatto Quotidiano, 2019)

Figure 4.1 displays the automatic scenario grouping obtained with Iramuteq. The lexical clustering performed by Iramuteq finds four to five word clouds, fairly distributed around the four corners of Figure 4.1.[6] These clusters are illustrated in Table 4.2, together with some of the most frequent words for each of them and the corresponding scenarios we identified through our manual analysis of the corpus.

The manual identification of scenarios finds a satisfying correspondence in the automatic clustering, despite some discrepancies in the grouping criteria: for example, unlike the software, we did not distinguish between discourses about national and international administration of migrations, since this distinction was not relevant to the purpose of our study. Furthermore, we included in our array three additional scenarios, based on our knowledge of the main topics in the Italian written media, which could have been interesting to monitor in relation to migrations (e.g. Climate change; Vigo 2017), and based on our further analytical interests (e.g. Quantity and Representation). In particular, Quantity and the 'number-game strategy' related to it (cf. our Introduction) play a crucial role in building the dehumanized portrait of refugees in which we are interested (cf. also the metaphor REFUGEES ARE NUMBERS discussed later).[7] Instead, the scenario Representation aims to take into account the extent to which refugees are given voice at all *in* the press for self-representation.

Table 4.1 Manually identified discourse scenarios

Scenario	Active/passive	Gloss	Example	Translation
Issue/administrative	P	All that concerns the administration of the 'refugee crisis', including internal as well as international political issues	*Via libera alla rete di enti locali per distribuire i richiedenti asilo*	'Green light to the municipalities network for allocating asylum seekers'
Welcome	P	(Un)willing reception of refugees by locals	*Il Pd all'esecutivo: apriamo le porte ai richiedenti asilo*	'Pd to the executive: let's open up our doors to asylum seekers'
Inclusion	P	Acts performed by local social groups or institutional representatives in order to prompt social inclusion of refugees	*La Cgil spiega diritti e doveri ai richiedenti asilo*	'Cgil explains rights and obligations to asylum seekers'
Representation	P	Overt (self-)depiction of refugees	*Storie di rifugiati: «Non una massa, sono una persona»*	'Stories of refugees: «Not a mass, I'm a person»'
Quantity	P	Information concerning refugees' quantification	*Germania. Nel 2015 i richiedenti asilo saranno 750.000*	'Germany. In 2015 there will be 750,000 asylum seekers'
Issue/economic	P	Economic implications of the 'refugee crisis'	*I profughi costano 21 miliardi*	'Refugees cost 21 billions'
Issue/deceit	P	Deceitful actions performed exploiting the 'refugee crisis'	*La truffa dei rifugiati, uno su due è falso*	'The refugee scam, one out of two is a fraud'
Abuse	P	Mistreatment of refugees, causing physical or psychological damages	*Profugo insultato e picchiato. Pietre sulle case dei rifugiati*	'Refugee insulted and beaten. Stones thrown at refugees' houses'
Charity	P	Acts of charity towards refugees	*Calcio: asta benefica per i rifugiati*	'Soccer: charity auction for refugees'
Encounter	P	Encounter of refugees with local social groups, institutional or religious representatives	*Mattarella nel campo profughi 'Dall'Etiopia a lezione all'Ue'*	'Mattarella in the refugee camp "From Ethiopia a lesson to the EU"'

Issue/public health	P	Implications related to public health of 'refugee crisis'	«Rischi sanitari, niente rifugiati in case private»	'«Sanitary risks, no to refugees in private houses»'
Death	P	Death of refugees	Rifugiato trovato morto nel centro di accoglienza	'Refugee found dead in the reception center'
Rescue	P	Rescue of refugees	«Così salvo i profughi che scappano dall'Isis»	'«This is how I save refugees running from Isis»'
Climate change	P	Climate change as a leading factor for asylum seeking	Più caldo farà, più rifugiati avremo	'The hotter it gets, the more refugees we'll have'
Crime	A	Crimes perpetrated by refugees	Richiedente asilo sorpreso mentre spaccia hashish	'Asylum seeker caught dealing hash'
Initiative	A	Manifestation of refugees' self-initiative	I rifugiati africani che operano accanto ai volontari	'The African refugees working alongside volunteers'
Demonstration	A	Protest actions performed by refugees	Richiedenti asilo in marcia da Busto Arsizio a Varese	'Asylum seekers marching from Busto Arsizio to Varese'
Arrival	A	Arrival of refugees into a territory (national or local)	Profughi, in arrivo una nuova ondata	'Refugees, a new wave is coming'
Escape	A	Escape of refugees	I rifugiati cristiani in fuga dai campi per le persecuzioni degli islamici	'Christian refugees fleeing camps because persecuted by Muslims'
Travel	A	Information concerning journeys of refugees	L'odissea senza fine dei rifugiati palestinesi	'The endless odyssey of Palestinian refugees'

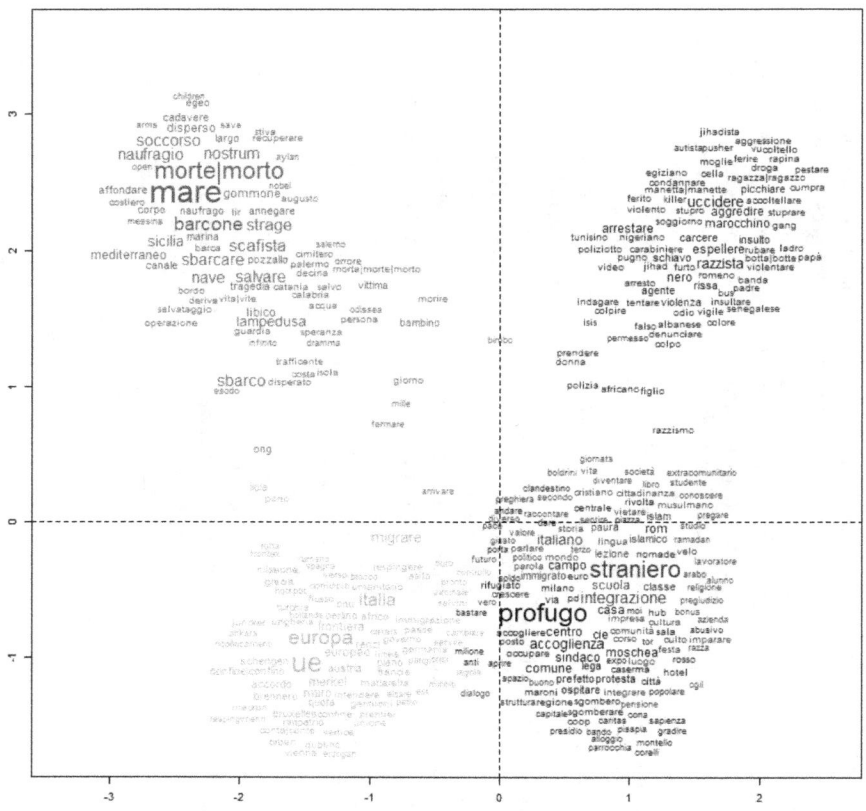

Figure 4.1 Automatic scenario detection performed with Iramuteq.

Table 4.2 Automatically and manually detected scenarios

Corner	Keywords	Corresponding scenarios
top-left	*mare* (see), *morto* (dead), *morte* (death), *barcone* (scow, barge)	Death, Rescue, Travel
top-right	*uccidere* (kill), *razzista* (racist), *marocchino* (Moroccan), *arrestare* (arrest)	Abuse, Crime, Demonstration
bottom-left	*Italia* (Italy), *Europa* (Europe), *UE* (EU), *frontiera* (frontier), *rimpatrio* (repatriation)	Issue/administration, Issue/deceit, Issue/economic
bottom-right (1)	*profugo* (refugee), *moschea* (mosque), *comune* (city hall), *accoglienza* (welcoming)	Issue/administration, Issue/deceit, Issue/economic, Issue/public health
bottom-right (2)	*italiano* (Italian), *straniero* (foreign), *scuola* (school), *integrazione* (integration), *sanità* (healthcare)	Charity, Encounter, Inclusion, Initiative, Welcome, Issue/public health

Conceptual Metaphors

Whenever headlines contain the metaphorical mapping of refugees onto other conceptual domains, we annotated the source domain. For example, in (4) refugees are mapped onto FLUIDS through the usage of the mass noun *ondata* (wave):

(4)   *Nuova* **ondata** *di profughi, in arrivo 50 persone* [REFUGEES ARE A FLUID]
   'New **wave** of refugees, 50 people coming' (Corriere del Trentino, 2014)

Quantitative Analysis: The Presence of Refugees in the Italian Press

We first took a close look at the frequencies of all terms referring to refugees in our overall corpus (93,934 headlines). Quantitative data is displayed in Table 4.3.

The frequency trend is initially increasing for all lexemes: in 2015, we registered a peak for *rifugiato* and *profugo*, while this occurs in 2014 for *immigrato* and in 2017 for *migrante* and *richiedente asilo*. Afterwards, occurrences of all lexemes decrease, except for *migrante*, which from 2016 onwards is by far the most frequently used term and whose usage starts growing again in 2019. Such usage trends can be interpreted, from an extra-linguistic perspective, in light with the events occurring around that time. From 2013 to 2016, Italy did register a strong immigration growth, which was followed by a remarkable increase in the news coverage of migrations, as shown in Figure 4.2. However, despite a reduction of arrivals after 2016, Italian media kept giving room to the migratory processes, as highlighted by the growing darker line in the chart as compared to the decreasing lighter one, representing arrivals.

The frequencies in Table 4.3 can also be observed in the light of their intra-linguistic-causing factors and implications. Comparing the frequency of *migrante* to that of the other terms, this lexeme seems to have partially substituted its alternatives in press use. In other terms, the semantic space of *migrante* results to be widened, partially covering also that of *rifugiato*, *profugo*, *richiedente asilo* and *immigrato*, which become dispreferred lexical choices. A possible explanation for the spread of *migrante* is its semantic underspecification as compared to the other lexemes: *migrante* literally means one who migrates, who moves, with no further details implied concerning the causes of the migration as for *profugo*, its juridical consequences as for *rifugiato*, or its direction as for *im-migrato*, which literally means 'one who migrated inwards', with the prefix *im-/in-* meaning 'towards, against, inside'. We argue that the underspecification of *migrante* makes this term more eligible for meaning/referential extension.

Table 4.3 Number of headlines containing *rifugiato, profugo, richiedente asilo, migrante* and *immigrato*

	Rifugiato	Δ%	Profugo	Δ%	Richiedente asilo	Δ%	Migrante	Δ%	Immigrato	Δ%
2013	79	—	231	—	5	—	359	—	451	—
2014	282	+257	1,212	+425	32	+540	1,182	+229	1,106	+145
2015	621	+120	2,542	+110	74	+131	2,442	+107	910	−18
2016	552	−11	2,053	−19	100	+35	2,412	−1	593	−35
2017	393	−29	1,502	−27	193	+93	2,841	+18	706	+19
2018	194	−51	527	−65	80	−59	1,794	−37	356	−50
2019	173	−11	338	−36	44	−45	1,926	+7	315	−12
TOTAL	2,294	—	8,405	—	526	—	12,956	—	4,437	—

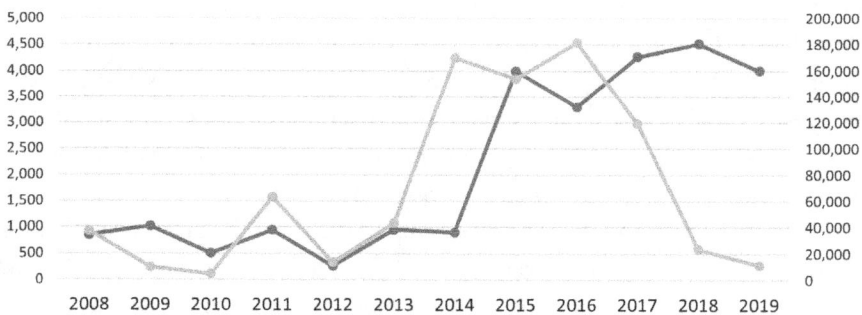

Figure 4.2 Arrivals of migrants vs. broadcast news coverage of migrations. The lighter line shows the arrivals of migrants; the darker line represents the trend of prime-time broadcast news on migrations (Rai, Mediaset, and La7). Data adapted from elaborations by ISMU and VII *Rapporto Carta di Roma*. https://www.ismu.org/wp-content/uploads/2019/12/SBARCHI_Anni-1997-2019.xls; https://www.cartadiroma.org/wp-content/uploads/2019/12/CdR-Report-2019_FInal.pdf (last access: 8 February 2022).

However, we observed that the boundaries of the meaning of other, more specific lexemes can vary, too. For instance, *rifugiato* properly refers to a person who, after entering a certain country, has obtained a specific juridical status. However, our corpus provides evidence that the term is used more widely: while it is not unexpected to read news about the arrival of *profughi*, headlines also report on the arrival of *rifugiati*, extending the use of the lexeme over its juridical specification. A hypothesis for the semantic extension of *rifugiato* is the influence of the international press on the Italian one (as mentioned in the introductory section). Thus, the extension of *rifugiato* to contexts where *profugo* would be more appropriate may be the result of a calque from the English 'refugee', which does not keep *profugo* and *rifugiato* distinct. With respect to this kind of meaning extension, *richiedente asilo* seems to be more stable: for instance, the inaccurate mention of the arrival of *richiedenti asilo* is only found once in our corpus:

(5)   *Richiedenti asilo, annunciati altri arrivi*
        'Asylum seekers, other arrivals announced' (Il Messaggero Pordenone, 2018)

The low overall frequency of *richiedente asilo*, indeed, may depend on its high degree of specification discouraging its meaning extension. Also, *richiedente asilo* is a multi-word expression and this, too, may disfavour its overuse in place of simpler alternatives. At any rate, our analysis confirms what Baker et al. (2008) highlighted for the British press, and specifically, the merging of the semantic concepts of migrants and asylum seekers/refugees.

Qualitative Analysis: Discursive Means of Dehumanization

In this section, we offer bivariate analyses of the parameters that we considered for our manual annotation. We first combine reference type with orientation; second, we analyse scenarios in relation with reference type and orientation; finally, we relate metaphors with orientation. Each combination of parameters is discussed concerning its dehumanizing effects in discourse.

Reference Type and Orientation

Now we look at the first two parameters: the orientation towards refugees expressed in news headlines and the kind of reference drawn by each lexeme. This data is displayed in Table 4.4.

In the reference-type column, we note that the vast majority of headlines refers to refugees as a category (69.8 per cent) or a topic (22.7 per cent), while reference to individuals is rather marginal (7.5 per cent). The preference for these types of reference itself shows that refugees tend to be depicted, in Italian press discourses, not as individuated, but rather as a category built up of generic and/or abstract entities, thus contributing to their dehumanization. This imbalance may be due to journalists being professionally more interested

Table 4.4 Orientation by lexeme and type of reference

	Rifugiato		Profugo		Richiedente asilo		Total/ reference type	
	Positive	Negative	Positive	Negative	Positive	Negative	Positive	Negative
Individuals	58.3%	41.7%	54%	46%	18.9%	81.1%	49.4%	50.6%
	base = 187		base = 124		base = 74		base = 385	
	(8.2%)		(5.4%)		(14%)		(7.5%)	
Category	56%	44%	40.4%	59.6%	52.2%	47.8%	48.8%	51.2%
	base = 1,653		base = 1,567		base = 347		base = 3,567	
	(72%)		(68.3%)		(66%)		(69.8%)	
Topic/ issue	43.2%	56.8%	35.7%	64.3%	41%	59%	39.1%	60.9%
	base = 454		base = 603		base = 105		base = 1,162	
	(19.8%)		(26.3%)		(20%)		(22.7%)	
Total/ each term	53.7%	46.3%	39.9%	60.1%	45.2%	54.8%	46.6%	53.4%
	base = 2,294		base = 2,294		base = 526		base = 5,114	
	(100%)		(100%)		(100%)		(100%)	

in giving information on administrative issues or on refugees in general, rather than in stories on individual migrants. However, the reasons for a representation do not erase its consequences and can strongly impact our way of talking and thinking about refugees, that is, as a category or as an issue. Table 4.4 also shows that headlines containing *rifugiato* are averagely more positively oriented (53.7 per cent) than those with *richiedente asilo* (45.2 per cent) and *profugo* (39.9 per cent), the latter registering the highest proportion of negative headlines. The predominance of negative orientation in headlines containing *profugo* may be explained with it being more subject to semantic manipulation, as *profugo* lacks any juridical nuances in its meaning (cf. earlier).

The lexeme with the highest proportion of reference to individuals is *richiedente asilo* (14 per cent), and a strikingly high percentage of these headlines display negative orientation (81.1 per cent). Our hypothesis for the relatively high proportion of headlines on individuated asylum seekers and for such a strong asymmetry in their orientation takes into account the outlined literal meaning of the lexeme: *richiedente* derives from *richiedere* (ask for), so that the lexeme itself expresses an action that can only be performed by an individual exerting agentivity and volitionality. Further, a *richiedente asilo* is someone who, under certain juridical circumstances, is asking for the permit to stay in another country under international protection but has not yet obtained such right. Therefore, if one wanted to prevent them – or to persuade the public opinion that they should be prevented – from getting to the 'next stage', the stage of becoming legally recognized refugees, then something could still be done. This could be achieved through discursively representing asylum seekers as potentially problematic, dangerous and undesirable, since the press is aware that public opinion is sensitive to alarmistic tones (cf. our Introduction and see example (27) later in the chapter).

Orientation of headlines varies among the three lexemes when they are used to refer to refugees as a category: orientation is positive in headlines containing *rifugiato*, slightly positive for *richiedente asilo*, and negative for *profugo*. When reference is made to refugees as a topic/issue, headlines tend to display negative orientation with all lexemes. In other words, the topic of refugees is most commonly the issue/problem of refugees.[8]

Discourse Scenarios, Orientation and Reference Type

The following figures capture the relation between scenarios and orientation (Figure 4.3), on the one hand, and between scenarios and reference type, on the other hand (Figure 4.4). The graphs in Figures 4.3 and 4.4 show that headlines depicting refugees as active beings are consistently less numerous than those in which they are treated as passive entities. Furthermore, there is a variety of topics addressed when giving a passive representation of refugees, whereas the assortment of scenarios with refugees playing the role of active agents is very limited.[9] We argue that the preference for reporting on events in which refugees are undergoers rather than active participants is another means of discourse construction through which refugees are given a dehumanized representation.

As shown in Figure 4.3, orientation of active scenarios is mainly negative: initiative is the only scenario with a predominantly positive orientation, while the most frequent active scenario is the distinctly negative Crime. Unsurprisingly, Crime is also the only scenario for which the reference type predominantly points at individual refugees (57.1 per cent), as reported in Figure 4.4 and exemplified in (6) (see also examples (1)b and (2)b previously):

(6)   *Pistoia. Molesta una tredicenne: arrestato richiedente asilo*
[Crime, individuals, negative]

'Pistoia. Harassing a 13-year-old girl: asylum seeker arrested' (Corriere Fiorentino, 2017)

This suggests that when refugees are depicted as individuated and active humans, they are crucially also portrayed as *bad* humans. The only additional

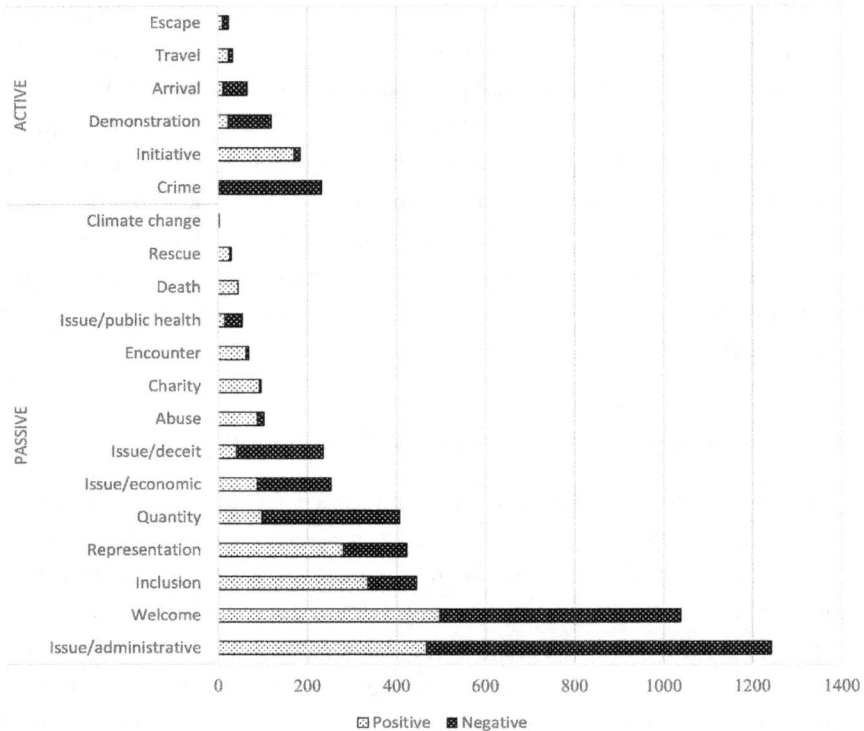

Figure 4.3 Active and passive scenarios with orientation.

scenario for which reference type is considerably, but still not predominantly, towards individuals is the passive Death (36.4 per cent; see example (3)b), which includes reports about refugees' death at sea, in refugee camps or under other circumstances. This is again unsurprising. Western media obviously has no interest in dramatizing the scale of these deaths, exploiting the so-called 'number-game strategy' (see Introduction) that is so common in the news about arrivals, as Western policies are all more or less directly involved and responsible for these deaths. Finally, for all other scenarios, the percentage of headlines that draw reference to individuals does not even reach 20 per cent.

Concerning the frequency distribution of each scenario, we see that Issue/administrative is by far the predominant one: if we add Issue/public health, Issue/deceit, Issue/economic to this count, we total 1,784 out of 5,114 headlines (viz. 34.9 per cent). This confirms that refugees are mostly conceptualized as an issue for the hosting country, rising problems in different key social areas: administration, economy and health.[10] Issue/deceit, in particular, captures the common and mostly, but not exclusively, right-winged rhetoric of 'fake refugees',

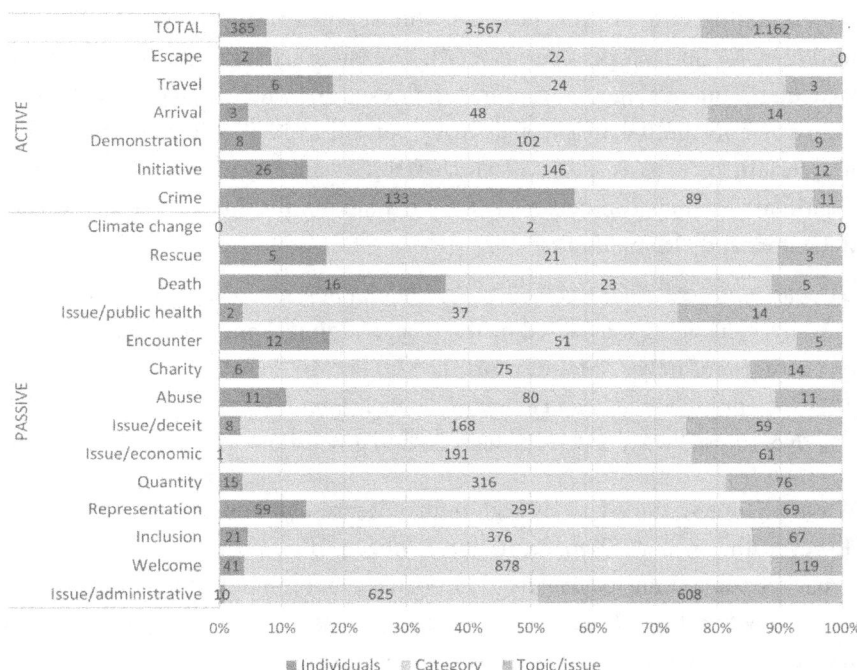

Figure 4.4 Active and passive scenarios with proportion of reference type.

which includes the following argumentations: (a) the NGOs and left-winged associations exploit the migratory phenomenon to be assigned funds by the government (cf. (7); see also (2)c previously and (15) later); (b) most so-called refugees are in fact not eligible for this juridical status (cf. (8)):[11]

(7) *Rifugiati, nei bandi anche coop che compaiono nell'inchiesta*
'Refugees, in the public calls there are also cooperatives that appear in the investigation' (Corriere della Sera Roma, 2015)
(8) *Finti profughi, la truffa dei passaporti*
'Fake refugees, the passports fraud' (Messaggero Udine, 2014)

Even if it is true that some criminal organizations or some individual scammers profit from refugees, this certainly does not constitute an argument against refugees, but rather against criminals that exploit them.

The second most frequent scenario is Welcome (1,038 headlines, viz. 20.3 per cent), almost evenly distributed between positively and negatively oriented headings, which respectively report on willing and unwilling reception of refugees by the citizens of the hosting country. The scenarios Inclusion and

Representation rank at third position, almost equal (respectively 444 and 423 headlines, 8.7 and 8.3 per cent of total). The latter scenario, Representation, is particularly interesting as it captures the extent to which refugees are directly given voice in the Italian press, as in (9), or are explicitly depicted as entities of a certain type, as in (10), in which refugees are negatively represented as illegitimate teachers (on negatively oriented human metaphors, see the section Metaphors and Orientation):

(9) «*Io, massacrato dal regime libico per l'Italia non sono rifugiato politico*»
'«Despite being massacred by the Libyan regime, I am not a political refugee for Italy»' (Mattino, 2013)

(10) *Ora i profughi salgono in cattedra a dare lezioni*
'Now refugees get on the teacher's desk to give lessons' (Libero Milano, 2018)

At a first glimpse, the relatively high rank of Representation seems encouraging. However, the scenario Representation is not even a fourth as frequent as the scenario Issue/administrative. In addition, it is predominantly found in headings that deal with refugees as an indistinct category, as in (10) (cf. Figure 4.4 for an overview), and it can moreover be negatively oriented.

The fourth most represented scenario in our corpus is Quantity (407 headings, 8 per cent), which, as displayed in Table 4.1, was used to tag newspaper articles that specifically focus on the scale of the migratory phenomenon in Italy. Obviously, other news headings, for example, those on Arrivals, may include numbers, too. Thus, the frequency of Quantity may well be rounded down and the total number of headings quantifying the migratory processes could be even greater. This granted, the majority of headlines attesting to the scenario Quantity are negatively oriented: as shown by previous studies (cf. Introduction), numbers and statistics have been proven to be exploited by media and politicians to dramatize the scale of migrations, thus triggering fear in the hosting country population. As a matter of fact, this manipulative usage of framing is frequently accompanied by other manipulative implicit devices (on which, see e.g. the summary in Lombardi Vallauri 2019), such as vague (example (11); see also (3) a) and scalar quantifiers (example (12); see also (4), (5), and (7) previously):

(11) *I rifugiati sono **metà** del popolo*
'Refugees are **half** the population' (Venerdì Repubblica, 2015)

(12) *Un **altro** regalo del governo: 1.500 profughi in Lombardia*
'**Another** gift from the government: 1,500 refugees in Lombardy' (Il Giornale Milano, 2014)

The heading in (11) does not provide the readers with exact numbers: we are just told that refugees are half of an unspecified population (e.g. of Italy? Of a certain city or village? If so, which one?), which is, however, presented as defined through the usage of *del*, composed of the preposition *di* (of) and the definite article *il* (the). The lead in (12) contains the adjective *altro* (another, additional). This quantifier, as well as similar scalar adjectives and adverbs, such as *nuovo* (new), *ennesimo* (umpteenth, further), *anche* (also), and *ancora* (again), activate the conventional implicature that, previously, other undesired events of the same type – here, refugees' arrivals – have occurred. Note that the exact number of these previous arrivals is, again, not provided. Thus, both explicitly framing migrations in a narrative that focuses on quantities and additionally enhancing this narrative through vagueness and implicatures contribute to dehumanizing refugees, by depicting them as high numbers (see also the following analysis of metaphors). Interestingly, the left-winged press at times reveals awareness of this unjust storytelling pattern:

(13) *I profughi sono **persone, non quote***
       'Refugees are **humans, not numbers**' (l'Unità, 2015)

Metaphors and Orientation

Example (13), in which the metaphorical conception of refugees as NUMBERS is explicitly criticized by the writer, drives us to the last section of this chapter, which is devoted to conceptual metaphors. As shown in Table 4.5, refugees are metaphorically mapped onto other entities in 1,387 out of 5,114 headings (viz. 27.1 per cent). In Table 4.5, source domains are divided into clusters and ordered along a continuum based on the assumed degree of dehumanizing portrait they trigger: the higher the group in the table, the more dehumanizing the metaphor.

In what follows, we will discuss examples for each source domain type. Example (14) contains the same metaphor as (13), specifically, REFUGEES ARE NUMBERS, which is counted among ABSTRACT ENTITIES metaphors in Table 4.5:

(14) «*Ecco come il Comune **moltiplicava** i profughi*»
       '«This is how the municipality **multiplied** the refugees»' (Il Tempo, 2015)

Headline (14) does not explicitly map REFUGEES onto NUMBERS, as (13) does. The metaphor is triggered by the verb *moltiplicare* (multiply): numbers can be multiplied, human beings cannot. In fact, conceptual metaphor usually works implicitly: it smuggles coherent views of the world without us being aware of it.[12]

Table 4.5 Source domain types

Source domain type	Occurrences	Orientation	
		Positive	Negative
ABSTRACT ENTITIES	222 (16%)	50 (23%)	172 (77%)
NATURAL MANIFESTATIONS	55 (4%)	6 (11%)	49 (89%)
INANIMATE PHYSICAL OBJECTS	314 (22.6%)	79 (25%)	235 (75%)
ANIMATE NON-HUMAN ENTITIES	27 (1.9%)	7 (26%)	20 (74%)
HUMAN/SUPERNATURAL	40 (2.9%)	24 (60%)	16 (40%)
HUMAN/NON-ADULT	53 (3.8%)	42 (79%)	11 (21%)
HUMAN/ADULT	680 (48.9%)	209 (31%)	471 (69%)
Total	1,391 (100%)	424 (30%)	967 (70%)

Similarly, in (15), the metaphor REFUGEES ARE FLUIDS is instantiated by the verb *arginare* (stem, contain) – see also example (4), in which the same metaphor is activated by *ondata* (wave):

(15) *Hanno un piano per **arginare** i profughi*
'They have a plan to **contain** refugees' (Libero, 2016)

Besides waves, refugees are also mapped to other NATURAL DISASTERS, as happens in (16) with *urto* (shock) and in (17) with *valanga* (avalanche). In Table 4.5, these are accounted for in the NATURAL MANIFESTATIONS category.

(16) *Trieste non regge l'urto dei profughi*
'Trieste cannot withstand the **shock** of refugees' (Il Piccolo, 2016)
(17) ***Valanga** di domande per lo status di rifugiato*
'A **flood** of applications for refugee status' (Gazzettino, 2015)

These metaphors are negatively connotated and map refugees onto inanimate and mass entities, such as water or snow, thus contributing to refugees' dehumanization at multiple levels. Going along the continuum of dehumanization of Table 4.5, refugees can also be mapped to countable INANIMATE PHYSICAL OBJECTS to be sorted (18) or managed (19):

(18) *Buttati altri 70 milioni per **smistare** i profughi nelle province lombarde*
'Further 70 million wasted to **sort** the refugees in the Lombard provinces' (Libero Milano, 2018)
(19) *Altri 90 profughi sono arrivati in città. Variati furioso: «**Gestiti come pacchi**»*
'Another 90 refugees have arrived in the city. Variati is furious: «**Managed like packages**»' (Corriere Veneto, 2014)

The given headlines have opposite orientation: (18) is negatively oriented towards refugees, while (19) is positively oriented and condemns the way refugees were handled like packages. As much as the report explicitly criticizes it, example (19) still uses a dehumanizing metaphor: as Lakoff (2004: 3) puts it, when one is arguing against the other side, one should avoid using their language, as 'their language picks out a frame – and it won't be the frame you want'. As in (18), the fact that refugees are objects and, as such, have a cost is emphasized in (20):

(20) *I profughi ci sono già **costati** 2.5 milioni*
'Refugees **costed** us 2.5 million already' (Libero Milano, 2014)

Other definitely negative metaphors belonging to this cluster are REFUGEES ARE TRASH (21) and the widespread REFUGEES ARE MEANS/WEAPONS, for example, to make illegal money ((22); in this respect, see also our analysis of the scenario 'issue/deceit') and to reach political/diplomatic goals in the national (23) or worldwide (24) arena.

(21) *Da eden a ghetto, Corcolle è la **discarica dei rifugiati***
'From eden to ghetto, Corcolle is the **refugee dump**' (Tempo, 2014)
(22) *«I rifiuti **rendono** più dei profughi»*
'«Waste **makes** more than refugees»' (La Verità, 2018)
(23) *Basta **usare** i profughi per fare politica*
'Stop **using** refugees to do politics' (La Stampa, 2018)
(24) *Erdogan '**schiera**' l'arma dei profughi*
'Erdogan **"deploys"** the refugee **weapon**' (Avvenire, 2018)

Note that in (22), given that incomes deriving from waste and refugees are compared, refugees are again paralleled to trash as in (21). As discussed earlier for the headline in (19), the metaphor in (23) acts as a resounding board of an unjust framing, though explicitly condemning it.

Refugees are also infrequently mapped to animate non-human entities, such as different types of animals (cf. Santa Ana 1999): (25) instantiate REFUGEES ARE RATS (and is related with REFUGEES ARE TRASH of (21) and (22)), (26) REFUGES ARE WILD ANIMALS, (27) REFUGEES ARE PREYS and (28) REFUGEES ARE BEES (Musolff 2015: 47 ff. thoroughly analyses the metaphor IMMIGRANTS ARE PARASITES, which also crucially emphasizes the idea that refugees suck economic resources of the hosting country, on which see further in this section). Different metaphors highlight diverse alleged similarities between refugees and animals: (i) dirtiness (25); (ii) dangerousness ((26), (28)); (iii) powerlessness (27).

(25) *Rifugiati e profughi «topi» dei cassonetti*
 'Refugees, dumpster «**rats**»' (Tempo, 2014)
(26) *A Calais, nella **giungla** dei rifugiati. Il Front trasforma la paura in voti*
 'In Calais, in the refugee **jungle**. The Front turns fear into votes' (Stampa, 2015)
(27) *Rifugiati in **trappola***
 '**Trapped** refugees' (Left, 2013)
(28) *Rifugiati, l'**arnia** di Mosca contro l'Europa*
 'Refugees, the **hive** of Moscow against Europe' (La Stampa, 2016)

The most frequent type of metaphors maps refugees onto different types of human beings: divine/supernatural entities (29); non-adult humans/pupils (30); adult, mostly dangerous, humans, such as ENEMIES (31) or, more generally, RIVALS (32) (van Dijk 1991; Reisigl and Wodak 2001; ter Wal 2002).

(29) *l Piemonte di Cerutti è **terra promessa** di rifugiati e profughi*
 'Cerutti's Piedmont is the **promised land** of refugees' (Il Giornale, 2016)
(30) *Ca' Foscari '**adotta**' 'studenti-rifugiati'*
 'Ca' Foscari "**adopts**" "student-refugees"' (Gazzettino, 2013)
(31) *«Noi **assediati** da zingari, immigrati e rifugiati»*
 '«We **besieged** by gypsies, immigrants and refugees»' (Tempo Roma, 2014)
(32) *Il Papa: «Ospitate i rifugiati» I dubbi dei parroci: e gli italiani?*
 'The Pope: «Host refugees» The doubts of parish priests: how about Italians?' (Il Giornale, 2015)

Thus, when refugees are depicted as human entities, they are also portrayed either as subject to the authority of a higher order entity (i.e. a god in (29), an instructor in (30)) or as a threat for life (31) and/or prosperity (32) of the citizens of the hosting country. In the latter case, Italy and Italians may even be described as REFUGEES-ENEMIES' VICTIMS in the right-winged press, up to the point that host citizens become the 'real refugees' (on 'fake refugees', cf. our analysis of discourse scenarios):

(33) *Ostaggi nelle città: **i veri profughi siamo diventati noi***
 'Hostages in the cities: **we have become the real refugees**' (Libero, 2014)

Conclusions

In this chapter, we showed how the Italian terms for refugees and asylum seekers, that is, *rifugiato*, *profugo* and *richiedente asilo*, lose some of their semantic traits in press discourse. Starting from the technical meanings of these terms, we carried out a quantitative analysis on a corpus of newspaper headings dating back from 2013 to 2019. We observed that, in line with what is happening in the international press, the concepts of migrants and refugees tend to blur: the misuse of these terms causes them to lose some of their specific semantic traits. Such bleaching occurs at different paces for the three lexemes. We explained these differences by taking into account the influence of the international press and the varying formal and semantic complexities of the terms, which make them more or less susceptible to manipulation. In addition, we measured the discursive means of dehumanization in a subcorpus of 5,114 headlines by operationalizing our theoretical assumptions in four parameters: (a) orientation; (b) reference type; (c) scenario; (d) metaphors.

Our bivariate analyses showed what follows. (i) Reference to individuals is generally rather marginal, apart for *richiedente asilo* in negatively oriented titles that tell about crimes perpetrated by asylum seekers. Thus, refugees are more frequently conceptualized as an indistinct category or as an abstract issue rather than as groups made up of distinct people, who may have their own painful stories and reasons for undertaking their migratory routes. (ii) Refugees tend to be depicted as passive undergoers rather than as active participants, thus being discursively deprived of their agentivity and intentionality. When they are portrayed as active individuals, they are also portrayed as criminals. (iii) Refugees are metaphorically conceptualized as non-human and non-adult entities (including numbers, natural manifestations, different kinds of objects, animals and children/pupils), thus as entities lacking individuation, agentivity and/or intentionality. Again, when refugees are instead described in terms of adult humans, they are also *dangerous* adult humans, such as enemies or rivals.

Our analyses also allowed for some interesting insights falling out of the precise scope of our research, but undoubtedly worthy of further investigation. For instance, unfavourable representation of refugees also occurs when they are grouped, for example, using list constructions, together with members of other categories that are deemed negative, that is, with *clandestini* (clandestines), *zingari* (gipsies) (cf. (31)) or *anarchici* (anarchists). Furthermore, we hinted at the fact that the use of scalar quantifiers, such as *altro/altri* (another/other), *nuovi* (new), *ancora* (again) and *ennesimo* (umpteenth, further), also confers a negative tone to news on refugees via the manipulative power of implicatures (on this, also see Zanchi et al. submitted). Finally, there are instances of *profugo* with metaphorical reference to someone finding themselves alone, having no one else to support them, also with derogatory evaluation (34) (cf. also example in (33)):

(34) *Lite sui richiedenti asilo. Con Fontana governatore **il vero «profugo»** è Sala*
'Fight over asylum seekers. With Fontana as governor **the real «refugee»** is Sala' (Libero Milano, 2018)

On the one hand, this usage undoubtedly shows the negative connotation assigned to *profugo* and the argued ease of its semantic broadening; on the other, it interacts with the mentioned right-winged rhetoric of fake versus real refugees, which also would deserve further investigation in future studies.

Notes

1 The following research was conducted within the crowdfunded project *Words Matter. Il peso delle parole nel dibattito pubblico* at University of Pavia. We would like to express our gratitude for all the funders who made this possible. We would also like to thank CARES_Osservatorio di Pavia for providing us with the initial corpus of headlines. This work is the result of the close cooperation of the two authors. For academic purposes, Serena Coschignano is responsible for sections *Quantitative Analysis: The Presence of Refugees in the Italian Press* and *Qualitative Analysis: Discursive Means of Dehumanization*, Chiara Zanchi for sections *Introduction, Theory and Methods* and *Conclusions*.
2 Cf. https://www.aljazeera.com/blogs/editors-blog/2015/08/al-jazeera-mediterranean-migrants-150820082226309.html (last access: 8 February 2022).
3 See, for instance, *La moglie di Ablyazov aveva il titolo di rifugiato in Inghilterra* (Ablyazov's wife used to have refugee status in England). Mukhtar Kabyluly Ablyazov is among co-founders and leaders of the unregistered, banned and deemed as extremist political party *Democratic Choice of Kazakhstan*.
4 Some headlines contain occurrences of more than one term – for example, **Profughi**, *a Drena una festa per conoscere le storie dei **rifugiati*** (Refugees, a party in Drena to get to know refugees' stories). In such cases, we independently analysed each lexeme.
5 Fifteen headlines only contain the term *richiedente* (seeker) without modifiers or in a different collocation from *richiedente asilo*, such as *richiedente protezione* (protection seeker). Since they are coreferential with *richiedente asilo*, we included such headlines in our analysis.

6   In the full-colour original diagram, it is evident that the bottom-right corner is occupied by two intertwined yet distinct word clouds. For this reason, we keep them separate in Table 4.2.
7   In another study (Zanchi et al. submitted), we elaborate on Quantification and its lexical activators – for example, numerals and indefinite quantifiers such as *altro/altri* (another/other), *nuovi* (new, additional) and *ennesimo* (umpteenth, further). These do not appear in Table 4.2 since they are classified as 'function words' in Iramuteq, while its thematic clustering is performed on 'lexical words' only.
8   The English 'refugee crisis' has no direct equivalent in Italian: in our corpus there are only eight instances of *crisi dei rifugiati* and four of *crisi (dei) profughi*. *Emergenza profughi* (refugee emergency) is more widespread and occurs thirty-two times; *emergenza rifugiati* (refugee emercengy) occurs twelve times, while *emergenza sbarchi* (landing emergency) and *emergenza immigrazione* (immigration emergency) only once.
9   We point out that we distinguished the scenario of 'escape' from those of 'travel' and of 'arrival', but they could also be considered different subparts of the same event, that is, moving from one place to another one; this merging would further reduce the already limited variety of active scenarios.
10 Our data does not cover the year 2020, in which, due to the spread of Covid-19, the association between refugees' arrivals and public health issue has become viral in the Italian mediatic and political discourse (cf. VIII Carta di Roma report: https://www.cartadiroma.org/wp-content/uploads/2020/12/Notizie-di-transito.pdf; last access: 8 February 2022).
11 Note that in (2)c the actual criminals who speculate on refugees are only vaguely referred to. Another example of vagueness as an implicit discursive means of manipulation is given in (11).
12 Words that activate metaphorical mappings are highlighted in bold in the examples.

References

Baker, Paul, Gabrielatos, Costas, KhosraviNik, Majid, Kryzanowski, Michal, McEnery, Tony, and Wodak, Ruth. 2008. A useful methodological synergy? Combining critical discourse analysis and corpus linguistics to examine discourses of refugees and asylum seekers in the UK press. *Discourse & Society* 19(3): 273–306.

Blommaert, Jan. 2001. Investigating narrative inequality: African asylum seekers in Belgium. *Discourse and Society* 12(4): 413–49.

Charteris-Black, Jonathan. 2004. *Corpus Approaches to Critical Metaphor Analysis*. Basingstoke: Palgrave Macmillan.

Chilton, Paul, and George, Lakoff. 1995. Foreign policy by metaphor. In: Schäffner, Christina, and Anita L. Wenden (eds), *Language and Peace*. Aldershot: Dartmouth, 37–60.

Clyne, Michael. 2005. The use of exclusionary language to manipulate opinion. *Journal of Language and Politics* 4(2): 173–96.

Coates, Linda, and Allan Wade. 2007. Language and violence: Analysis of four discursive operations. *Journal of Family Violence* 22: 511–22.

Colombo, Monica (ed.). 2013. *Discourse and Politics of Migration in Italy. The Production and Reproduction of Ethnic Dominance and Exclusion [Special Issue of Journal of Language and Politics 12(2)]*. Amsterdam: Benjamins.

Fairclough, Norman. 1989. *Language and Power*. London & New York: Longman.

Fairclough, Norman. 2015. *Language and Power* (3 suppl.). London & New York: Routledge.

Flowerdew, John, Li, David C.S., and Tran, Sarah. 2002. Discriminatory news discourse: Some Hong Kong data. *Discourse and Society* 13(3): 319–45.

Grimm, Scott. 2018. Grammatical number and the scale of individuation. *Language* 94(3): 527–74.

Hart, Christopher. 2011. Force-interactive patterns in immigration discourse: A cognitive linguistic approach to CDA. *Discourse & Society* 22(3): 269–86.

Hart, Chistopher. 2015. Cognitive linguistics and critical discourse analysis. In: Dabrowska, Ewa, and Divjak, Dagmar (eds), *Handbook of Cognitive Linguistics*. Berlin: De Gruyter, 322–45.

Hart, Christopher. 2021. Animals vs. armies: Resistance to extreme metaphors in antiimmigration discourse. *Journal of Language and Politics* 20(2): 226–53.

KhosraviNik, Majid. 2009. The representation of refugees, asylum seekers and immigrants in British newspapers during the Balkan conflict (1999) and the British general election (2005). *Discourse and Society* 20(4): 477–98.

KhosraviNik, Majid. 2010. Actor descriptions, action attributes, and argumentation: Towards a systematisation of CDA analytical categories in the representation of social groups. *Critical Discourse Studies* 7(1): 55–72.

Lakoff, George. 2004. *Don't Think of an Elephant*. White River Junction (VT): Chelsea Green Publishing Company.

Lakoff, George, and Johnson, Mark. 1980. *Metaphors We Live By*. Chicago: University of Chicago Press.

Meyers, Marian. 1997. *News Coverage of Violence against Women: Engendering Blame*. London: SAGE.

Mollica, Fabio, and Wilke, Beatrice. 2017. Metaphor and conceptualization of migration in the German and Italian press. In: Erica Pinelli, and Annalisa Baicchi (eds), *Cognitive Modelling in Language and Discourse across Cultures*, 233–48. Cambridge: Cambridge Scholars Publishing.

Musolff, Andreas. 2015. Dehumanizing metaphors in UK immigrant debates in press and online media. *Journal of Language aggression and Conflict* 3(1): 41–56.

Orrù, Paolo. 2017. *Il discorso sulle migrazioni nell'Italia contemporanea. Un'analisi linguistico-discorsiva sulla stampa (2000–2010)*. Milano: Franco Angeli.

Pietikainen, Sari. 2003. Indigenous identity in print: Representations of the Sami discourse. *Discourse and Society* 14(5): 581–609.

Reisigl, Martin, and Wodak, Ruth. 2001. *Discourse and Discrimination: Rhetorics of Racism and Anti-Semitism*. London and New York: Routledge.

Rydgren, Jens. 2008. Immigration sceptics, xenophobes or racists? radical right-wing voting in six west European countries. *European Journal of Political Research* 47: 737–65.

Santa Ana, Otto. 1999. Like an animal I was treated: Anti-immigrant metaphor in US public discourse. *Discourse and Society* 10(2): 191–224.

Scott, James C. 1990. *Domination and the Arts of Resistance*. New Haven, CT: Yale University Press.

Taylor, C., and Marchi, A. 2018. *Corpus Approaches to Discourse: A Critical Review*. Oxon: Routledge.

Teo, Peter. 2000. Racism in the news: A critical discourse analysis of news reporting in two Australian newspapers. *Discourse and Society* 11(1): 7–49.

ter Wal, Jessika (ed.) 2002. *Racism and Cultural Diversity in the Mass Media: An Overview of Research and Examples of Good Practice in the EU Member States, 1995–2000*. Vienna: European Monitoring Centre on Racism and Xenophobia.

Tileaga, Cristian. 2005. Accounting for extreme prejudice and legitimating blame in the talk about the Romanies. *Discourse and Society* 16(5): 603–24.

van der Valk, Ineke. 2000. Interruption in French parliamentary debates on immigration. In: Reisigl, Martin, and Wodak, Ruth (eds), *The Semiotics of Racism, Approaches in Critical Discourse Analysis*, 105–28. Vienna: Passagen.

van Dijk, Teun A. 1984. *Prejudice in Discourse*. Amsterdam: Benjamins.

van Dijk, Teun A. 1991. *Racism and the Press*. London: Routledge.

van Dijk, Teun A. 1998. *Ideology*. London: SAGE.

van Dijk, Teun A. 1999. Racism, monitoring and the media. In: Nordenstreng, Kaarle, and Griffin, Michael (eds), *International Media Monitoring*, 307–16. Cresskill, NJ: Hampton.

van Dijk, Teun A. 2003. The discourse and knowledge interface. In: Weiss, Gilbert, and Wodak, Ruth (eds), *Critical Discourse Analysis; Theory and Interdisciplinarity*, 85–109. Palgrave: Macmillan.

van Dijk, Teun A. 2004 [2000], *Ideologie. Discorso e costruzione sociale del pregiudizio*. Roma: Carocci.

van Dijk, Teun A. 2005. *Racism and Discourse in Spain and Latin America*. Amsterdam: Benjamins.

van Leeuwen, Theo, and Wodak, Ruth. 1999. Legitimizing immigration control: A discourse-historical analysis. *Discourse Studies* 1(1): 83–118.

Verhoeven, Elisabeth. 2017. Scales or features in verb meaning? Verb classes as predictors of syntactic behavior. *Belgian Journal of Linguistics* 31: 164–93.

Vigo, Francesca. 2017. Climate-induced migration and infotainment: The ultimate edge of news construction?. *Anglistica AION* 21(2): 113–29.

Vihman, Virve-Anneli, and Nelson, Diane. 2019. Effects of animacy in grammar and cognition: Introduction to special issue. *Open Linguistics* 5(1): 260–67.

Weiss, Gilbert, and Wodak, Ruth (eds) 2003. *Critical Discourse Analysis: Theory and Interdisciplinary*. Basingstoke, UK: Palgrave.

Wodak, Ruth. 2015. *The Politics of Fear: What Right-Wing Populist Discourses Mean*. London: SAGE.

Zanchi, Chiara, Coschignano, Serena, and Minnema, Gosse. Submitted. Explaining the distribution of implicit means of misrepresentation: A case study on Italian immigration discourse. *Journal of Pragmatics*.

Part II

Constructing Emotion in Internet Discourses

5

A Comparative Study of Donald J. Trump and Matteo Salvini's Populist Strategies in the Representation of Immigrants and Refugees on Twitter

Ester Di Silvestro

Introduction

The election of President Donald J. Trump in 2016 highlighted the growth of a phenomenon that seems to be unstoppable. Populism is a heterogeneous phenomenon capable of adapting to different contexts and political situations (Mudde and Kaltwasser 2017: 1). The phenomenon was born in the nineteenth century in Russia (Canovan 1981: 96) and since then it has spread around the globe. The current rise and revival of populism – especially in Europe and America – is due to several reasons, particularly the precarious socio-economic situation caused by the financial crisis of 2008 (Tormey 2019). In addition to the unstable economic situation, it is also important to take into consideration the immigration phenomenon and all the terrorist attacks that followed 9/11 since they are strategically exploited by far-right populist politicians in order to amplify both fear and instability. Indeed, far-right politicians usually present a polarized vision of the world based on the dichotomy *us versus them* (Wodak 2015; Tormey 2019).

Populist politicians are well known for their discursive strategies that aim to trigger people's emotions (Wahl-Jorgensen 2018) in order to gain consensus. Even the fundamental dichotomy *people versus elite* is based upon a feeling of dissatisfaction that the people feel towards the elite. In this situation characterized by general dissatisfaction, populist leaders try to gain people's consensus through the feeling of trust; for this reason, populist leaders represent themselves as being part of the people and as the *vox populi* (de la Torre 2019: 2; Mudde and Kaltwasser 2017: 68) that will take back power. Another crucial aspect to highlight is that far-right populist politicians' attitude towards immigration is combined with Islam because these politicians aim to trigger the emotion of fear that is inevitably connected to racism, xenophobia and Islamophobia.

Nowadays social media play a crucial role in the strategies of politicians because they are part of our everyday life and, most importantly, they are part of the political sphere. Specifically, social media are particularly useful for populist politicians since they facilitate the unmediated and direct relationship between the populist leader and the people. Indeed, politicians are able to address the electorate directly and without the help of traditional media (Enli 2017; Van Kessel and Castelein 2016) and to disseminate their ideologies very easily (Kreis 2017). More precisely, Twitter is the social media that has a perfect synergy with populist discourse (Ott 2017) mainly because of its technological constrains (such as the limitation of characters) that can favour the direct and aggressive populist style of communication.

Even though this case study is part of a larger research project about populist discourse in Italy and in the United States, it focuses mainly on how populist politicians are able to trigger some emotions through the employment of specific linguistic strategies. The following section describes the collection of the data and how the corpora were built. The methodology and the research questions are presented in Section 3. Section 4 is dedicated to the results of the qualitative analysis and their discussion. The results of the quantitative analysis are showed and discussed in Section 5. The last section is dedicated to conclusions and further research.

Collection of Data and Corpora Building

The data were collected in the time span that covers – for both politicians – the last three months of electoral campaign and the following seven months. The time span was chosen to investigate both campaign and institutional communication. More precisely, the time span of Trump's data goes from 1 September 2016 to 31 July 2017. The time span of Salvini's data goes from 1 January 2018 to 31 October 2018.

Donald Trump's tweets were collected on the website *Trump Twitter Archive* and were organized in a corpus (Trump Tweets Corpus) that counts 2,253 tweets. In order to analyse the tweets qualitatively, I created a subcorpus that counts fifty tweets. I reduced the original corpus through specific keywords such as 'Europe',

'EU', 'west', 'border', 'immigration', 'immigrant/s', 'ISIS', 'refugee/s', 'Mexico' and 'wall'. Trump's traditional speeches were collected on the website *The American Presidency Project* and were organized in a corpus (Trump Traditional Speeches) that counts ten traditional speeches.

Matteo Salvini's tweets were collected through a Google Chrome tool called Data Miner on Salvini's official Twitter account @matteosalvinimi and were organized in a corpus (Salvini Tweets Corpus) that counts 1,597 tweets. Even in this case, I created a subcorpus that counts fifty tweets through the keywords *immigrazione* (immigration), *immigrato/i* (immigrant/s) and *Europa* (Europe). The traditional speeches were collected through videos available on Salvini's official Facebook page. I transcribed all the speeches except for one speech that I found already transcribed on the Italian Senate website. The Salvini Traditional Corpus counts ten traditional speeches as well.

To sum up, all the data were organized into four corpora and two subcorpora:

1. Trump Tweet Corpus (2,253 tweets and 49,694 tokens)
   Trump Tweet Corpus for UAM Corpus Tool (50 tweets)
2. Trump Traditional Corpus (10 speeches and 39,075 tokens)
3. Salvini Tweet Corpus (1,597 tweets and 59,112 tokens)
   Salvini Tweet Corpus for UAM Corpus Tool (50 tweets)
4. Salvini Traditional Corpus (10 speeches and 43,631 tokens)

Methodology

The data were analysed with a combination of critical discourse analysis and corpus linguistics approaches. The qualitative part of the analysis (Machin and Mayr 2012) was carried out through the employment of the software UAM Corpus Tool (O'Donnell 2008). Specifically, both tweets (the subcorpora of fifty tweets) and traditional speeches were uploaded on UAM Corpus Tool and were annotated. The qualitative analysis focused on three major aspects: metaphors (Lakoff and Johnson 1980), *topoi* (Wodak 2015) and representational strategies (van Leeuwen 1996, 2008; van Dijk 1998). I decided to take into consideration these three main aspects because their combination provides a clear and (almost) complete picture about the representation of refugees and immigrants. It is also necessary to specify that although immigrants and refugees have two different legal statuses, during the analysis they were considered as one category because the distinction between immigrants and refugees is often ambiguous and blurred (Baker et al. 2008). First, the qualitative analysis focused on the source domains used by Trump and Salvini. The importance of metaphors is due to the fact that they are so deeply embedded in our everyday language and sometimes they are even used unconsciously (Lakoff and Johnson 1980). Moreover, metaphorical expressions help us to shape and understand the world around us since they provide a source for the process of conceptualization (Chilton 2004: 51). Second, *topoi* are argumentative strategies theorized by Wodak (2015) in her Discourse Historical Approach. They can be defined as *content-related warrants* that connect an argument to a conclusion and at the same time justify this connection (Wodak 2015: 76). For this reason, *topoi* can facilitate the production and the legitimation of some statements concerning specific social actors such as the dangerousness of immigrants and refugees. Third, I followed van Leeuwen's approach (2008) regarding social actors' representational strategies – especially his seminal classification based upon a socio-semantic perspective (van Leeuwen 2008: 23) – and van Dijk's (1998) approach concerning legitimation and delegitimation strategies.

The quantitative part of the analysis (Baker 2006; Partington et al. 2013) was supported by the software Sketch Engine (Kilgariff et al. 2014) where I uploaded both tweets and traditional speeches. The corpus linguistics approach was used mainly to verify the results of the qualitative analysis. For this reason, the quantitative approach focused on the analysis of the concordances and the co-occurrences of specific words connected to each source domain, *topos* and representational strategy identified during the qualitative analysis. Starting from these methodological premises, the present analysis aims to answer the following research questions:

1. What are the – similar or different – strategies that Donald Trump and Matteo Salvini use in order to create a lack of empathy in the representation of refugees and immigrants?
2. Are there any similarities or differences between the linguistic strategies that Trump and Salvini employ in tweets and traditional speeches?

Qualitative Analysis

The qualitative part of the analysis is based on the results of the annotations carried out through the software UAM Corpus Tool.[1] It is important to specify that all the percentages shown in the tables of this section include the results of both tweets and traditional speeches.

Metaphors

The analysis of metaphors identified three source domains that are employed by Trump and Salvini in the representation of immigrants and refugees. Metaphors related to migration were not frequently found as Trump's corpora count just one occurrence and Salvini's corpora count nine occurrences (Table 5.1).

1. I am going to end illegal immigration, stop the **massive inflow of refugees**, keep jobs from pouring out of our country, renegotiate our disastrous trade deals, and massively reduce taxes and regulations on our workers and our small businesses. [emphasis added] (Remarks at Prescott Valley Event Center in Prescott Valley, Arizona 4 October 2016)
2. [. . .] and this rosary was made by an exploited woman, by one of those women who had been deluded that in Italy there were homes and jobs for everyone. **She was uprooted from her land**. [emphasis added] (Salvini's Speech, Pontida 7 July 2018)[2]
3. Today the ship Sea Watch 3, a German NGO flying the flag of Holland, is off the coast of Libya too, waiting **to carry out the umpteenth load of immigrants** to bring to Italy. Italy has stopped to bend the head and to obey, this time THERE IS SOMEONE WHO SAYS NO. #closetheharbours [emphasis added] (Salvini's tweet, 11 June 2018)[3]

Example 1 shows the only metaphor found in Trump's corpora; it is a water metaphor that is very common in the description of these social actors since water is an unpredictable force of nature. As a result, refugees are perceived as an uncontrollable threat that needs to be stopped. According to the qualitative results, Salvini uses the nature, and the object and merchandise source domains. The first one is showed in example 2 where the then Italian Minister of the Interior compares a woman to a plant that was uprooted from her native land. It is also interesting to emphasize how he describes this woman as a completely passive social actor without any type of human agency. Example 3 shows the source domain that Salvini uses the most. It is a dehumanizing metaphor that represents immigrants as a load of inanimate objects that are loaded in the

Table 5.1 Source domain percentages

Source domain	Donald Trump	Matteo Salvini
Nature	—	22%
Objects and merchandise	—	78%
Water	100%	—

Mediterranean Sea by NGOs and unloaded in the coasts of Italy. Specifically, in example 3, Salvini blames NGOs for immigrants' dehumanization in order to discredit NGOs but at the same time to legitimize his immigration policies. Trump's only occurrence of metaphors was found in the traditional speeches; on the other hand, Salvini uses the source domain of object and merchandise in both corpora and the source domain of nature just in his Traditional Corpus.

Topoi

In addition to metaphors, Trump and Salvini use *topoi* as well in the representation of both immigrants and refugees. Specifically, during the analysis I have identified four types of *topoi*: burden, danger, threat and fear, invasion and victim. Trump's *topoi* occurrences are thirty, while Salvini's occurrences are sixty-eight; their distribution can be found in Table 5.2.

4. Wow, just came out on secret tape that Crooked Hillary **wants to take in as many Syrians as possible. We cannot let this happen – ISIS!** [emphasis added] (Trump's Tweet, 24 October 2016)
5. A couple of months ago the prosecutor of Agrigento (the one who is investigating me) said: '**there is a high risk of terrorists' presence on board of immigrants' boats**' Has he changed his mind? For me the problem is the same even TODAY. [emphasis added] (Salvini's Tweet, 26 August 2018)[4]
6. **Thousands of refugees are being admitted, with no way to screen them**, and **are instantly made eligible for welfare and free healthcare** – even as our own Veterans die waiting for the medical care they need. [emphasis added] (Remarks at Prescott Valley Event Center in Prescott Valley, Arizona 4 October 2016)

Example 4 shows a combination of the danger, threat and fear and the invasion *topoi*. The wording *as many Syrians as possible* suggests an indefinite huge

Table 5.2 *Topoi* percentages

Topoi	Donald Trump	Matteo Salvini
Burden	10%	28%
Danger, threat and fear	83%	44%
Invasion	7%	12%
Victim	—	16%

number of people coming into the United States who – according to Trump – have a connection with radical Islamic terrorism. In this regard, it is crucial to underline how Trump implies that all Syrians are affiliated to ISIS; indeed, the tweet ends simply with the word 'ISIS!' that Trump uses to warn his followers and to justify his immigration policies. Similarly, Salvini employs the same strategy by talking about the potential presence of terrorists on immigrants' boats in example 5. Example 6 shows how refugees can be perceived as an economic burden (especially if they are compared to other suffering groups of people such as veterans) because they have free access to healthcare. Consequently, these social actors are described as having privileges that they should not have. In this tweet there are other two *topoi*. First, the *topos* of invasion since Trump talks about thousands of refugees who are entering into the United States. Second, it is the *topos* of danger, threat and fear because he claims that all these refugees are being admitted into the country without any control or screening. Finally, example 2 shows how Salvini uses the *topos* of the victim to describe immigrants. Specifically, he presents himself as a compassionate man who does not blame immigrants but rather the elites (such as the European Union and his Italian political opponents) for wrong immigration policies that cause suffering to both immigrants and Italians. Salvini employs the *topos* of the victim especially referring to the ones that he calls 'true' refugees. Few women, boys and children who escape from war and who should not be confused with illegal immigrants. However, the *topos* of the victim is used by Salvini mainly to describe Italians who suffer reverse racism (see example 12). Trump and Salvini employ each type of *topos* (except for the victim *topos*) in both corpora. The only exception is Trump's burden *topos* that was found just in the Traditional Corpus.

Representational Strategies

Donald Trump and Matteo Salvini employ several types of representational strategies, summarized in Table 5.3, but they mainly use the connection to crime and terrorism, the aggregation and the opposition strategies. Trump's corpora count fifty-six occurrences, while Salvini's corpora count ninety-one occurrences.

7. **ISIS is taking credit for the terrible stabbing attack** at Ohio State University by **a Somali refugee** who should not have been in our country. [emphasis added] (Trump's Tweet, 30 November 2016)

Table 5.3 Representational strategies percentages

Representational strategies	Donald Trump	Matteo Salvini
Aggregation	32%	40%
Crime and terrorism	41%	33%
Genericization	11%	11%
Opposition	11%	15%
Specification	—	1%
Suppression	5%	—

8. **Mexico** was just ranked **the second deadliest country in the world**, after only Syria. **Drug trade** is largely the cause. **We will BUILD THE WALL!** [emphasis added] (Trump's Tweet, 23 June 2017)
9. Hillary has called for **550% more Syrian immigrants**, but won't even mention **'radical Islamic terrorists'**. #Debate #BigLeagueTruth. [emphasis added] (Trump's Tweet, 23 June 2017)
10. During the last week, @poliziadistato has arrested 528 people, of whom **more than a half are immigrants**, and reported 2,478 people, of whom **over 50% are immigrants. More immigration means more criminality**: having reduced disembarkations and arrivals, despite complaints, is a source of pride for me! [emphasis added] (Salvini's Tweet, 7 September 2018)[5]
11. **Who thinks that the woman has less rights than man stays at home because Italy is not fit for him.** [. . .] and if you want to **cover her with carpets** you do it at your home, because I do not want in Italy people dressed in a **Batman suit**. [emphasis added] (Salvini's speech, Pinzolo 25 August 2018)[6]
12. #Diciotti immigrants on hunger-strike? Do as they please. **In Italy 5 millions of people live in absolute POVERTY (1.2 millions of CHILDREN)**, who go on hunger-strike every day, in the silence of do-gooders, journalists and various comrades. #Italiansfirst [emphasis added] (Salvini's Tweet, 24 August 2018)[7]
13. ISIS is on the run & will soon be wiped out of Syria & Iraq, <u>**illegal border crossings**</u> **are way down (75%)** & MS 13 gangs are being removed. [emphasis added] (Trump's Tweet, 12 July 2017)

In example 7, Trump combines the association to terrorism with genericization talking about *a* generic *Somali refugee*. As a result, Trump leads his followers to believe that all (Somali) refugees are potential threats who can be affiliated to ISIS. In example 8, he implicitly associates immigration (Southern American immigration and especially Mexican immigration) to crime. In this way, he wants to legitimize his immigration policies (in this specific case the construction of the wall) that include a physical exclusion of both immigrants and refugees. In both examples 9 and 10, Trump and Salvini combine the aggregation strategy with the association to crime and terrorism. It is important to mention that the strategy that connects these social actors to crime and terrorism is strictly connected to the *topos* of danger, threat and fear. Consequently, during the analysis this association was useful in the identification of the *topos* and vice versa. The aggregation strategy is also present in other examples such as examples 6 and 13. This is one of the most important strategies used by both politicians because immigrants and refugees are not perceived as human beings since they are represented through the employment of numbers, percentages and statistics. Example 11 shows a traditional type of opposition strategy based on culture and religion that highlights the impossibility of integration; indeed, Salvini – during his speech in Pinzolo in occasion of a League Party – talks in a derogatory way about the condition of Islamic women comparing the burqa to a Batman suit. However, in example 12, it is possible to find a type of opposition strategy that the leader of the League definitely prefers to use. Specifically, he opposes two suffering groups of social actors. In this case, immigrants are opposed to suffering Italian people. According to Salvini, Italian people should feel more empathetic towards their poor suffering compatriots rather than towards immigrants who are represented as ungrateful and capricious protesters. Trump employs this type of opposition strategy as well; more precisely, in example 6, he opposes the privileged refugees (who have free access to healthcare) to suffering veterans (who still wait for the same assistance). In both cases, it is clear that this strategy aims to shift people's empathy and trigger anger towards an unfair situation. Lastly, the suppression strategy – that is used just by Trump according to the qualitative results – completely suppresses the existence of these human beings that are assimilated to criminals and are reduced to *illegal border crossings*. The connection to crime and terrorism, the aggregation and the genericization strategies are present in both politicians' Tweet and Traditional Corpora. On the one hand, Trump uses the opposition strategy just in traditional speeches. On the other hand, he employs the suppression strategy just in tweets. Finally, the only (there is just one occurrence) specification strategy used by Salvini was found in his Tweets Corpus.

Hashtags

In addition to the strategies previously mentioned, the employment of specific hashtags must be highlighted. The first reason why is because hashtags are an essential feature of Twitter since they connect people who do not know each other (Murthy, 2013: 3) but who can share the same values (Zappavigna, 2014: 142). Second, they are potentially viral. This characteristic can be used by politicians to spread their ideologies that are summarized in well-structured and well-thought-out hashtags.

14. [...] the wall is not built, which it will be, the drug situation will NEVER be fixed the way it should be! **#BuildTheWall** [emphasis added] (Trump's Tweet, 24 April 2017)
15. **#Stopinvasion**. My aim is to stop large and small boats, it is to set up counters in African countries in order to decide who has and who has not the right to leave following the Australian model. Business for traffickers? #NOWAY! [emphasis added] (Salvini's Tweet, 23 August 2018)[8]
16. Today Mattarella has reminded that 'nobody is above the law'. He is right. For this reason, I closed and I will close the harbours to human traffickers respecting the law, the Constitution, and the commitment I made with the Italians. Investigate me, I go ahead! **#closedharbours** and **#openhearts** [emphasis added] (Salvini's Tweet, 12 September 2018)[9]

#BuildtheWall is the hashtag that summarizes Trump's immigration policies. Indeed, during and after the electoral campaign in 2016, he always talked about the construction of Trump Wall, a barrier that should have kept the United States safe from Southern American immigration and crime. The then President of the United States showed the same attitude towards immigrants and refugees from other parts of the world with the hashtag #travelban. This specific hashtag was used when in 2017 Trump imposed – through a series of executive orders – a ban for people who come from certain countries (such as Iran, Libya, Nigeria, Somalia) to travel in the United States. In example 15, Salvini's hashtag #Stopinvasion is clearly linked to the *topos* of invasion and aims to represent the phenomenon of immigration as an emergency that needs to be under control. In example 16, it is possible to notice an interesting combination of two hashtags: #closedharbours and #openhearts. There is a clear contradiction since #closedharbours summarizes strict immigration policies and #openhearts suggests an opening and hospitality. Moreover, it is necessary to highlight that these two hashtags co-occur often. The quantitative results show that the hashtag #closedharbours has eight occurrences in Salvini Tweet Corpus and it co-occurs four times with the hashtag #openhearts (that occurs in the corpus just in combination with #closedharbours). Salvini's strategy consists in the representation of himself as a compassionate and religious man, but at the same time as a strong leader that protects his nation and his compatriots. For this reason, another common hashtag used by Salvini is #Italiansfirst (example 12). In addition to #closedharbours, he uses the hashtag #closetheharbours (example 3) as well.

It is possible to compare the employment of some hashtags that are used very similarly by both politicians. #Americafirst and #Italiansfirst are employed similarly to sum up their immigration policies. However, Trump talks about America as a nation because this hashtag is used more generally to reaffirm the geopolitical and economic hegemonic position of the United States in the world. Salvini employs the hashtag mainly when he talks about immigration but also about Europe; as a result, he does not mention Italy as a country and he rather mentions the Italian people who come first in comparison to immigrants, refugees and all the other European citizens. Moreover, the hashtags #BuildTheWall and #closetheharbours (or #closedharbours) have the same function since they summarize these politicians' immigration policies. Even though the construction of a wall and the closure of the harbours are different processes, the consequences of these actions are the same. It is impossible to build a wall in the middle of the Mediterranean Sea but the closure of the harbours has the same effect because it means to create a barrier, an invisible wall that *the others* cannot go through. These immigration policies clearly aim to restore security creating a physical exclusion of immigrants and refugees. In this regard, we should highlight that American and Italian people feel insecure because both Trump and Salvini always trigger fear through the representation of immigrants and refugees as threats.

Quantitative Analysis

Corpus linguistic was used mainly to verify the results of the qualitative analysis. For this reason, the quantitative part of the analysis investigates the concordances and the co-occurrences of specific words connected to each source domain, *topos* and representational strategy identified during the qualitative analysis.

Source Domains

The quantitative results of the analysis on the whole corpora reveal that Trump is not the only one who uses the water source domain. Salvini employs this source domain too in his Tweet Corpus where there are two occurrences of the words *flussi migratori* (*migratory flows*) and one occurrence of the words *flussi della morte* (*flows of the death*). In addition, I tried to identify other water metaphors through the research of specific words such as 'sea' (*mare*), 'ocean' (*oceano*) and 'tide' (*marea*) but none of them were connected to immigrants and refugees. The only exception is the word 'pour' that is employed by Trump (especially in his Tweet Corpus) to represent ambiguously immigrants entering into the United States. Specifically, this word counts eight occurrences in Trump Tweet Corpus and twelve occurrences in Trump Traditional Corpus. The concordances reveal that not all of the occurrences concern immigrants and refugees, and that Trump uses the word 'pour' for several purposes such as to indicate an economic revival of the United States (e.g. *jobs will start pouring again in the country*). However, this word is also employed to represent the dangerous access of criminals and drugs from Mexico (e.g. *drug, dangerous, illegal, stop, border, cartel* and *criminal*). It is important to mention again that immigrants who come from South America – and more precisely from Mexico – are associated implicitly to crime; consequently, they are often linked to the macro-category of criminals. Indeed, Trump associates the word 'pour' to the words 'illegals' and 'dangerous people'. These two words are very generic and could comprehend ambiguously both criminals and immigrants. The impossibility to distinguish the two categories is used strategically by the then President of the United States to remark the connection between immigration and criminality and to represent every immigrant as a potential threat. The quantitative approach confirms that Salvini is the only one who employs the source domain of nature to represent immigrants and refugees. The analysis of concordances and co-occurrences of the words 'roots' (*radici*), 'uproot/eradicate' (*sradicare*) and 'plant' (*piantare*) reveals that Trump employs the natural source domain just to talk about the removal of criminals and terrorists from the United States. Finally, the quantitative results verify that Trump does not use the source domain of object and merchandise to represent immigrants and refugees in a dehumanizing way. Specifically, I looked for the concordances and co-occurrences of the words 'load' (*carico*), 'unload' (*scaricare*) and *discharged (scaricare)* that confirm and expand Salvini's employment of this source domain.

Table 5.4 Occurrences and co-occurrences of *load* in Salvini's corpora

Corpora	Occurrences	Co-occurrences of *load*
Salvini Tweet Corpus	6	*immigrato* (immigrant) (4), Aquarius (1), *mediterraneo* (Mediterranean) (1), *clandestino* (illegal) (1)
Salvini Traditional Corpus	7	*barcone* (immigrants' boat) (2), *immigrato* (immigrant) (1)

Table 5.4 shows that the co-occurrences of the word 'load' are often associated with immigrants and their boats. For instance, the word 'Aquarius' is the name of an NGO that caused an immigration crisis in the summer of 2018. On the other hand, the word 'unload' counts four occurrences just in the Salvini Tweet Corpus and even in this case this word is associated to immigrants. In addition, the co-occurrences list includes the words 'Brussels' and 'Macron' that signal tensions between Italy, Europe and France about the immigration topic, especially regarding the distribution of immigrants and refugees among European countries. Moreover, Table 5.12 shows the co-occurrences (especially in Salvini Tweet Corpus) of the word 'immigrant' that are clearly linked to this source domain such as *take back, unload, load, fill* and *take*.

Topos of Danger, Threat and Fear – Association to Crime and Terrorism

The *topos* of danger, threat and fear is strictly connected to the representational strategy that associates immigrants and refugees to terrorism and crime. For this reason, I investigated quantitatively both strategies through the research of specific words such as 'terrorism' *(terrorismo)*, 'terrorist' *(terrorista)*, 'ISIS', 'attack' *(attacco/attentato)*, 'invasion' *(invasion)*, 'criminality' *(criminalità)*, 'criminal' *(criminale)*, 'arrest' *(arrestare)*, 'capture' *(catturare)*, 'detain' *(detenere)*, 'incarcerate' *(incarcerare)*, 'seize' *(sequestrare)*, 'illegal immigrant' *(clandestino)*, 'rape' *(struprare/ stupro)*, 'robber/thief' *(rapinatore)*, 'drug dealer' *(spacciatore)*, 'kill' *(ammazzare)* and 'murder' *(omicidio/uccidere)*. Tables 5.5 and 5.6 show how Trump tends to associate immigrants and refugees to terrorism more often than Salvini.

More precisely, it is possible to notice – through the co-occurrences of the words 'terrorism' and 'terrorist' – that Trump talks exclusively about radical Islamic terrorism. He focuses on terrorist attacks that happened in Europe and expresses his concern about new possible Islamic threats that the United States have to face since immigrants and – especially – refugees from the Middle East

Table 5.5 Occurrences and co-occurrences of *terrorism*

Corpora	Occurrences of *terrorism*	Co-occurrences of *terrorism*
Trump Tweet Corpus	10	Islamic (3), radical (3), threat (2), eradicate (1), extremism (1), horror (1), evil (1), extreme (1), safety (1), ISIS (1), terrorist (1), stop (1), fight (1), security (1)
Trump Traditional Corpus	22	threat (3), extremist (2), Islamic (2), radical (2), defeat (2), crush (1), combat (1), Muslim (1), spread (1), ideology (1), enemy (1), ISIS (1), battle (1), protect (2), fight (2), allow (1), nation (3), attack (1), immigration (1)
Salvini Tweet Corpus	9	islamico (Islamic) (7), cosa nostra ('our thing') (1), uccidere (kill) (1), richiedente (asylum seeker) (1), arresto (arrest) (2), minaccia (threat) (1), problema (problem) (1), Europa (Europe) (1), immigrato (immigrant) (1), Italian (Italy) (1)
Salvini Traditional Corpus	0	

Table 5.6 Occurrences and co-occurrences of *terrorist*

Corpora	Occurrences of *terrorist*	Co-occurrences of *terrorist*
Trump Tweet Corpus	16	radical (4), Islamic (4), attack (4), kill (2), destroy (1), Egypt (1), London (1), war (1), potential (1), Paris (1), keep (2), terrorism (1), security (1), our (5)
Trump Traditional Corpus	12	radical (3), Islamic (3), attack (4), keep (4), endure (1), crush (1), another (2), immigration (1), foreign (1), country (4), our (4)
Salvini Tweet Corpus	9	#battisti (2), rosso (red) (2), barcone (immigrants' boat) (2), importare (import) (1), islamico (Islamic) (2), rischio (risk) (1), reato (crime) (1), mafioso (1), Italia (Italy) (3)
Salvini Traditional Corpus	0	

enter in the country with no screening. As mentioned before, Salvini uses this connection less frequently. He talks about Islamic terrorism (sometimes in connection to Italian organized crime as it is signalled by the word 'our thing' that indicates Sicilian mafia) but he focuses on other aspects as well. For instance,

Table 5.7 Occurrences and co-occurrences of *criminal*

Corpora	Occurrences of *criminal*	Co-occurrences of *criminal*
Trump Tweet Corpus	10	deport (1), investigation (2), illegal (2), drug (1), immigration (1)
Trump Traditional Corpus	10	cartel (2), removal (2), alien (2), scandal (1), ringleader (1), killer (1), corrupt (1), drug (1), immigrant (1), open (1), pour (1), illegal (1), our (4)
Salvini Tweet Corpus	10	Romania (1), episodio (episode) (1), spacciatore (drug dealer) (2), illegalità (illegality) (1), schifoso (disgusting) (1), rischio (risk) (1), reato (crime) (1), clandestino (illegal immigrant) (1)
Salvini Traditional Corpus	4	Boldrini (2), Saviano (1), invasion (invasion) (1), Renzi (1)

the words #battisti and #red refer to far-left Italian political terrorism. Moreover, the connection to terrorism is absent in his Traditional Corpus.

As shown in Table 5.7, there are no particular quantitative differences in the way these politicians use the word 'criminal' in connection to immigrants and refugees. However, the co-occurrences of this word reveal Trump and Salvini's slightly different approach. Trump – in both Traditional and Tweet Corpora – connects criminality to Mexican criminal cartels and implicitly to immigration that comes from South America. Instead, the words 'scandal' and 'ringleader' are employed to delegitimize Hillary Clinton. Salvini's co-occurrences – in his Tweet Corpus – show that he has a similar approach but the word 'Romania' remarks the League's xenophobic tendencies (Salvini specifies very often the ethnicity of immigrants and refugees). We should notice that – even this time – he prefers to use this strategy in his Tweet Corpus. Indeed, in the Traditional Corpus Salvini focuses more on delegitimizing the political and cultural elite.

In addition to the word 'criminal', there are also other words such as 'arrest', 'illegal immigrant' and 'rape' that confirm Salvini's tendency to associate more immigrants and refugees to criminality in comparison to Trump. In this regard, there are some quantitative data that are worth mentioning. The word 'arrest' has forty occurrences in the Salvini Tweet Corpus (he does not use this word in the Traditional Corpus) and its co-occurrences (such as 'illegal immigrant' and immigrants' ethnicities) reveal that he associates this word mainly to immigrants, but as the then Minister of the Interior he talks about the Italian organized crime as well. In the Trump Traditional Corpus, the word 'arrest' has just two occurrences and they are not linked to immigrants or refugees. The word 'illegal immigrant' (*clandestino*) has forty occurrences in the Salvini Tweet Corpus and just one occurrence in his Traditional Corpus. Trump counts two occurrences in his Tweet Corpus and seven occurrences in his Traditional Corpus. The co-occurrences of the word 'illegal immigrant' show that both politicians use this strategy in a similar way; however, it is important to highlight that Salvini is the one who employs this strategy massively in his Twitter account. As a result, it is clear that he prefers to employ this connection (rather than the connection to terrorism) to trigger fear and represents immigrants and refugees as threats. Finally, Salvini Tweet Corpus counts eleven occurrences for the word *stuprare* ('to rape') and eight occurrences for the word *stupro* ('rape'). Both words occur once in his Traditional Corpus and indicate mainly rapes perpetrated by immigrants. On the other hand, Trump has just one occurrence in his Tweet Corpus but he mentions a rape accusation against Bill Clinton in an attempt to delegitimize Hillary Clinton once again.

Topos of Invasion and the Aggregation Strategy

Even for these strategies, I carried out a unified quantitative analysis since the *topos* of invasion inevitably involves the use of numbers. More precisely, I looked for the concordances and co-occurrences of numbers, percentages, statistics and the words 'allow into/enter' (*entrare*) and *barcone* (immigrants' boat). Numbers are one of the most important aspects of identifying both the aggregation strategy and the *topos* of invasion. Table 5.8 shows that Trump and Salvini use more numbers in their tweets rather than in their traditional speeches. Moreover, Salvini's corpora count more numbers in comparison to Trump's. From the analysis of co-occurrences, it is possible to notice (through the words 'illegal immigrant', 'asylum seeker', 'refugee', 'foreigner' and 'Tunisian') that Salvini is more focused on immigrants and refugees.

Specifically, the words 'ship', 'host', 'disembark', 'rescue' and 'Mediterranean' refer to immigrants' voyage towards Italy and their arrival. The words 'take back' and 'take' refer to immigrants as well and they are strictly connected to the dehumanizing source domain of object and merchandise. In addition, numbers are predictably connected to money (e.g. *euro*). The hashtag *#Italiansfirst* and the word *Italian* signal that Salvini talks about the Italian people in terms of numbers as well. Although Salvini usually employs numbers to dehumanize people, he employs this strategy to highlight how many Italians have difficulties (especially in comparison to immigrants) and to remark the importance of

Table 5.8 Occurrences and co-occurrences of [number]

Corpora	Occurrences	Co-occurrences of [number]
Trump Tweet Corpus	474	Clinton (25), Hillary (19), #draintheswamp (13), billion (11), million (11), people (13), country (10), our (12), American (9), control (6), #makeamericagreatagain (6), murder (3), refugee (3), victim (3), #americafirst (3), terror (2), ms-13 (1), immigrant (1), Syrian (1)
Trump Traditional Corpus	170	billion (9), million (9), African American (4), Clinton (4), border (2), people (5), America (4), American (4), homicide (3), victim (2), refugee (2), Muslim (1)
Salvini Tweet Corpus	555	milione (million) (35), immigrato (immigrant) (27), euro (26), italiano (Italian) (25), sbarcare (12), straniero (foreigner) (8), clandestino (illegal immigrant) (7), #primagliitaliani (#Italiansfirst) (6), nave (ship) (6), Rom (Gipsy) (5), riportare (take back) (5), immigrazione (immigration) (5)
Salvini Traditional Corpus	243	italiano (Italian) (24), milione (million) (22), euro (17), persona (person) (12), immigrato (immigrant) (7), accogliere (host) (5), miliardo (billion) (3), sbarcare (disembark) (3), prendere (take) (3), salvataggio (rescue) (2), migrare (migrate) (2), mediterraneo (Mediterranean) (2), mantenere (support) (2), richiedente (asylum seeker) (1), rifugiato (refugee) (1), tunisino (Tunisian) (1), umano (human) (1)

the Italian people (against the European elite). Trump uses numbers similarly regarding immigrants and refugees, and regarding the American people (he also focuses on minorities, e.g. *African Americans*). However, in Trump's co-occurrences, there are some connections to terrorism (e.g. *terror*) and crime (e.g. *ms-13*, *murder* and *homicide*). In this way, he remarks the *topos* of danger, threat and fear; indeed, the *topos* of invasion can be considered as a subcategory of the former.

Topos of Burden

In order to investigate this *topos* form a quantitative perspective, I focused my attention on the words 'money' (*soldi/denaro*), 'hotel' (*albergo*), 'cost' (*costo/ costare*) and 'pay' (*pagare/mantenere*). Table 5.9 shows that both Trump and Salvini use the word 'pay' primarily for other topics such as to talk about taxes. Furthermore, the co-occurrences highlight that Trump focuses more on the

Table 5.9 Occurrences and co-occurrences of *pay*

Corpora	Occurrences	Co-occurrences of *pay*
Trump Tweet Corpus	30	wall (6), Mexico (6), tax (3)
Trump Traditional Corpus	24	US (3), bill (4), wall (2), tax (2), Mexico (1), immigration (1)
Salvini Tweet Corpus	57	tassa (tax) (11), pensione (pension) (8), spacciare (push) (2), immigrare (to immigrate) (2), droga (drug) (2), colazione (breakfast) (1), pranzo (lunch) (1), cena (dinner) (1), albergo (hotel) (1), immigrazione (immigration) (1)
Salvini Traditional Corpus	38	tassa (tax) (7), colazione (breakfast) (1), pranzo (lunch) (1), cena (dinner) (1), albergo (hotel) (1)

Wall and especially on the fact that it will be paid by Mexico. On the other hand, Salvini highlights that immigrants are a social cost because they are paid – according to him by Italian citizens – to push drugs and to live in hotels.

The overall quantitative analysis confirms that Salvini uses more of this *topos* in comparison to Trump. Specifically, the then Italian Minister of the Interior relies a lot on the fake news that depicts all immigrants as criminal deadbeats who live in Italy at the expense of the Italian people.

Topos of the Victim and the Opposition Strategy

The *topos* of the victim was quantitatively analysed through the research of the words 'victim' (*vittima*), 'children' (*bambino/ bimbo*), 'human being' (*essere umano*), 'poor' (*povero/povertà*), 'innocent' (*innocente*), 'save' (*salvare*), 'help' (*aiutare*), 'escape/runaway' (*scappare*), 'suffer' (*soffrire*) and 'assistance' (*assistenza*). Table 5.10 highlights that both politicians use the word 'victim' to indicate the American, Italian and European victims of criminal actions perpetrated by refugees or illegal immigrants, and victims of terrorist attacks. The quantitative results (especially the co-occurrences of the words 'children' and 'human beings') confirm that Salvini is the only one who employs this type of *topos* to represent immigrants and refugees (see example 2). Even though Salvini seems to recognize that there are actually some people who escape from their own country for good reasons, he usually employs this *topos* to describe Italians who suffer because of economic matters linked to his opponents' policies

Table 5.10 Occurrences and co-occurrences of *victim*

Corpora	Occurrences	Co-occurrences of *victim*
Trump Tweet Corpus	7	mourn (2), murder (1), shooting (1), family (2), France (1), healthcare (1), Obamacare (1)
Trump Traditional Corpus	5	murder (1), gun (1), custody (1), Obamacare (1), American (1)
Salvini Tweet Corpus	16	preghiera (pray) (3), parente (relative) (2), violenza (violence) (2), Pamela (1), #francia (#france) (1), ragazza (girl) (1), razzismo (racism) (1), immigrazione (immigration) (1), clandestino (illegal immigrant) (1), italiano (Italian) (1)
Salvini Traditional Corpus	5	tassa (tax) (1), razzismo (racism) (1), norma (law) (1), giudice (judge) (1), mafia (1), guerra (war) (1)

Table 5.11 Occurrences and co-occurrences of *Islamic*

Corpora	Occurrences	Co-occurrences of *Islamic*
Trump Tweet Corpus	8	radical (7), terrorist (4), terrorism (3), threat (1), extreme (1)
Trump Traditional Corpus	5	radical (5), terrorist (3), terrorism (2), attack (1), illegal (1), immigration (1), out (2), protect (1)
Salvini Tweet Corpus	28	terrorismo (terrorism) (7), estremista (extremist) (2), regime (2), dichiarazione (declaration) (2), ospedale (hospital) (2), terrorista (terrorist) (2), donna (woman) (3), presenza (presence) (1), imbarcare (embark) (1)
Salvini Traditional Corpus	3	omosessualità (homosexuality) (1), animale (animal) (1), permettere (allow) (1), immigrazione (immigration) (1)

or European financial laws, but most important because they suffer from reverse racism (see example 12). Indeed, this is a crucial step in Salvini's employment of the opposition strategy since he wants to create an empathy shift.

Regarding the opposition strategy, I looked for the words 'religion/religious' (*religione/religioso*), 'culture/cultural' (*cultura/culturale*), 'tradition' (*tradizione*), 'Islam/Islamic' (*Islam/Islamico*) and 'Christian' (*cristiano*). The analysis of concordances and co-occurrences of the word 'Islamic' (Table 5.11) – and of the other words previously mentioned – confirms that both politicians connect Islam to terrorism. On the one hand, Salvini remarks the (religious and cultural) incompatibility describing Islamic people as unrespectful and intolerant. On the other hand, Trump wants to highlight how important it is to preserve religious liberty (threatened by Islamic extremism). Concerning the type of opposition strategy that opposes two suffering groups, I analysed the concordances and the co-occurrences of the words 'American people', 'Italians' *(Italiani)*, 'veterans', 'children' *(bambino/bimbo)*, 'suffering' *(sofferenza)* and 'difficulty' *(difficoltà)*.

This analysis confirms that Salvini is the one who employs more of this type of opposition strategy in order to create a shift of empathy towards poor Italians – who suffer, have difficulties and live in poverty – rather than towards immigrants or refugees.

Table 5.12 Occurrences and co-occurrences of *Immigrant*

Corpora	Occurrences	Co-occurrences of *Immigrant*
Trump Tweet Corpus	4	eastern (1), Sweden (1), Syrian (1), Australia (1), thousand (1), middle (1), illegal (1), % (1), take (1), more (1), from (1), [number] (1)
Trump Traditional Corpus	11	illegal (7), kill (3), charge (2), deport (1), gun (1), gang (1), release (1), murder (1), ISIS (1), criminal (1), hundred (1)
Salvini Tweet Corpus	129	clandestino (illegal immigrant) (11), regolare (legal immigrant) (6), bordo (on board) (6), più (more) (14), [number] (25), nave (ship) (6), riportare (take back) (5), scaricare (unload) (4), carico (load) (4), gommone (inflatable boat) (4), perbene (decent) (4), altro (other) (6), Italia (Italy) (12), meno (less) (4), sbarcare (disembark) (4), pensione (pension) (4), integrato (integrated) (3), irregolare (illegal) (3), riempire (fill) (3), portare (take) (4), Libia (Libya) (3), asilo (asylum) (3), altri (others) (3), milione (million) (3), 700mila (700 thousands) (2), rimpatrio (repatriation) (2), richiedente (seeker) (2), Gambia (1), Mohamed (1) molestatore (molester) (1), Senegalese (1), tunisino (Tunisian) (1), africano (African) (1), nigeriano (Nigerian) (1)
Salvini Traditional Corpus	31	accogliere (host) (4), alcuni (some) (4), albergo (hotel) (2), riempire (fill) (2), sbarcare (disembark) (2), nave (ship) (2), raccogliere (pick up) (1), mare (sea) (1), rifugiato (refugee) (1), carico (load) (1), droga (drug) (1), clandestino (illegal immigrant) (1), perbene (decent) (1), portare (take) (2), [number] (6), milione (million) (1), problema (problem) (1)

Specification, Genericization and Suppression

The strategies of specification and genericization were analysed through the research of the concordances and the co-occurrences of the words 'immigrant' (*immigrato*), 'refugee' (*rifugiato/profugo*) and 'asylum seeker' (*richiedente asilo*). The quantitative analysis confirms that Salvini is the only one who – on very few occasions – uses the specification strategy (e.g. *Mohamed* in Table 5.12). The quantitative results also confirm that Salvini employs more the genericization strategy in comparison to Trump, especially in his Tweet Corpus. It is also necessary to specify that the genericization includes very often the ethnicity of these people as is shown in Table 5.12 (e.g. *Tunisian, African, Nigerian*). Lastly, the strategy of suppression was investigated through the words 'repatriation' (*rimpatrio*), 'expulsion' (*espulsione*), 'border crossing' (*attraversamento*) and 'disembarkation' (*sbarco*). The quantitative analysis reveals – in contrast with the qualitative results – not only that Salvini uses this strategy as well, but also that he employs suppression more than Trump through the words *espulsione* ('expulsion') and *sbarco* ('disembarkation').

In addition to these words, the suppression strategy is pervasive in both politicians' tweets and traditional speeches since information about immigrants and refugees is completely absent. There is no mention about their stories, their lives, why did they decide to move or how much they suffered before, during and after the migration. This suppression is crucial in the dehumanizing process because it is impossible to empathize with immigrants and refugees without knowing what their feelings are. Instead, we perceive just one side of the story which is the one told by politicians who represent these people just as potential threats, criminals and terrorists.

Conclusions

The results of the analysis show that Donald Trump and Matteo Salvini employ several strategies in order to create a lack of empathy in the representation of immigrants and refugees. First of all, these politicians use dehumanizing metaphors. Both politicians use the source domain of water that metaphorically depicts immigrants and refugees as a dangerous and unstoppable force of nature that needs to be stopped and controlled. Moreover, Salvini prefers to employ the object and merchandise source domain to create a lack of empathy describing immigrants and refugees as inanimate objects that NGOs load in the Mediterranean Sea and discharge in Italy. In addition to metaphors, the aggregation strategy (strictly connected to the *topos* of invasion) is another dehumanizing strategy since it is very difficult to emphasize with numbers, percentages or statistics. Second, immigrants and refugees are represented by these politicians combining the *topos* of danger, threat and fear, the association to crime and terrorism, and the genericization strategy. This combination aims to trigger fear because immigrants and refugees are depicted as human beings but at the same time as potential threats. Consequently, it is difficult to empathize with people that are described and perceived as being dangerous. Third, the *topos* of burden can trigger a feeling of injustice and dissatisfaction towards the elites and anger since immigrants and refugees are represented as a social cost. Indeed, the feeling of anger is mainly due to the fact that people believe that they have to pay and contribute for the presence of these social actors in their countries. Lastly, the opposition strategy that opposes people from a cultural and religious perspective aims obviously to trigger fear of *the other* and to highlight the impossibility of inclusion because of cultural and religious incompatibilities. On the other hand, the other type of opposition strategy that focuses on opposing two suffering groups of people can create an empathy shift. For instance, Salvini – who uses this type of opposition more than Trump – encourages Italians to be more empathetic towards other Italians – who live in poverty or have some difficulties – rather than towards immigrants and refugees.

Regarding the different employment of the strategies in tweets and traditional speeches, the main differences are due to the constrains and peculiarities of Twitter such as the limitations of characters and the employment of hashtags and pictures. For this reason, during the qualitative analysis I paid attention to the pictures attached to tweets as well. These pictures can convey additional meanings to the main ones present in the written texts or simply reinforce the messages already present in the tweets. In addition to these main differences, the quantitative analysis highlighted a different approach regarding the association to crime and terrorism. Trump prefers to associate immigrants and refugees to terrorism, while Salvini prefers to associate them to crime. This difference could be explained through the different historical backgrounds of the United States and Italy. Trump is easily able to trigger fear through the association to terrorism after 9/11. This association could be more complicated and less effective for Salvini because in Italy there is a history of far-right and far-left political terrorism. For this reason, Salvini probably prefers to highlight criminal actions perpetrated by immigrants and refugees in order to represent them as dangerous people. Furthermore, the analysis revealed that some strategies are not present in certain corpora. For instance, Salvini does not use the source domain of water and the association to terrorism in his Traditional Corpus.

Further research will investigate the possible reasons why some strategies are not employed in traditional speeches or in tweets. This will be helpful in order to comprehend even better the overall populist phenomenon, and more precisely, to fully investigate the impact that populism has on current political communication.

Notes

1 It is a software that allows users to annotate texts through the creation of layers.
2 The original Italian version of Salvini's tweets and traditional extracts is provided here in the notes.
   [. . .] ed è stato confezionato questo rosario da una donna sfruttata, da una di quelle donne che erano state illuse che in Italia c'era il bengodi, che in Italia c'era casa e lavoro per tutti ed è stata sradicata dalla sua terra.
3 Oggi anche la nave Sea Watch 3, di Ong tedesca e battente bandiera olandese, è al largo delle coste libiche in attesa di effettuare l'ennesimo carico di immigrati, da portare in Italia. L'Italia ha smesso di chinare il capo e di ubbidire, stavolta C'È CHI DICE NO. #chiudiamoiporti
4 Qualche mese fa il procuratore di Agrigento (quello che mi sta indagando) diceva: 'Il rischio di terroristi a bordo dei barconi è alto.' Ha cambiato idea? Per me il problema rimane lo stesso anche OGGI.
5 Nell'ultima settimana la @poliziadistato ha arrestato 528 persone, di cui più della metà immigrati, e ne ha denunciate 2.478, di cui oltre il 50% immigrati. Più immigrazione significa più delinquenza: aver ridotto sbarchi e arrivi, nonostante denunce, è per me motivo di orgoglio!
6 Chi ritiene che la donna ha meno diritti dell'uomo stia a casa sua perché l'Italia non è il paese che fa per lui [. . .] e se vuoi coprirla con i tappeti lo fai a casa tua, perché io di gente che va vestita in giro da Batman in Italia non ne voglio.
7 Immigrati della #Diciotti in sciopero della fame? Facciano come credono. In Italia vivono 5 milioni di persone in POVERTÀ assoluta (1.2 milioni di BAMBINI) che lo sciopero della fame lo fanno tutti i giorni, nel silenzio di buonisti, giornalisti e compagni vari. #primagliitaliani
8 #Stopinvasione. Il mio obiettivo è bloccare barconi e barchini, è organizzare nei Paesi africani degli sportelli che decidano chi ha diritto di partire e chi no, seguendo il modello australiano. Business per gli scafisti? #NOWAY!
9 Mattarella oggi ha ricordato che 'nessuno è al di sopra della legge'. Ha ragione. Per questo io, rispettando legge, Costituzione e impegno preso con Italiani, ho chiuso e chiuderò i porti a trafficanti di esseri umani. Indagatemi, io vado avanti! #portichiusi e #cuoriaperti

References

Baker, P. (2006), *Using Corpora in Discourse Analysis*, London and New York: Continuum.

Baker, P., et al. (2008), 'A useful methodological synergy? Combining critical discourse analysis and corpus linguistics to examine discourses of refugees and asylum seekers in the UK press', *Discourse & Society*, 19(3), 273–306. doi: https://doi.org/10.1177/0957926508088962

Canovan, M. (1981), *Populism*, New York and London: Harcourt Brace Jovanovich.

Chilton, P. (2004), *Analysing Political Discourse. Theory and Practice*, London and New York: Routledge. doi: https://doi.org/10.1017/S0047404506230136

de la Torre, C. (2019), 'Global populism: Histories, trajectories, problems, and challenges', in de la Torre, C. (ed.), *Routledge Handbook of Global Populism*, 1–27, London and New York: Routledge. doi: https://doi.org/10.4324/9781315226446

Enli, G. (2017), 'Twitter as an arena of the authentic outsider: exploring the social media campaign of Trump and Clinton in the 2016 US presidential election', *European Journal of Communication*, 32 (I), 50–61. doi: https://doi.org/10.1177/0267323116682802

Kilgarriff, A., et al. (2014) 'The sketch engine: Ten years on', *Lexicography* 1, 7–36.

Kreis, R. (2017), 'The "tweet politics" of president Trump', *Journal of Language and Politics*, 16(4), 607–18. doi: https://doi.org/10.1075/jlp.17032.kre

Lakoff, G., and M. Johnson (1980), *Metaphors We Live By*, Chicago: University of Chicago Press.

Machin, D., and A. Mayr (2012), *How to Do a Critical Discourse Analysis. A Multimodal Introduction*, London: Sage.

Mudde, C., and C. R. Kaltwasser (2017), *Populism: A Very Short Introduction*, Oxford: Oxford University Press.

Murthy, D. (2013), *Twitter: Social Communication in the Twitter Age*, Cambridge and Malden: Polity Press.

O'Donnell, M. (2008), 'Demonstration of the UAM CorpusTool for text and image annotation', Proceedings of the ACL-08:HLT Demo Session (CompanionVolume). Columbus, Ohio, June 2008. Association for Computational Linguistics, 13–16.

Ott, B. L. (2017), 'The age of Twitter: Donald J. Trump and the politics of debasement', *Critical Studies in Media Communication*, 34(1), 59–68. doi: https://doi.org/10.1080/15295036.2016.1266686

Partington, A., A. Duguid, and C. Taylor (2013), *Patterns and Meanings in Discourse: Theory and practice in corpus-assisted discourse studies (CADS)*, Amsterdam and Philadelphia: John Benjamins Publishing Company. doi: https://doi.org/10.1075/scl.55

The American Presidency Project. https://www.presidency.ucsb.edu/ (accessed 31 January 2021).

Tormey, S. (2019), *Populism. A Beginner's Guide*, London: Oneworld Publications.

Trump Twitter Archive. http://www.trumptwitterarchive.com/ (accessed 31 January 2021).

Van Kessel, S., and R. Castelein (2016), '"Shifting the blame: Populist politicians" use of Twitter as a tool of opposition', *Journal of Contemporary European Research*, 12 (2), 594–614.

van Dijk, T. A. (1998), *Ideology: A Multidisciplinary Approach*, London: Sage. doi: http://dx.doi.org/10.4135/9781446217856

van Leeuwen, T. (1996), 'The representation of social actors', in Caldas-Coulthard, C. R., and M. Coulthard (eds), *Texts and Practices: Readings in Critical Discourse Analysis*, 32–70, London: Routledge. doi: https://doi.org/10.4324/9780203431382

van Leeuwen, T. (2008), *Discourse and Practice: New Tools for Critical Discourse Analysis*, Oxford: Oxford University Press. doi: 10.1093/acprof:oso/9780195323306.001.0001

Wahl-Jorgensen, K. (2018), 'Media coverage of shifting emotional regimes: Donald Trump's angry populism', *Media, Culture & Society*, 40(5), 766–78. doi: https://doi.org/10.1177/0163443718772190

Wodak, R. (2015), *The Politics of Fear: What Right-Wing Populist Discourses Mean*, London: Sage. doi: http://dx.doi.org/10.4135/9781446270073

Zappavigna, M. (2014), 'CoffeeTweets: Bonding around the bean on Twitter', in Seargeant, P., and C. Tagg (eds), *The Language of Social Media: Identity and Community on the Internet*, 139–60, London: Palgrave Macmillan UK. doi: 10.1057/9781137029317

Collective Identities and Emotions in Online Contexts

Barbara Lewandowska-Tomaszczyk and Paul A. Wilson

Research Focus

The chapter focuses on types of and differences in collective group identity patterns that evolve from the analysis of discourse materials from Polish and English public internet space. The examples discussed involve recent social and political matters as presented in online discussions as well as emotionality dynamics that accompany them. The interpretation of collective group identity is driven by the culture-specific character of online interactions, which act as a stimulus of emergent group formation. The main part of the chapter presents and discusses two different possible formats, namely cooperation and conflict, as the major driving forces of such activities, with a number of various emotion clusters functioning in terms of intermediate conditioning.

Structure of the Chapter

The first part of the chapter discusses the concept of identity and presents the cultural background of Polish and English communities. Examples of online newspaper comments are discussed and the discourse-based dynamics of the particular events is presented, making reference to the dimensions proposed by Hofstede (1980) and Triandis (1995, 2001) that are relevant to the English and Polish cultural models.

Research Methods: Linguistic Exponents of Identity

The research methodology used involves a contrastive analysis of Polish and English collective identity profiles, analysed in terms of varying online discourse strategies and their linguistic realisation. The topic of collective actions in social networks is analysed frequently in contemporary media research (e.g. Hui, Lin and Cui 2015). The data are extracted from internet materials (Lewandowska-Tomaszczyk 2015) and mapped on a typology of communication patterns.

One of the interpretations of the concept of identity can be based on the available corpus materials by generating a discourse distribution and the semantic relationships between the term 'identity' and other relevant forms which are used in the discourses and measured in terms of the distance (word slots) between the focal term and the neighbouring forms. Lexical proximity reflects conceptual propinquity as can be conjectured by the cognitive principle of form-meaning iconicity. The same principle is relevant in searching for the relevant *distribution* of *collocations*, that is, such word combinations which are more frequent in texts than other, chance, lexical combinations. The partly overlapping areas of concept ranges, not necessarily predictable from definitions but motivated by conventions of usage, contain the forms which are used in close neighbourhood to the concept of *identity* in corpus materials of the British National Corpus (Lewandowska-Tomaszczyk 2015), such as *participation* and *involvement*, *community* and social *roles*, personal traits of *integrity* with a set of its foundational components (*honesty, courage, honour*, etc.) as well as *culture, ethnicity, religion, class* and *gender*. Each one of these sets of properties can be considered the basis of and reference to the self- and other-categorisation group identity category, particularly with respect to collective identity, emerging in the context of web-based group goals. Both qualitative and quantitative methodologies are used in the present study to analyse these phenomena. Authentic discourse samples (concordances) and their frequencies, as well as the frequencies of use and clustering of forms, are generated using PELCRA corpus tools developed at the University of Łódź (Pęzik 2014). Discourse-analytic instruments are applied to infer lexical analytic and structural patterns of language, which indicate both the dynamic emotionality axis, commentators' collective identity traits and interactional properties of exchange. These analytic findings are part of what is called participants' *Online Discourse Activity*, whose main component is the *Online Interconnectivity Value/Index* (Lewandowska-Tomaszczyk 2015), which identifies the *type and number* of interactive links among discussion participants. *Interconnectivity Values*, accompanied by the use of particular forms of address, metaphor as well as other figurative uses, selected discourse structure and lexical choices underlie the processes of group emotionality and identity-building dynamics.

There are three main communicative strategies identified in online discussions by Lewandowska-Tomaszczyk (2015). The first, *snowball communication*, is a paragon of categories which most strongly demonstrates collective (group) identity emergence and consolidation. *Snowball* communication has a more consistently determined communicative profile than any of the two others (*ping-pong* and *flying kite* or *loose-balloon*) and involves a clearly defined objective, typically addressed at an external opponent. The other communication type – ping-pong communication – has a strongly confrontational one-to-one or group-to-group profile, targeted towards two polar, often contradictory, judgements. Framed in an argumentative and often aggressive dialogic debate type, this strategy frequently represents two opposing worldviews and judgements, characteristic of two opposing group identities.

It is only members of the third of the communication types, *loose balloons* communication, who discuss the topic from their personal, experiential point of view, are typically less directly involved in a conflict scenario and tend to pass less emotional and more reflective judgements.

Identity is not a static or homogenous concept (Lewandowska-Tomaszczyk and Tomaszczyk 2012) and can rather be perceived as a constant process of becoming. And yet, as defended in Lewandowska-Tomaszczyk (2015), this conception does not exclude a certain more stable, core set of properties which underlie a central or prototypical category, developed in childhood experiences and based on psycho-physical predispositions of an individual, to which speakers and interactants can refer in various contexts. These more stable properties, mapped onto a more general frame, function as a more constant *tertium comparationis* for other – transitional – identity attributes which are constructed and dynamic.

Collective group identity is characterised by varying periods of duration. In real life, personal identities shift from the identification of one social role and function to another (Gaertner et al. 1993). In internet-based activities, particularly in discussion fora, the sense of *projected identity* and group membership is likely to be consistent in a particular thread. As emphasised by various scholars, identity is a multifaceted concept involving the process of the social construction of reality, which covers the shared properties that differentiate one group from another (e.g. Berting and Villain-Gandossi 1995: 19).

It should also be noted that group members make a distinction between the in-group and out-group properties which may differ considerably and can be treated by the group either as positive or negative in various contexts.

Leadership Function

It needs to be emphasised that one of the major properties in online identity formation is the role of online users that are the most active. To determine the most characteristic identity properties of the leading commentators and leadership in particular Computer-Mediated Communication (CMC) exchanges, it is argued (Lewandowska-Tomaszczyk 2016) that to achieve leadership in online discussion, what is crucial is to maintain online (*anonymous*) *visibility* (see i.a., Graham and Wright 2014) among the groups of commentators in a thread. Considering the absence of visual clues in internet exchanges, it is language and discourse strategies that play a decisive role in visibility management. Among a number of quantitative and qualitative strategies used by leaders in online discussions, such as a high frequency of posts, clear expression of assertiveness, high emotionality and a high Interconnectivity Index, Lewandowska-Tomaszczyk's study (2016) reveals Polish and English differences in leadership models: a positive *companionate leadership model* in English, and a negative *war leadership* model in Polish. On the basis of Hofstede's cultural dimensions patterns (Hofstede 1980), in which Poland is argued to be more collectivistic than the UK, Polish collectivism can be considered to be a special type, restricted to and engaging small family and companionate circles of community members on the one hand, or embracing a very large, nation-centred, historical-patriotic type of community on the other. What is missing in the picture is a rich intermediate level in group identity development. The present chapter clearly shows a dynamic identity axis, moving – in the Polish context – towards a more and more individualistic pole, while – in the case of UK culture – towards absorbing some properties of collectivistic attributes.

Driving Forces of Collective Identity Formation

Apart from the role of leadership in group identity formation, a central tenet that is proposed and supported in Lewandowska-Tomaszczyk and Wilson (2019) is that it is the motivation involving attempts to achieve the state of *well-being* that is at the heart of engagement in collective movements. In agreement with self-determination theory (e.g. Deci and Ryan 2000) it might be conjectured, as Lewandowska-Tomaszczyk and Wilson (2019) do, that one's interconnectedness to other individuals, the degree of autonomy that one perceives oneself to have, and ability to achieve success through one's actions are all conducive to collective identity formation and, through that – to the ultimate goal of human activities in terms of the achievement of the state of well-being, that is happiness and success (Howell et al. 2017). This places well-being at the heart of actions pertaining to engagement in protest movements in a number of ways.

To achieve the state of well-being, groups and individuals reach for various strategies. These can either involve *cooperation* on a different scale, or *conflict* and *fight* at the emergent, opposing group level (Lewandowska-Tomaszczyk and Wilson 2019; Diers-Lawson 2017).

The commentators' intention in online exchanges is typically to create a persuasive effect in the addressee or to get the addressee to do something in the real world. It is claimed in the present chapter that the persuasive force of the utterance in online discussions depends on a number of factors, both inherent to the commentator and the addressee but also, to a large extent, on the type of CMC interaction, the argumentation structure as used in the language of the interactants and the degree of emotionality both with the commentator and with the addressee. While the social–biological profile of commentators is not easy, or not always possible to determine, the circumstantial properties and online discourse behaviour can be subject to analytical scrutiny.

It is argued in the present chapter, and confirmed by a number of other findings (e.g. Lewandowska-Tomaszczyk 2017b), that there is more mitigating force, less abuse and more substantial argumentation in UK than Polish online comments. In other words, in terms of politeness theory (Brown and Levinson 1987), whereas British online comments conform to the *negative politeness strategies* identified in this culture (i.e. non-imposition type of verbal preferences rather than expressing oneself), Polish online comments are consistent with the positive politeness that has been demonstrated to be more present in individuals from this culture (Lewandowska-Tomaszczyk 2020).

Cooperation, as an action of working together towards one uniform end for common or mutual benefit, is manifested in a number of various cooperative online actions. It may involve crowdsourcing, that is engagement of various people, who contribute to putting the action goal in practice by paid or unpaid service, by their money or some other goods transferred to those in need, or alternatively by expressing their support and/or by clicking the relevant option.

Cooperation is typically connected with positive feelings, and, as Rheingold (1993: 15) calls it, 'gift economy' in which no 'direct, immediate quid-pro-quo' (lit. Latin 'something for something') is expected. To refer to Rheingold's theory again (1993: 15), we need to look for motivation in the processes of constituting what the author calls *a good group*. He identifies five of such properties: (1) ongoing interaction, (2) identity persistence, (3) knowledge of previous interactions to maintain identity across interactions, (4) online visibility, discussed in the preceding section and (5) definite group boundaries. The sense of fruitful cooperation is intimately connected with the feeling of satisfaction, and, eventually, increases the experiencer's well-being.

Conflict and fight are intimately linked with feelings of disappointment and its emotion cluster members such as hate and hostility (Wilson 2017). However, such actions typically involve cases of the fight for the well-being of community members and strong elements of conflict and cooperation are both manifested. In both Polish and English, what is observed at present is a strong radicalisation of opinions and attitudes (Rzepnikowska 2019; Lewandowska-Tomaszczyk 2020). However, while the Polish case demonstrates a more direct fight (interactional, etc.), the English case presents a more general movement of support in the cases of fights against existing injustice or decisions (viz. Brexit). If direct conflict is observed between commentators holding different opinions, the vocabulary used is more tempered and non-vulgar in English when juxtaposed with Polish. And yet, in both cases, the rising of emotionality is observed and, for example, the use of negative and abusive *ad personam* remarks to online interactants (cf. Lewandowska-Tomaszczyk 2017a) is much more often used in current comment discourses, which was not found in such numbers in English comments before 2015.

However, in both types of scenario what is especially evident, particularly in the Polish online discourse data, is the urge to secure online visibility (Lewandowska-Tomaszczyk 2017a), with some of the commentators' evident narcissism and aggression directed at one of the interaction sides.

Individualism versus Collectivism

The extent to which one views oneself as relatively less or more socially integrated and connected with others is an important feature of collective online identities. An important cultural dimension in this respect is the cultural dimension of individualism versus collectivism advanced by Hofstede (1980). Individualism emphasises one's autonomy with personal goals, which optimises the self as opposed to the in-group in terms of achieving success and fulfilling one's potential. There is also greater focus on individual emotions, values and thoughts compared with those shared by the in-group, and lifesatisfaction is more central to self-construal. Additionally, there is a greater focus on rights and more detachment from in-groups; individuals are more responsible for themselves, have fewer duties towards the in-group and are freer to make individual choices. In contrast, in-groups and out-groups are viewed as more distinct and separate in collectivistic cultures, with more of an impermeable border between them. Rather than individual autonomy, there are stronger interpersonal relations in the in-group that centre on equality and principles based on generosity. Satisfaction and contentment are determined by a construal of the self that is based on the successful execution of social roles and duties that are in turn derived from common aims and harmonious relations in in-groups. In addition, there is relatively more regulation of the outward expression of emotions to preserve harmonious in-group relationships.

In the light of the contrastive analysis of Polish and English online collective identity profiles in British English and Polish in the present study, it is important to narrow our focus on these two cultures. In cross-cultural research, Poland is often described as a collectivistic culture (e.g. Szarota et al. 2015). However, despite a score of 60 on the individualism–collectivism scale, which shows that Poland is clearly more collectivistic in relative terms than individualistic Britain with a score of 89 in Hofstede's dimensions, it can be questioned whether Poland should be deemed to have a collectivistic status that is on a par with countries typically considered in such terms, such as China with an individualism–collectivism score of 20 (Hofstede 1980). However, the point to note here is that the individualism–collectivism scale allows the relative comparison of countries on this dimension, and Poland is clearly more collectivistic in comparison to Britain on this scale.

English and Polish Emotion Profiles

Emotions are central to engagement in collective online movements. An understanding of the complexities of the influence of emotions in this respect involves a number of elements including well-being, the nature of emotion clusters and culture.

In terms of self-determination theory (e.g. Deci and Ryan 2000), well-being is directly influenced by online movement activity. This posits that well-being is determined by one's interconnectedness to other individuals, the degree of autonomy that one perceives oneself to have, and level of competence, that is, one's ability to achieve success through one's actions. These psychological needs are important determinants of well-being as they bridge an important connection between action that is taken by individuals and levels of happiness and contentment (Howell et al. 2017). This is directly relevant to active participation in online movements as the very nature of the collective action enhances the development of interrelationships with the aim of achieving a shared goal. Activity in such an endeavour can also highlight one's own individual, autonomous competence that contributed to the group's success.

Within the context of engagement in online group action, it is important to investigate a number of both positive and negative emotions that have a bearing on the psychological needs of interconnectedness, autonomy and competence that self-determination theory links with well-being. The first point to note is that the proposed conceptual architecture of emotions we advance is organised as clusters of emotions that are relatively more distant or closer in proximity (Wilson and Lewandowska-Tomaszczyk 2019). The meaning of specific emotions is based on relationships between and within emotion clusters and additionally how these clusters interact with each other. We argue that clusters of emotions, similar to concepts of a more concrete nature, are organised in terms of their prototypicality, with fuzzy boundaries and a graded structure (Rosch 1973). We further argue that this conceptual organisation of emotion clusters is at the heart of the variability in emotion profiles across languages and cultures and that this has a direct impact on the positive and negative emotions that are relevant to the feelings of well-being of individuals in different cultures who engage in collective online activity.

The very nature of well-being highlights an obvious association with positive emotions, which has a direct relevance to the cultural variability in emotions experienced by individuals cooperating in the online sphere. This is underscored by one of our recent studies showing that the Polish, being relatively more collectivistic than the British (Hofstede 1980), base their contentment, fulfilment, serenity, happiness and joy on the quality and harmony of their close interpersonal relationships (Lewandowska-Tomaszczyk and Wilson 2015). Consistent results have been obtained in other studies. For example, Pflug (2009) observed that the more collectivistic South African participants in his study characterised happiness in terms of close family bonds and harmonious interpersonal relations. Uchida and Kitayama (2009) similarly report that their Japanese respondents associated hedonic experience with social harmony. In contrast, the emphasis on achieving success through one's actions pertains to the individualistic feature of personal goal achievement that is an inherent feature of personal satisfaction (e.g. Diener and Diener 1995). Therefore, in individualistic societies such as Britain, one's level of competence takes priority over interpersonal connections, meaning that one's well-being is enhanced when one's actions result in success. There are a number of studies that support this. For example, emphasising the self-fulfilment element in happiness, Uchida and Kitayama (2009) observed that their American sample characterised positive hedonic experience in terms of personal achievement. Uchida, Norasakkunkit and Kitayama (2004) similarly concur that happiness in European-American cultures is often defined in terms of personal achievement.

From the viewpoint of self-determination theory, it is interesting to compare how the variability in emotions pertaining to collectivism and individualism is relevant to collective online action in these cultures. A major feature in this respect is the foregrounding of interpersonal harmony in in-groups vis-à-vis out-groups. It is easy to see, in terms of self-determination theory, how this emphasis placed on in-group harmony by collectivists would be particularly likely to increase the well-being they derive from online in-groups. Furthermore, as pondered in Lewandowska-Tomaszczyk and Wilson (2019), a collectivist who gains well-being and a sense of contentment, fulfilment or happiness from the strong ties of an online in-group might strive to maintain this through criticism of the out-group, who are therefore more likely to be viewed as enemies than contenders. In contrast, we argue that the main features of individualism that are relevant to internet discourse, namely autonomy, personal goal achievement, and greater freedom from in-groups, are more conducive to online collective action in these cultures when there is relatively low interconnectedness. In such circumstances, an individualist is likely to view opponents in the out-group adversaries or contenders rather than enemies as they are relatively less likely to feel strong personal ties to the in-group vis-à-vis the out-group. As a consequence of this, the discourse between opponents is likely to be more measured and less extreme.

It is additionally important to underscore the role of negative emotions with respect to well-being in online group action, such as anxiety and anger. It would appear that ANXIETY cluster emotions, such as anxiety, concern and worry, are relevant to aspects of both collectivism and individualism in this regard. In terms of collectivism, there is a clear prosocial element to online social campaigns that lessen the anxiety of others. However, witnessing the plight of others also has a more individualistic inward focus as it has been shown to evoke vicarious distress in an observer, who is motivated to reduce this in a similar way that one desires to lessen one's own distress (Piliavin et al. 1981). It is clear to see that if one engages in a collective action to reduce the suffering of another individual then it is possible that there will be a decrease in the levels of one's own anxiety. In terms of self-determination theory, although a successful outcome in this regard depends largely on the interconnectedness involved in collective group action, we argue that it is the personal awareness that one has contributed to such a positive result that increases one's own sense of competence, which increases personal well-being via the reduction of ANXIETY cluster emotions. Therefore, the underlying motivation would be based on the more individualistic element of personal gain rather than prosocial concerns.

Another important emotion to consider in terms of cultural differences with respect to well-being in online group action is anger. Many studies have identified the maintenance of social harmony as the key basis to the variation in the representation of anger in collectivistic versus individualistic cultures. Specifically, whereas the expression of anger is viewed more negatively by collectivistic individuals as it is seen as a threat to the quality of interpersonal relations (Ngwayuh 2017), in more individualistic societies, which place relatively more importance on the self as opposed to social relationships, outward manifestations of anger are more accepted. Results consistent with this were demonstrated by Ogarkova, Soriano and Lehr (2012), in a study in which participants from two relatively more collectivistic cultures, Russia and Spain, were compared with those from three more individualistic cultures, Britain Germany and France, in their labelling of different emotional experiences pertaining to four emotion categories (anger, shame, guilt and pride). The specific results pertaining to anger showed that the most frequent label used by the Russian sample to refer to the anger situations was the lower intensity emotion, *razdrazhenie* 'irritation', and that similarly there was a high usage of the label *impotencia* 'impotence'/'powerlessness' by the Spanish sample for the anger situations. This restriction of anger has also been observed in more collectivistic Asian cultures by Cole, Bruschi and Tamang (2002) who note the threat it poses to relationship harmony. The intermediate position of Poland between Asian and Western cultures in terms of aggression has been shown by Forbes et al. (2009). Consistent with its intermediate position in terms of individualism–collectivism, the Polish sample had lower aggression than the US sample, but higher aggression than the Chinese sample. Crucially, the important point to be noted with regard to the present study is that the Polish participants had lower aggression than the more individualistic US participants. As aggression is closely related to the expression of anger, these results have a similar pattern to those of a study by Soriano (2013), which showed that the relatively more individualistic American English participants rated *anger* higher on GRID features pertaining to *desire to act* than the corresponding ratings by the more collectivistic Spanish participants for the Spanish equivalent to anger, *ira*.

English and Polish Comments

Rheingold proposes (1993: 3) that 'people in virtual communities do just about everything they do in real life, but we leave our bodies behind'. This quote suggests that the internet is a particular communal medium, enhancing cooperation, 'conviviality and understanding' (Rheingold 1993: 3). On the other hand, it is also treated as a platform of conflict and expression of negative emotions. Due to the fact that in virtual reality what we hear are only our voices, words and symbols – it is precisely the reason why this medium plays a particular role in the expression of conflict and cooperation online.

A few representative examples that are presented here have been selected from a number of various online cooperative and argumentative conflict exchange types in both languages.

Cooperation

Cooperation cases on the internet are often connected with financial support for somebody who cannot afford some goods and can be considered synonymous with helping victims of some disasters or posting verbal expression of support, which may eventually bring positive legal, administrative support to the victims. In other words, cooperation in such cases is linked with the feeling of compassion and urge to help.

Cooperative Scenarios
Polish

Examples of Polish cooperative scenarios typically focus either on giving professional information or advice or involve calls to help others in need. A few examples of the latter can be observed on the following websites:

(1) Help-others organizations and websites *Pomaganie innym pozwala pomóc sobie samemu* 'Helping others makes you help yourself' 12 February 2018 https://pieknoumyslu.com/pomaganie-innym-pomoc-sobie/

(2) Action dissemination in social media *Facebook* post: 11 March 2019
(3) Polish Humanitarian Action https://www.facebook.com/PolishHumanit arianAction/posts/823808751298764

What is necessary for maintaining health?
To know the rules of hygienic safety! 💪✊
✓See how our hygiene promoters educate Korijo IDPs in South Sudan about keeping good hygiene in difficult conditions, when access to water and sanitary facilities is very limited!

The internet posts calling for aid do not always meet with global support (e.g. there are as few as eighteen Facebook likes for (2)). As reported in Lewandowska-Tomaszczyk and Wilson (2019: 215), an opinion on Polish people's involvement in humanitarian actions by Janina Ochojska, [president of the Polish Humanitarian Action] is moderate: 'The Poles help willingly, but they are selective [. . .] it's the easiest to collect money or victims of natural catastrophes [. . .] But e.g., for aid for the victims of the Syrian war, that's a different matter. [. . .] I'm also surprised by weak interest in the action of buying food Pajacyk for Children.'[1] In contrast, one can be surprised by the extraordinary success of the annual initiative, instigated by Jerzy Owsiak, *Wielka Orkiestra Świątecznej Pomocy* 'Great Orchestra of Christmas Charity'. It is the biggest, non-governmental, non-profit charity organisation in Poland, running various programmes, offering professional and general courses, such as first-aid, and purchasing equipment for medical institutions, hospital wards and individual people on a large scale. These activities are supported exclusively by money raised in public collections.

We might also hypothesise that the mass positive reaction is not pure altruism but maybe connected with political preferences of the donors. The Orchestra's achievements and mass popularity, as well as a charismatic leader, are not particularly appreciated by the current governing party political leaders, so the donors, looking broadly, might treat their acts (also) as a manifesto of their political preferences. In this sense, it can be seen that this identity is based both on the negative as well as positive forces of collective identity formation.

English
There are hundreds of humanitarian and charity organizations in the UK, addressing sometimes small segments of society; for example, activities described at the Facebook profile of the Obsessive Compulsive Disorder (OCD) support group at https://www.facebook.com/groups/887884195319532.

Other support societies, for example Victim Support (VS) at https://www.victimsupport.org.uk/, boast thousands of active supporters and thousands of people who are offered help (814,000 in 2018). There are numerous charity funds in the UK, as reported at https://www.theguardian.com/commentisfree/2018/mar/04/the-guardian-view-on-charity-dont-turn-away. Some of them are very highly evaluated, as can be seen at https://www.consumerreports.org/charities/best-charities-for-your-donations/.

One of the most active non-profit social campaign organizations in the UK is 38 Degrees (https://en.wikipedia.org/wiki/38_Degrees (Wilson 2013)). It was established with the aim to strive for peaceful solutions, promote human rights and fairness, protect the environment and advance democratic procedures. And yet, even the oldest and best known, as, for example, the Salvation Army, one of the best charities according to consumer reports, can also meet with severe criticism on the part of some other consumers.[2]

Negative Cooperation

Internet snowball effects can involve people's cooperation with regard to negative cooperative cases, such as rejection of government proposals in acts of civil disobedience, protests, as in (2–4) later. All the commentators unite in a group and fight to reject the government's regulation, and each of the comments adds a new negative point to oppose the regulation. The group identity that emerges in the discussion is homogenous and provides strong counterbalance to the official regulation. The emotionality dynamics develops in terms of negative, also abusive, vocabulary, pessimistic scenarios and sarcastic comments, addressed to individuals considered particularly harmful in the relevant exophoric contexts. The use of rich punctuation is characteristic for expressions of emotionality.

(2)

Ustawa o Naczelnej Izbie Aptekarskiej 'Regulation on Chief Pharmacy Chamber
http://www.rynekaptek.pl/marketing-i-zarzadzanie/ustawy-o-zawodzie-farmaceuty-podpisz-petycje,30281.html[3]
C1[4]: Nic nie podpisywac bo to cyrograf!! Obecne NRA dziala z premedytacja na szkodetysiecyfarmaceutow i tak samo jest z tym bublem!! Wierchuszka za zlamanie statutu powinna trafic na niedole, teraz by sobie z Misiem przynajmniej pogrypsowali na fachowe tematy.

C2: Czy oni tam, z tej NIA, to tak na poważnie?
C3: Kazdy kto to podpisze pokaze jedynie ze jest idiota co podpisuje cokolwiek bez czytania. [. . .] Chyba izba ma cos do ukrycia albo ma czlonkow za baranow skoro poleca podpisywac nie pokazujac co szczegolnie ze to wazna ustawa.
C1: Cala ustawe zmiescilbym na 2 kartkach A4. Bedzie to kolejny martwy i niezyciowy bubel a la kodeks etyki aptekarskiej. Po co kasjerowi i sprzedawcy lekow ustawa? 15 lat temu nie bylo ustawy i kazdy dobrze zyl, niedlugo baba w miesnym zazada ustawy
Niedlugo NRA zrobi zbiorke na Misiewicza zeby biedak w niedoli cos w kantynie mogl upic.

English Translation of (2)

Bill on the Supreme Chamber of Pharmacists
C1: do not sign (the petition), it's a pact with the devil. The current Chamber means harm to thousands of pharmacists and this bill is no different. The top echelon of the profession should be jailed for breaking the profession's constitution – they would thus get a chance to talk shop with Teddy Bear (nickname of former vice defence minister, who is now in jail)
C2: are the Supreme Chamber guys serious about it?
C3: anyone who signs it will show himself to be a nitwit who signs things without reading them. Either the Chamber guys have something to hide or they treat us members as a bunch of idiots, expecting us to sign it without telling us exactly why it is so important.
C1: the whole bill could be reduced to two A4 pages. It will be another piece of dead and useless trash, just like the code of pharmacists' ethics. What's the use of the law for the seller or the person at the cash register? Next thing you know a lady at the meat store will demand a law. Before you know it the Chamber will start raising money for Teddy Bear so the poor wretch can buy something at the prison shop.

In the web discourse scenarios we analyse all concern matters that take place in the real world. Apart from the cooperative scenarios of the positive and negative types discussed in Sections 8.1.1 and 8.1.2, the former representing people who perform activities of the approach – cumulative type, and the latter – uniting those who disagree with public, often official, plans or acts and fight together to overturn them, there are also other large, if not the largest, groups of internet users in conflict we address further in Section 8.1.3, who fight against each other internally, within online spaces. Such scenarios may overcome internet discourse boundaries and gain an authentic presence in offline contexts in, for example, the threatening cases of devirtualization we refer to in Section 9.

Interactional Conflict Scenario

Interactional conflict scenarios are typically structured in terms of a ping-pong communication type. In sample (3) further, the commentators form two opposing groups with clear collective identities concerning the Brexit conflict in the UK: Remainers and Leavers. However, their collective identity links are less clearly evident when contrasted with Polish samples in (2) and (4).

English

(3)   10 March 2019
https://www.telegraph.co.uk/politics/2019/03/10/analysis-does-eu-stand-lose-no-deal-brexit/#comments
C1: The EU is ten times the size of Britain, its economy was worth about 20 trillion dollars last year. That's 20,000 billion dollars for you Brexiteer slow learners. The 39 billion pounds is peanuts. The British contribution of some £9 billion is even less than peanuts. Wake up, give up your delusions, and face reality of what Britain is proposing.
C2: That's the economy not the EU budget which is *c.* 145 billion stupid. The size of an economy is irrelevant.
C1: 'give up'? That's for people such as retainers who have no strength of spirit.
C2: money money money
C3: The last paragraph of the article is the obvious solution to the Irish border problem – a customs border between the ROI and the rest of the EU.
It is no concern of the UK if the Irish have to go that route. None at all.
C4: So you want to play chicken, you pound shop napoleon lush?
C5: 'The UK has agreed to pay approximately £39 billion but Theresa May and many other senior figures in the Government have hinted Britain would not pay all of that if no agreement was struck.'
Wow, 2 big lies in one sentence! You can't even lie without contradicting yourselves. If the government 'hinted' it won't pay 'all of that' then the EU is not bound to lose the £39 billion. Only the part the government 'hinted' it won't pay. You can spin it as much as you like but the reality is that the EU is not impressed and don't seem to be willing to compromise.
C3: We will pay when the EU provides an invoice.

C5: But if you think we're paying for nothing think again. Oh and can you ask the EU to break it down for us.
C2: Once the Leavers die off we let the UK back in for 50 bill
C1: As the Leavers die off they are replaced with maturing Remainers who see the EU for what it is and become ... Leavers.
C2: no you Leavers will all die off in April
C1: Gotta love it hehehe
C2: idiot

Polish

Polish internet comments, generally similar to the British ones, focus on the relationship between national – country – interests – and the role and position of the European Union.

(4)

http://wiadomosci.gazeta.pl/wiadomosci/7,114884,24524610,nowy-sondaz-na-wybory-do-pe-cztery-partie-z-europoslami-schetyna.html
C1: prawie 40% chce pełzającego wyjścia z Unii? To skąd potem będzie na 500+? Na remonty szpitali, zabytkowych kościołów, pieniądze dla rolników i na czym tam jeszcze zależy wyborcom pisu?
C2: stąd co dzisiaj – z podatków ... Unia niedługo będzie nas więcej kosztować niż daje
C1: według was kłamcy od samego początku niby więcej nas kosztuje a jakoś setki milionów euro Polska jest na plusie. A z podatków naiwniaku to trzeba spłacać dług publiczny nabijany codziennie przez morawieckiego i nie będzie na żadne inwestycje
C2: Troche mieszasz fakty.
Schetyna chce organizowac referendum na temat wyjscia z UE.
To oboz polityczny Schetyny mowil, ze 'piniedzy nie ma na 500+'; to tak tylko w gwoli trzymania siefaktow.
C3: Na razie to Schetyna rzucil swego czasu temat o referendum unijnym ;)
C1: słowa klucze – swego czasu. Nie liczą się słówka bez znaczenia, tylko działania. Te wskazują wprost – pis chce nas wyprowadzić z UE bo patrzy im na ręce jak zawłaszczają państwo i kasę
C2: Wszystko można powiedzieć o Kaczyńskim, ale na pewno nie to że jest głupcem. Jemu się wyjście z UE NIE OPŁACA! Przerażające jest to, ze tylu matołów powtarza te brednie o polexicie!

C3: A gdzie w programie PiSowcy maja punkt: wyjscie z EU albo chocby referendum?
Podpisuje sie pod tym, ze wszystko mozna o Kaczorze powiedziec ale wyjscia EU nie poprze, przykladchocy ilu prominentnych działaczy PiS walczy i Bruksele
C1: oczywiście po to aby po pierwsze nachłapać się kasy, a po drugie mataczyć i jątrzyć na Tuska i totalną opozycję także w EU
C2: s-f proponuje pisac :))) Policz nie wplaty z UE i wplaty do UE ale dolicz koszty dostosywania PL firm do przepisow UE , policz koszty zwiekszonej biurokracji . . . A za chwile bedziemy jeszcze platnikiem netto . . . Myslisz ze taka UE daje nam $$$$ za frajer, z dobroci serce?!?!? :))) Naprawdejestes tak naiwny? :)
C4: Rzont [rząd] da. Przecież to jasne.
C2: UE daje nam za frajer?
C1: Ale się tu wyroiło od trolipisowskich po 0,2 zł za wpis. [. . .]
No pisie pachołki- na miejsca, gotowi?? START . . . Bolszewia się słania, ale parę pisich rubelków jeszcze wpadnie za wiernopoddańcze posty. Do dzieła towarzysze . . . [. . .]
To teraz piss ogłosi 500+ na planowane dziecko i jabol + dla rodziców

English Translation of (4)
C1: close to 40 per cent (of us) want Poland to get out of the EU. If that happens where will money be coming from for welfare giveaways and farming subsidies, to maintain hospitals and historic churches, and whatever else is important for PiS (Law and Justice, ruling party) voters?
C2: from taxes, just as today. Soon enough (membership in) the EU will start costing us more than we get from it.
C1: according to you, liars, it's been costing us more from the very beginning, so how come the country has been a net beneficiary to the tune of several hundred million Euros a year. And the tax money, you simpleton, is eaten up by public debt that keeps being inflated by Morawiecki (the PM) and nothing is left for investment projects.
C2: you've got your facts wrong. It is Schetyna (opposition leader) who wants to hold a referendum on Polexit. It's Schetyna's crowd who say there is no money for welfare spending, just for the sake of facts
C3: so far it's only been Schetyna who raised (lit. tossed) the topic of EU referendum

C1: key words, some time ago. Words without substance don't matter, only deeds count. And those make it clear PiS wants to pull us out of the EU because the EU is watching them taking over the state and the money.
C2: you can say anything about Kaczyński (PiS leader) but definitely not that he is a fool. Leaving the EU IS NOT IN HIS INTEREST. It's astonishing that so many morons keep talking this Polexit rubbish.
C3: where in their programme do the PiS crowd talk of 'leaving the EU' or 'membership referendum'? I quite agree, you can say anything about the Duck (the nickname of the leader of PiS) but he will not support Poland leaving the Union, just look how many PiS top guns are scrambling for MEP jobs.
C1: they are, aren't they! First to line their pockets and then to go on with their monkey business, putting down Tusk and (Poland's parliamentary) opposition also in Brussels.
C2: I suggest you take up sf writing :)))) Count not what is paid out and in but add in the expenses Polish companies incur having to adjust to EU standards, add in burgeoning bureaucracy. And very soon we will become a net contributor. Do you really think the EU is giving us $$$$ for nothing, out of the goodness of their heart!?!?!?!? Are you really that naïve?:).
C4: The government will, isn't that obvious?
C2: the EU is giving us money for nothing?
C1: look at the swarm of PiS trolls, at 5 eurocents a post [...]
now PiS lackeys, ready, set, GO! The Bolsheviks are reeling but a few roubles can be earned for servile posts. So get to work, comrades [...]
Now PiS will announce another handout for each planned baby, and a bottle of plonk for the parents.

When compared with the English samples what is striking is a structural – ping-pong – discourse organisation resemblance between Polish (examples 3, 5) |and the English discourse structure as presented in example (4). However, the Polish discourse displays higher emotionality – it contains more derogatory and abusive expressions than the English one, with more direct expression of slight and contempt, insulting and denigrating the interactional addressee. This observation is conformant with the findings reported in Lewandowska-Tomaszczyk (2017a, b) and the *Interconnectivity* profiles generated for the materials discussed there but, at the same time, judging both Polish and British data, it can be considered a sign of more global radicalisation of internet exchange. The division into opposing camps, or 'tribes' as some would call them, is more and more visible in the comments. Although the interactive abuse in the

British comments is weaker, in both groups a tribal division is seen, making the two discourses structurally – and semantically – alike.

Future Directions: Conflict Devirtualization

Although social media can offer online spaces within which individuals can launch protests that can be less restricted by offline societal restraints, the blurred boundary between these two spheres, the permeability of which is dependent on many potential contextual factors, means that the total separation of the two is to some extent illusory. Specifically, a pertinent question in this respect relating to our contrastive analysis of British versus Polish online collective identities and expanding it to a broader cultural context is to determine the differences between factors that influence such online activity vis-à-vis a devirtualized offline presence, that is, when individuals or groups are forced or choose to move their activity from an online to an offline space, particularly as this issue has received relatively little scholarly attention. A key element of collective action in a devirtualized space is the extent to which it is accepted within different societies that take a lenient or oppressive stance to real-world protest. Protests concerning feminine rights can serve a good example in this respect. For example, Newsom and Lenge (2012), commenting on online Arab feminist activity in the revolutions in Tunisia (December 2010 to January 2011) and Egypt (January to February 2011), observes that because "online activism occurs in a liminal "third space", a place where traditional rules governing society can be set aside" (p. 32), it only constitutes contained empowerment. This means that although it has the potential to attract global attention and hence encourage involvement, the potential power gained from this is constrained within local, traditional power structures that need to be negotiated with if such global support is to be recognised and accepted in this offline space. The role of anonymity is foregrounded in the case of Muslim women who use it as a means of apparent protection in protests against the patriarchal online society that oppresses them. However, such anonymity is often illusory, as can be seen in the case study of the Pakistani social media celebrity Fouzia Azeem, who adopted an online, defiant strategy against the unfair treatment of women using her online social media pseudonym, Qandeel Baloch. However, the exposure of her true identity by traditional online led to her enforced devirtualization and she fled in fear to her family home where she was tragically murdered by her brother in an honour killing due to his sense of shame (Wilson and Lewandowska-Tomaszczyk 2021).

This can be contrasted with the successful offline, devirtualized 'Black Monday Protest' (Pol. Czarny Protest, cf. internet sources in the bibliography) in Poland on 3 October 2016, in which thousands of women protested against a total ban on abortion following initial online opposition to the proposed anti-abortion ban regulations (Lewandowska-Tomaszczyk and Wilson 2019).[5] Within the context of self-determination theory (e.g. Deci and Ryan 2000), it is likely that the social harmony and well-being derived from the online 'Black Monday Protest' remained a key feature of its offline, devirtualized space, especially when one considers the certain degree of collectivism in this culture.

Conclusions

While well-being is in fact the ultimate consequence of helping others and is linked to a cluster of other positive emotions, which is visible in cooperative practices in both British and Polish cultures, it is negative emotionality that is typically stronger and provides a more intensive sense of satisfaction when it has an outlet for expression. It significantly releases the experiencer's negative emotionality pressure in such cases (Tice, Bratslavsky, and Baumeister 2001), and is thus likely to provide a more satisfactory outcome to him/her than positive emotions (Lewandowska-Tomaszczyk 2017a, b, 2020). Higher interconnectedness in collectivistic societies develops this relation of satisfaction mainly with regard to their in-group members. These societal bonds between members of in-groups are stronger than in the case of individualistic societies. As noted earlier, appreciation of the well-being gained from this might lead collectivists to more harshly oppose the out-group in comparison with individualists who, on the basis of their less social interconnectivity to the in-group compared with the out-group, are less likely to view opponents in the out-group as enemies in favour of adversaries. And yet, the fluctuation of the individualistic versus collectivistic cultural criteria are observed in both – Polish and British – online interactions, making the collectivistic–individualistic axis differentiation in the two cultures flatter and less conspicuous.

However, while, as Lewandowska-Tomaszczyk and Wilson (2019) propose, a member of an individualistic society is less likely to feel pressure to determine their own identity in terms of in- and out-groups, for collectivistic cultures this is precisely the case. The formation of virtual communities, as phrased by Goodwin (2004: 102 [1993]), may give a chance to revitalise the public sphere, which, to follow Rheingold (1993, 14), is necessary to 'revitalise citizen-based democracy [. . .] to put it back in the hands of the public'. The public, however, are not only groups of individuals within localities but they are such individuals who also develop their online collective identities at a higher and higher degree, within Europe, or beyond, converging towards stronger and stronger agency in both internet discourse, as well as in real-world radicalisation.

Notes

1. http://weekend.gazeta.pl/weekend/1,152121,19445997,czy-polacy-potrafia-i-chca-pomagac-innym-szefowie-organizacji.html.
   Czy Polacy pomagają innym? Szefowie organizacji charytatywnych mają na ten temat różne opinie.
2. https://www.whatpeoplesay.org/salvation-army-article-newspaper-article.
   The Starvation Army: twelve reasons to reject the Salvation Army.
   Twelve reasons why you should think twice about supporting the Salvation Army.
   salvation army letter March 2019
   https://www.whatpeoplesay.org/salvation-army-letter-march-2019.
3. The original spelling is retained in the posts.
4. C 'Commentator'.
5. www. 'To sztuczna definicja człowieka' Prof. Monika Płatek o ustawie Ordo Iuris rozmawia z Renatą Kim – komentarze.

Bibliography

Berting, J., and Ch. Villain-Gandossi. 1995. The role and significance of national stereotypes in international relations: An interdisciplinary approach. In: T. Walas (ed.), *Stereotypes and Nations*. Cracow: The International Cultural Centre, 13–27.

Brown, P., and S. C. Levinson. 1987. *Politeness: Some Universals in Language Usage*. Cambridge: Cambridge University Press.

Cole, P. M., C. J. Bruschi, and B. L. Tamang. 2002. Cultural differences in children's emotional reactions to difficult situations. *Child Development* 73(3), 983–96.

Deci, E. L., and R. M. Ryan. 2000. The "what" and "why" of goal pursuits: Human needs and the self-determination of behavior. *Psychological Inquiry* 11(4), 227–68.

Diener, E., and M. Diener. 1995. Cross-cultural correlates of life satisfaction and self-esteem. *Journal of Personality and Social Psychology* 68, 653–63.

Diers-Lawson, A. 2017. Antecedents and indicators of strong emotional reactions to crises among stakeholders. In: S. Croucher, B. Lewandowska-Tomaszczyk, and P. Wilson (eds), *Conflict, Mediated Message and Group Dynamics: Intersections of Communication*, 81–136. USA: Rowman & Littlefield.

Forbes, G., Z. Xiaoying, K. Doroszewicz, and K. Haas. 2009. Relationships between individualism–collectivism, gender, and direct or indirect aggression: A study in China, Poland, and the US. *Aggressive Behavior* 35, 24–30.

Gaertner, S. L., J. F. Dovidio, P. A. Anastasio, B. A. Bachman, and M. C. Rust. 1993. The common ingroup identity model: Recategorization and the reduction of intergroup bias. *European Review of Social Psychology* 4, 1–26.

Goodwin, I. 2004 [1993]. *Review of Rheingold 1993. Westminster Papers in Communication and Culture* © *2004*. University of Westminster, London, Vol. 1 (1), 103–9.

Graham, T., and S. Wright. 2014. Discursive equality and everyday talk online: The impact of "superparticipants". *Journal of Computer-Mediated Communication* 19, 625–42.

Hofstede, G. 1980. *Culture's Consequences: International Differences in Work-Related Values*. Beverly Hills: Sage.

Howell, R. T., M. Ksendzova, E. Nestingen, C. Verahian, and R. Iyer. 2017. Your personality on a good day: How trait and state personality predict daily well-being. *Journal of Research in Personality* 69, 250–63.

Hu, H-H., J. Lin, and W. Cui. 2015. Cultural differences and collective action: A social network perspective. *Complexity* 20(4), 68–77.

Lewandowska-Tomaszczyk, B. 2015. Emergent group identity construal in online discussions: A linguistic perspective. In F. Zeller, C. Ponte, and B. O'Neill (eds), *Revitalising Audience Research: Innovations in European Audience Research*. Abington, UK: Routledge, 80–105.

Lewandowska-Tomaszczyk, B. 2016. Language, leadership and visibility in online discussions. In: K. Ciepiela (ed.), *Identity in Communicative Contexts*. Frankfurt am Main: Peter Lang, 57–80.

Lewandowska-Tomaszczyk, B. 2017a. Conflict radicalization and emotions in English and Polish online discourses on immigration and refugees. In: S. Croucher, B. Lewandowska-Tomaszczyk, and P. Wilson (eds), *Conflict, Mediated Message and Group Dynamics: Intersections of Communication*. USA: Rowman & Littlefield, 1–24.

Lewandowska-Tomaszczyk, B. 2017b. Identity, emotions and cultural differences in English and Polish online comments. *Journal of Language and Culture* 4(1), 47–71.

Lewandowska-Tomaszczyk, B. 2020. Culture-driven emotional profiles and online discourse extremism. *Pragmatics and Society* 11(2), 262–92.

Lewandowska-Tomaszczyk, B., and J. Tomaszczyk. 2012. We in the union: A Polish perspective on identity. In P. Bayley, and G. Williams (eds), *European Identity: What the Media Say*. Oxford: Oxford University Press, 224–57.

Lewandowska-Tomaszczyk, B., and P. A. Wilson. 2015. It's a date: Love and romance in time and space. Paper delivered at International Workshop: Love and Time at University of Haifa, 8th–10th March.

Lewandowska-Tomaszczyk, B., and P. A. Wilson. 2019. Well-being and collective identity in Polish and English contexts. In B. Lewandowska-Tomaszczyk (ed.), *Contacts & Contrasts in Culture and Language*. Springer, 193–220.

Newsom, V. A., and L. Lenge. 2012. Arab women, social media, and the Arab spring: Applying the framework of digital reflexivity to analyze gender and online activism. *Journal of International Women's Studies* 13(5), 31–45.

Ngwayuh, E. 2017. Immigrant threat, prejudice and the growing refugee crisis. In: S. Croucher, B. Lewandowska-Tomaszczyk, and P. Wilson (eds), *Conflict, Mediated Message and Group Dynamics: Intersections of Communication*, 137–52. USA: Rowman & Littlefield.

Ogarkova, A., C. Soriano, and C. Lehr. 2012. "Naming feeling: Exploring the equivalence of emotion terms in five European languages." In P. A. Wilson (ed.), *Dynamicity in Emotion Concepts. Lodz Studies in Language*, vol. 27, 253–84. Frankfurt a. Main: Peter Lang.

Pęzik, P. 2014. Graph-based analysis of collocational profiles. In V. Jesenšek, and P. Grzybek (eds), *Phraseologieimwörterbuch und Korpus (Phraseology in dictionaries and corpora)*. ZORA 97. Maribor, Bielsko–Biała, Budapest, Kansas, Praha: Filozofskafakuteta, 227–43.

Pflug, J. 2009. Folk theories of happiness: A cross-cultural comparison of conceptions of happiness in Germany and South Africa. *Social Indicators Research* 92(3), 551–63.

Piliavin, J. A., J. F. Dovidio, S. L. Gaertner, and R. D., III Clark. 1981. *Emergency Intervention*. New York: Academic Press.

Rheingold, H. 1993. *The Virtual Community: Homesteading on the Electronic Frontier*. New York: Addison-Wesley.

Rosch, E. 1973. Natural categories. *Cognitive Psychology* 4, 328–50.

Rzepnikowska, A. 2019. Racism and xenophobia experienced by Polish migrants in the UK before and after Brexit vote. *Journal of Ethnic and Migration Studies* 45(1), 61–77.

Soriano, C. 2013. Conceptual metaphor theory and the GRID paradigm in the study of anger in English and Spanish. In J. J. R. Fontaine, K. R. Scherer, and C. Soriano (eds), *Components of Emotional Meaning: A Sourcebook*. Oxford: Oxford University Press, 410–24.

Szarota, P., K. Cantarero, and D. Matsumoto. 2015. Emotional frankness and friendship in Polish culture. *Polish Psychological Bulletin* 46(2), 181–5.

Tice, D. M., E. Bratslavsky, and R. F. Baumeister. 2001. Emotional distress regulation takes precedence over impulse control. *Personality and Social Psychology* 80(1), 53–67.

Triandis, H. C. 1995. *Individualism and Collectivism*. Boulder, CO: Westview Press.

Triandis, H. C. 2001. Individualism-collectivism and personality. *Journal of Personality* 69, 907–24.

Uchida, Y., and S. Kitayama. 2009. Happiness and unhappiness in east and west: Themes and variations. *Emotion* 9, 441–56.

Uchida, Y., V. Norasakkunkit, and S. Kitayama. 2004. Cultural constructions of happiness: Theory and empirical evidence. *Journal of Happiness Studies* 5(3), 223–39.

Wilson, P. A. 2013. 38 Degrees: green shoots of a new democratic process? Paper delivered at New Media, New Audiences workshop at the University of Lodz, 13th April.

Wilson, P. A. 2017. The role of shame in conflict: A cross-cultural perspective. In: B. Lewandowska-Tomaszczyk, P. A. Wilson, and S. Croucher (eds), *Approaches to Conflict: Theoretical, Interpersonal, and Discursive Dynamics*. USA: Rowman & Littlefield, 55–78.

Wilson, P. A., and B. Lewandowska-Tomaszczyk. 2019. Cognitive structure and conceptual clusters of emotion terms. *FILOZOFIA I NAUKA Studia filozoficzne I interdyscyplinarne Tom 7, część 1*, 91–123.

Wilson, P. A., and B. Lewandowska-Tomaszczyk. 2021. Real-world consequences of devirtualization from online to offline spaces; The role of shame as a resource in the honor-killing of Qandeel Baloch. In: C-H. Mayer, E. Vanderheiden, and P. Wong (eds), *From Shame to Well-Being in Industry 4.0*, 455–74. Switzerland: Springer.

Internet sources

38 Degrees
https://en.wikipedia.org/wiki/38_Degrees

Czarny Protest – ustawa antyaborcyjna
www. 'To sztuczna definicja człowieka' Prof. Monika Płatek o ustawie Ordo Iuris rozmawia z Renatą Kim – komentarze

Czy Polacy pomagają innym?
http://weekend.gazeta.pl/weekend/1,152121,19445997,czy-polacy-potrafia-i-chca-pomagac-innym-szefowie-organizacji.htmlCzy Polacy pomagają innym? Szefowie organizacji charytatywnych mają na ten temat różne opinie.

Online Newspaper Comments

http://www.theguardian.com/commentisfree/2016/jan/22/the-guardian-view-on-the-refugee-crisis-dial-down-the-rhetoric-and-have-the-difficult-debate#comments

https://www.telegraph.co.uk/politics/2019/03/10/analysis-does-eu-stand-lose-no-deal-brexit/#comments

http://www.rynekaptek.pl/marketing-i-zarzadzanie/ustawy-o-zawodzie-farmaceuty-podpisz-petycje,30281.html

http://wiadomosci.gazeta.pl/wiadomosci/7,114884,24524610,nowy-sondaz-na-wybory-do-pe-cztery-partie-z-europoslami-schetyna.html

https://pieknoumyslu.com/pomaganie-innym-pomoc-sobie/

https://www.facebook.com/PolishHumanitarianAction/posts/823808751298764

https://www.facebook.com/groups/887884195319532

https://www.victimsupport.org.uk/

https://www.theguardian.com/commentisfree/2018/mar/04/the-guardian-view-on-charity-dont-turn-away

https://www.consumerreports.org/charities/best-charities-for-your-donations/

https://www.whatpeoplesay.org/salvation-army-article-newspaper-article

https://www.whatpeoplesay.org/salvation-army-letter-march-2019

A Phraseological Perspective on Evaluation

The Covid-19 Vaccination in Polish Web-Based News

Mikołaj Deckert, Krzysztof Hejduk and Piotr Pęzik

Introduction

As of June 2022, when this chapter was completed, Covid-19 vaccines were not mandatory in Poland.[1] Since obligatory Covid-19 vaccination is controversial, some outlets and journalists, especially when publishing on the internet, regularly resort to a range of argumentative devices when expressing stance on this issue. One potentially productive source of argumentative innovations is the coverage of public opinion polls on Covid-19 vaccination mandates. Reports and commentaries on such results can be biased evaluatively, often in ways that are only partly congruent with how the poll was originally designed and used.

Polling the Public about Vaccine Mandates

To identify news reports and commentaries on Covid-19 vaccination opinion polls, we retrieved a set of 343 titles of news articles found in the Monco PL corpus using a query which matched any conjunction of the noun *sondaż* (poll) and either the noun *szczepienie* (vaccination) or *szczepionka* (vaccine) published until 1 March 2022. Within this initial pool of articles, we found a smaller set of thirty-four unique titles about public polls on a hypothetical situation in which any vaccinations (including those against Covid-19) were to be made mandatory in Poland. Twenty-seven out of these titles used the noun *obowiązek* (mandate). The titles used this lexeme in contexts which were relatively positive (e.g. 'More than 64 per cent of pensioners want mandatory vaccinations introduced'[2]), neutral (e.g. 'Poll: Should vaccinations be mandatory?'[3]), mixed (e.g. 'The Left wants mandatory vaccinations and penalties for the unvaccinated'[4]) and negative (e.g. 'Poles want neither mandatory vaccinations, nor nationwide restrictions.'[5]). Our particular interest was in the remaining seven cases. Table 7.1 provides an overview of expressions used to describe the results of a given poll, which are juxtaposed with the original phrasing of the poll question.

Positions 57, 100 and 122 exemplify the use of the noun *przymus* and the adjective *przymusowe* in the poll reports. This is in contrast to the original poll questions referred to by the reports, which used the noun *obowiązek* and the adjective *obowiązkowe* to describe the vaccination mandate. Although at some level of lexicographic description all of these words could be considered to denote a sense of being compelled to do something, there are arguably significant differences in how they function. The latter expression is regularly translated into English as 'obligation', 'duty', 'responsibility', 'burden', 'mandatory' and 'compulsory', whereas the former – as '(en)forced', 'involuntary', 'coercive', 'hard', 'duress' and 'compulsion'.[6] For the sake of clarity and consistency, throughout this chapter we will translate *obowiązkowy* as 'mandatory' and *przymusowy* as 'coercive'.

The supposition behind this chapter is, therefore, that we may be dealing with a regular divergence in evaluation whereby the polling question utilizes a more neutral word like *obowiązek* and journalists report the polling results using a more affectively charged word like *przymusowy*. To shed light on this hypothesized evaluative mismatch, we investigate the semantic-prosodic qualities (cf. Zhang 2010: 190) of these two lexemes and how they are utilized in the context of vaccination. Our aim is to better understand how apparently subtle evaluative marking in a message may shape the message itself. Another envisaged outcome of this analysis is the observation that phraseology formation is an important aspect of language change. In public discourse, such change is often driven by the evaluative function of language.

As the aforementioned seven cases of poll results coverage (see Table 7.1) seem to suggest a degree of politicization of the context, especially with *przymusowy* (coercive) being used in major right-wing Polish political outlets, our analysis concentrates on political discourse. The differences in the evaluative potential of the two adjectives can be revealed by tapping into a representative corpus such as Monco PL. The corpus is used in this chapter to aggregate patterns of evaluation, following Louw (1993: 157) who observes that '[o]ne consequence of the advent of large corpora has been their increased potential for revealing consistencies in the influence of collocation on the behaviour of particular linguistic forms.

Table 7.1 Selected polls on the reception of possible Covid-19 vaccination mandate

#	Poll provider	Poll commission	Report source and date	Lexeme used in the poll question	Lexeme used in the report's title
57	SW Research (not stated in the report)	*RP.pl* (Szaniawski 2018)	*Do Rzeczy* (19 February 2018)	'Obowiązkowe' (not stated in the report)	'Przymusowych' (*Do Rzeczy* 2018a)
100	SW Research	*RP.pl* (Bartkiewicz 2021)	*Epoznan.pl* (28 August 2021)	'Obowiązkowe' (not stated in the report)	'Przymusu' (*S.K.* 2021)
122	Social Changes	*wPolityce.pl* (Szymański 2021)	*wPolityce.pl* (14 May 2021)	'Obowiązku'	'Przymusowe' (Szymański 2021)
171	(not available)	*Wysokie Obcasy* (Pacewicz 2018)	*300polityka.pl* (5 October 2018)	'Ma prawo'	'Ma prawo' (Mężyk 2018)
191	Estymator (CAWI)	*Do Rzeczy* (*Do Rzeczy* 2018c)	*Do Rzeczy* (19 October 2018)	'Dobrowolność' (not explicitly stated)	'Chce wolności' (*Do Rzeczy* 2018c)
196	Centrum B-R BioStat (CAWI)	*(does not apply)* (*K.M.* 2021)	*Wirtualne Media* (2 August 2021)	'Ograniczenia' + 'niezaszczepiony'	'Ograniczenia' + 'niezaszczepiony' (*K.M.* 2021)
203	'Instytut Badania Opinii Demos'	*La Repubblica* (*A.A.P.* 2021)	*Najwyższy Czas* (4 September 2021)	(not explicitly stated in the report)	'Obowiązek' + 'segregacja' (*A.A.P.* 2021)

[...] Semantic prosodies have been largely inaccessible to human intuition about language and they cannot be retrieved reliably through introspection'. Drawing on collocation analysis, we look at the possible convergence of idiomaticity and affective–ideological framing, using the above-discussed polling questions as a point of departure, to detect patterns of evaluation in Polish political discourse centred on vaccination.

Evaluation through Language

Judgements, especially axiological ones, may be expressed in language, supplying the recipient of a given message with a certain ready-made evaluation from the creator of such messages. In a paper on argumentative uses of emotive language, Macagno and Walton (2010: 1; 7) exemplify the traditional use of 'argumentation tactics that exploit emotive language' – while importantly distinguishing between using them as tools of persuasion and using them to deceive and manipulate – with the account from Quintilian's *Institutio Oratoria* (c. 95 CE): 'we may say that a man who was beaten was murdered, or that a dishonest fellow is a robber'; 'we may say that one who struck another merely touched him' (Book VIII; 4, 1 – eds. Butler 1922). Establishing this idea further, Martin and White open their monograph *The Language of Evaluation: Appraisal in English* with the following premise: 'writers/speakers approve and disapprove, enthuse and abhor, applaud and criticise, and [. . .] position their readers/listeners to do likewise' (2005: 1). Similarly, Liu (2015/2020: 6) opines on this function of language in the internet era that 'we have witnessed how opinionated posts on social media sites have helped [. . .] sway public sentiment, profoundly impacting our social and political lives'.

Such an attitudinal or perspectival variable can be observed to function saliently not only on the document or sentence levels (cf. Lin et al. 2006), as some scholars believe them to manifest themselves on the level of lexico-grammatical units. Deckert et al. (2016: 1), for instance, exemplify that with the case of word co-occurrence patterns. The connotative profile and the semantic prosody of a given lexeme is dependent on its 'habitual collocates', that is, quantifiably most frequent ones (Louw 1993: 158; Deckert et al. 2016: 1). Collocates triggering evaluative connotations can endow a given node word with non-neutral prosody (cf. Zhang 2010: 190–2 for an overview). This can even occur in relation to expressions usually considered neutral when decontextualized, as in the case of the negatively prosodic lexeme 'cause' (Stubbs 1995) or 'utterly' (Louw 1993: 160), whose concordances (e.g. 'utterly stupid', 'utterly demolished', 'utterly insensible') show 'an overwhelmingly "bad" prosody and there are few "good" right-collocates' (Louw 1993).

Another relevant construct to be referred to in this setting is sentiment analysis. One definition of 'sentiment analysis or opinion mining' can be found in the *Handbook of Natural Language Processing*: a process attempting to 'infer people's sentiments based on their language expressions' (Liu 2010: 633). This field, however, seems to be connected with more than just the extraction of 'opinions expressed in text' and the analysis of 'the entailed sentiments and emotions', involving 'many overlapping concepts and sub-tasks', such as 'classification [. . .], summarization, sentiment retrieval, etc.' – each with 'multiple solution paths' (Zhao et al. 2016: 1). In this chapter, we come to understand 'sentiment' following Liu's (2015/2020: 2) usage of the term, 'to mean the underlying positive or negative feeling implied by an opinion', the latter being defined (2015/2020) as the concept of 'evaluation, appraisal, or attitude and associated information'.

It should be noted that subjectivity can be expressed more explicitly or more indirectly, with varying intensity across cases. Mejova (2016) illustrates this point utilizing computational techniques for sentiment analysis in news coverage. Her findings indicate that news agencies can moderate highly emotional language, but certain agencies are willing to utilize 'emotion-laden and biased rhetoric'.[7] Her text observes that during the 2013 analysis across fifteen large US news media organizations, 'bias terms' as well as negative lexemes in general were more likely to be used in controversial topics, while 'strong emotional words' were less likely (Mejova 2016).

Covid-19 and Language

Corpora can serve to quantify pre-existing co-occurrence patterns across contexts and produce 'a seed list of opinion words to find other opinion words in a large corpus' (Liu 2010: 642). The reasoning for that can be summarized as follows: '[i]t is difficult for a human reader to find relevant sources, extract related sentences with opinions, read them, summarize them, and organize them into usable forms' (Liu 2010). A famous formulation of the methodological intuition behind such procedures was provided by Sinclair, who observes that 'language looks rather different when you look at a lot of it at once' (1991/2001: 100). As a relevant example of a corpus-based approach, Augustyn and Prażmo (2020: 209) conducted a cognitively oriented corpus analysis to examine English-language internet discourse relating to the SARS-CoV-2 disease. Among their findings, they suggested that 'the reader's interpretation of a given expression [. . .] can be guided by the author's aims and the way they are linguistically encoded in the discourse' (Augustyn and Prażmo 2020: 225). This observation is also relevant to our analysis of semantic prosody in Polish Covid-19 vaccine political discourse.

A number of studies have attempted to broaden our understanding of particular linguistic phenomena observed in Covid-19 discourse by concentrating on the English-speaking populations, and also by focusing on other languages and studying local lingua-cultural contexts. Mesthrie (2020: 1) argues in the journal commentary tellingly titled *More eyes on COVID-19: Pay attention to how people are talking about the pandemic in different languages* that '[c]ommunication of meaning does not rest with the scientists, health specialists or presidents alone', and so 'it is important to listen to the voices of those affected most' across time and cultures. Equally, Jarynowski et al. (2020) present an example of a quantitative study of data-mined perception of the coronavirus in Poland from social media. They find their data to have 'reflected the structural division of the Polish political sphere' (2020: 1), identifying the communities which approve of the governing party and those supporting the political opposition.

Premises and Methodology

A key characteristic of language use which needs to be clarified at this point is its formulaicity. As noted by Pawley and Syder, 'native speakers do not exercise the creative potential of syntactic rules to anything like their full extent, and [. . .] if they did do so they would not be accepted as exhibiting nativelike control of the language' (1983: 193). Pęzik (2019: 318) suggests that what it entails is that (native-like) language use to a large extent comprised of selected prefabricated phraseological units (phrasemes), which can naturally vary in length and frequency of use, and which serve a variety of purposes and registers of communication. In contrast, compositional constructions (syntagms) are 'original' in the sense that they are not 'solidified' in language. This is also why they can be seen as more 'impromptu' in comparison to phrasemes. The exact ratio of use between those two, however, is difficult to estimate, with the sheer amount of possible structure combinations and the relative difficulty of verifying the boundary between the two types appearing to be the most prominent reasons. The only currently known way of approximating the ratio of formulaic versus compositional language is through the use of corpora. The exploration of formulaicity can be coupled with aggregation of bibliographic and sociolinguistic annotation available in most reference corpora. For this reason, Monco PL (monco.frazeo.pl), a publicly available monitor-reference corpus, and its search engine were chosen as the primary tool for our purposes. As part of our methodology, we first extracted collocation profiles of the lexemes in question, including possible Polish grammatical variants, case, gender and plural markings. These results were then supplemented with a qualitative concordance-based discussion aimed to offer contextualization for our comparative analysis.

An important characteristic of the corpus used in this study is that through constant and open monitoring of language variation from a large list of sources, which itself entails an increasing rate of flow and great referential potential (Pęzik 2020: 133–4), it makes it possible to observe certain language trends as they occur. Another important asset of Monco PL is that it is a densely time-sampled corpus with tens of thousands of sentences added to it every day. As a corpus of over seven billion words covering the developments of the Covid-19 pandemic in Polish news websites, it can be used to find rare but significant collocations relevant to this topic and explain even subtle differences in their evaluative potential.

Data Selection

In the subsequent analysis, we used a subset of Monco PL covering the period of 4 January 2020 to 1 March 2022. The beginning of this sampling frame is marked by the report of World's Health Organisation's involvement in the then unknown-cause emergent cases of pneumonia in Wuhan, China – according to WHO's Listings of response to Covid-19.[8]

Classification of Sources

Since our preliminary analysis of the use of *przymusowy* (coercive) suggested that evaluation may be dependent on political orientation, we have decided to create two distinct subcorpora for the two basic political affiliations (left-leaning and right-leaning), grouping the sources into two distinct categories, so as to be able to look at them either jointly or individually. Each group was assigned four sources. The left-leaning group consists of 'strajk.pl', 'trybuna.eu', 'tygodnikprzeglad.pl', 'gazeta.pl'. The right-leaning – 'dorzeczy.pl', 'naszdziennik.pl', 'wpolityce.pl' and 'nczas.com'. Certainly, other outlets (many of which are also parsed by Monco PL) could be eligible for our classification. However, the political bias in the context of journalism is a relatively sensitive issue, and political orientation can essentially be viewed as a context-dependent and gradably subjective construct. Therefore, for the purposes of this study, we utilize only sources whose political orientation was publicly stated or we judge to be widely recognized in credible sources.

Generally, the selected sources were hesitant to state their affiliation using the basic left-right axis. Certain sources, however, only used it to refer to themselves – even large outlets, like *Do Rzeczy* in 2018: 'a leader among the portals of the right';[9] or *wPolityce* in 2015: 'a definitive leader among the conservative-right-wing news services'.[10] Similarly, *Najwyższy Czas* referred to itself as 'the first right-wing magazine in Poland' in 2019.[11] From the political left-wing, the descriptions available on the Facebook page of *STRAJK.eu* state: 'homepage of the Polish left'.[12] Contrariwise, the official website of *Przegląd* affiliates it more indirectly, stating that their work is 'oriented towards readers of leftist and centrist views',[13] although it can also be found quoted in a positive context as definitively 'secular and left-wing'.[14] Equally, the subscription of the *Trybuna* newspaper is officially advertised using the phrase 'a newspaper with strict, targeted views of the left-wing nature'.[15] The remaining sources, the liberal-leaning *Gazeta* – previously an online site for the left-leaning *Gazeta Wyborcza* – and the Catholic *Nasz Dziennik*, can be found in certain scholarly works (e.g. Krupa 2021: 55) as exemplary polar perspectives when it comes to the two-pronged political axis.

Analysis

Adjectival Collocates

We first checked whether the adjectives *przymusowy* (coercive) over *obowiązkowy* (mandatory) tend to be used as modifiers of the nouns 'vaccination' and 'vaccine' across the political spectrum of the Covid-19 Polish press coverage. Table 7.2 provides the highest-ranked adjectival collocates of *szczepienie* and *szczepionka* (vaccination). We generally inspect all potential collocates which have four or more occurrences in Monco, but they are additionally sorted by Dice score[16] as a measure of association strength.

As Table 7.2 shows, *obowiązkowy* (mandatory) is the highest-ranking adjectival collocate in the right-leaning subcorpus. The lexeme is also prominent in the left-leaning subcorpus, even if it is clearly lower on the list (adj5). However, a conspicuous asymmetry surfaces with *przymusowe* (coercive) being remarkably high on the right-leaning list (adj4) and completely absent from the left-leaning one. This, among other implications, reaffirms our intuition that the selectional preference in question is somehow mediated by political orientation.

Table 7.2 Highest-ranked right-wing adjectival collocates of *szczepienie**|szczepionka*** query (Monco PL)

	Left-wing subcorpus			Right-wing subcorpus		
#	Collocate	Freq.	Dice	Collocate	Freq.	Dice
adj1	zaszczepić (innoculate)	27	0.0039	obowiązkowy (*mandatory*)	211	0.0135
adj2	2021	21	0.0038	kliniczny (clinical)	75	0.0132
adj3	masowy (mass)	124	0.0036	skuteczny (effective)	171	0.0114
adj4	ochronny (protective)	26	0.0021	przymusowy (*coercive*)	58	0.0107
adj5	obowiązkowy (mandatory)	116	0.0019	uboczny (side)	44	0.0096
adj6	wektorowy (vector)	6	0.0017	masowy (mass)	83	0.0081
adj7	uboczny (side)	11	0.0016	ochronny (protective)	43	0.0075
adj8	16-	6	0.0016	potencjalny (prospective)	81	0.0069
adj9	Majówkowy ((May) long-weekend)	6	0.0016	farmaceutyczny (pharmaceutical)	33	0.0055
adj10	szczepionkowy (vaccinal)	5	0.0014	wynaleźć (devise)	23	0.0055
adj11	kliniczny (clinical)	17	0.0014	bezpieczny (safe)	91	0.0054
adj12	rozmrozić (defreeze)	5	0.0014	opracowywać (develop)	28	0.0049
adj13	powszechny (popular)	58	0.0013	eksperymentalny (experimental)	23	0.0048
adj14	populacyjny (populational)	5	0.0012	19	396	0.0045
adj15	Covidowych	4	0.0012	dostępny (available)	127	0.0044
adj16	Kubańskich (Cuban)	4	0.0012	2021	18	0.0041
adj17	Jednodawkową (single-dose)	4	0.0012	immunologiczny (immunological)	17	0.0041
adj18	spiskowy (conspiratorial)	7	0.0011	opracować (develop)	51	0.0037
adj19	19	478	0.0011	dobrowolny (volitional)	56	0.0037
adj20	odporny (immune)	11	0.0011	przebadać (examine)	21	0.0037
adj21	węzłowy (nodal)	4	0.0011	testować (to trial)	29	0.0036
adj22	zachęcający (encouraging)	8	0.0011	powszechny (popular)	38	0.0032
adj23	skuteczny (effective)	62	0.0011	genetyczny (genetic)	18	0.0032
adj24	niepożądany (adverse)	6	0.0009	wirusowy (viral)	14	0.0032
adj25	immunologiczny (immunological)	4	0.0009	zaszczepić (innoculate)	14	0.003

A qualitative review of the occurrences of the collocation in the right-leaning subcorpus makes it possible to account for the asymmetry. As demonstrated by the selection of instances in Table 7.3, qualifying vaccination as *przymusowe* (coercive) serves the purpose of construing it negatively.

For instance, let us consider the concordance in position 293 assuming that the message intends to portray Chancellor Merkel's decision as rational. One way to reinforce such a portrayal would be through negative framing of the rejected entity (in this case, mandatory vaccination). Accepting this, *przymusowy* (coercive) could have been selected by the author of the message as a more negatively marked alternative to *obowiązkowy* (mandatory), to match the sentiment of the categorical ('in any form') rejection of this entity. Moreover,

Table 7.3 Selection of concordances (right-wing) for the *Przymusowy*** (adjective) query on Monco PL

#	Left-side context	Match	Right-side context
293	Merkel odrzuciła (Merkel rejected)	przymusowe (coercive)	szczepienia w jakiejkolwiek formie. (vaccination in any form)[a]
331	Każdy – czyli na przykład zagonienie przez wojsko na stadion i (Everyone – so that includes herding into a stadium by the military and performing)	przymusowe (coercive)	szczepienia wyrywających się ludzi też? (vaccinations as people try to wrestle away, too?)[b]
866	W naszym nieszczęśliwym kraju może być to jednak *obowiązkowe*, w ostatnim czasie koalicji PiS-PO-PSL-Lewica zagłosowali 'za' nowelizacją przepisów otwierającą furtkę do (In our miserable country, however, this may be *mandatory*, (as) the recent PiS-PO-PSL-Lewica (the Polish political parties) coalition voted in favour of an amendment to the law, which creates a loophole enabling)	przymusowych (coercive)	szczepień (vaccination)[c]

[a] *wPolityce* (2021). Retrieved from: wPolityce.pl (accessed 1 March 2022). Date of corpus capture: 13 July 2021.
[b] Warzecha (2021). Retrieved from: DoRzeczy.pl (accessed 1 March 2022). Date of corpus capture: 1 December 2021.
[c] RP (2020). Retrieved from: nCzas.com (accessed 1 March 2022). Date of corpus capture: 2020-10-31.

Table 7.4 A selected case of concordance (right-wing) for the *Przymusowy*** adjective query on Monco PL

#	Left-side context	Match	Right-side context
283	SONDAŻ: Czy Polacy zaakceptowaliby (POLL: Would the Polish people accept)	przymusowe (coercive)	szczepienia przeciwko koronawirusowi? (vaccinations against the coronavirus?)[a]

[a] Szymański (2021). Retrieved from: wPolityce.pl (accessed 1 March 2022). Date of corpus capture: 15 May 2021.

position 866 is particularly conspicuous as it juxtaposes *obowiązkowe* and *przymusowe*, foregrounding the evaluative mismatch between the two, where the latter is arguably more negatively marked.

Notably, as evidenced in yet another occurrence of the collocation in the right-leaning data set (see Table 7.4), questions could be carrying evaluation and likely eliciting emotions by activating certain concepts, even if the speaker's attitude is not openly coded. This exemplifies a powerful discursive strategy of putting forward an idea or argument whereby it does not necessarily need to be true or relevant. By extension, the speaker can put that idea or argument on the table and withdraw or negate it later, but that idea or argument cannot be 'unseen'.

Noun Collocates

The adjectival results are then reinforced by findings from noun collocates (see Table 7.5).

In the right-leaning subcorpus, the noun *przymus* (coercion) is again high on the list (position n12), while it is not found on the analogous list corresponding to the left-leaning data set. We, therefore, see that the lexeme once more strongly – and asymmetrically across orientations – collocates with *szczepienie* (vaccination)/*szczepionka* (vaccine).

Investigating the particular contexts (see Table 7.6) in which the lexeme *przymus* (coercion) collocates with *szczepienie* (vaccination) provides further material to conclude that the word is used pejoratively, expressing negative attitude towards (mandatory) vaccination in the right-wing as opposed to the left-wing subcorpus. This is congruent with what we found in the case of *przymusowy* (coercive) (see Tables 7.3 and 7.4).

Table 7.5 Highest-ranked noun collocates (right-wing) of *Szczepienie***|*Szczepionka*** query (Monco PL)

#	Left-wing subcorpus			Right-wing subcorpus		
	Collocate	Freq.	Dice	Collocate	Freq.	Dice
n1	Covid	526	0.1521	Koronawirusa (the coronavirus)	560	0.1419
n2	Koronawirusa (the coronavirus)	229	0.065	Covid	300	0.0763
n3	dawka (dose)	328	0.0223	grypa (flu)	378	0.0618
n4	AstraZeneca	74	0.0208	Covid	217	0.0552
n5	Covid	61	0.0176	szczepionka (vaccine)	144	0.0263
n6	Covid	60	0.0174	dawka (dose)	152	0.0246
n7	Pfizera (of Pfizer)	41	0.0116	WhatsApp	83	0.02
n8	grypa (flu)	154	0.0107	Gates	76	0.0174
n9	pandemia (pandemic)	36	0.009	skuteczność (efficacy)	124	0.015
n10	Pfizer	32	0.0084	koronawirusowi (of the coronavirus)	52	0.0132
n11	Dworczyk	27	0.0069	Pfizer	52	0.013
n12	Sputnik	30	0.0063	*przymus (coercion)*	59	0.0121
n13	Johnson	63	0.0061	wirus (virus)	93	0.0117
n14	Koronawirusowi (of the coronavirus)	19	0.0055	AstraZeneca	46	0.0116
n15	Opolszczyzna (the region)	50	0.0053	pandemia (pandemic)	47	0.0116
n16	szczepionka (vaccine)	57	0.0051	szczepienie (innoculation)	59	0.0096
n17	Medyk	35	0.0048	lek (medicine/cure)	149	0.0093
n18	Moderna	28	0.0048	gruźlica (tuberculosis)	38	0.0087
n19	WUM (the University)	17	0.0047	SARS-CoV-2	34	0.0086
n20	szczepienie (vaccinating)	65	0.0045	Sputnik	35	0.0083
n21	AstraZeneki	15	0.0043	odporność (immunity)	41	0.0078
n22	mRNA	15	0.0043	Szumowski	33	0.0077
n23	Podlaskiem (the region)	22	0.0038	NCZAS (the source)	30	0.0075
n24	Antyszczepionkowców (anti-vaxxers)	10	0.0029	test	124	0.0073
n25	Koronawirusem (the coronavirus)	10	0.0029	SARS-CoV	28	0.0071

Table 7.6 Selection of concordances (right-wing) for the *Przymus*** (noun) query on Monco PL

#	Left-side context	Match	Right-side context
700	Ustępujący prezydent Andrzej Duda podczas swojego wystąpienia w telewizji, które nazwano debatą, sprawiał wrażenie przeciwnego (The outgoing *(originally perhaps a pun on 'yielding')* Polish President Andrzej Duda, during his televised address, which was called a debate, gave the impression of being against the)	przymusowi (coercion)	szczepień. (of vaccination.)[a]
782	Dziennikarz, łowca hipokryzji w swym zajęczym sercu niewolnika nie jest w stanie zrozumieć, że można dać się zaszczepić i być jednocześnie przeciwko (That journalist, a hypocrisy-hunter, with their slavish yellow belly is unable to understand that a person can have themselves vaccinated and simultaneously be against the)	przymusowi (coercion)	szczepień. (of vaccination.)[b]
789	Podkreślił, że nie będzie (He stressed that there will be no)	przymusu (coercion)	szczepień, a jeśli zajdzie taka potrzeba, punkty szczepień zorganizowane zostaną w szkołach. (of vaccination, and if necessary, that vaccination sites/centres will be organized at schools.)[c]

[a] S.G. (2020). Retrieved from: nCzas.com (accessed 1 March 2022). Date of corpus capture: 7 July 2020.
[b] Karwelis (2022). Retrieved from: DoRzeczy.pl (accessed 1 March 2022). Date of corpus capture: 27 January 2022.
[c] A.B. (2021). Retrieved from: NaszDziennik.pl (accessed 1 March 2022). Date of corpus capture: 19 August 2021.

Interestingly, the view presented in instance 782 above also seems to validate our assumption that vaccinations may be framed negatively through semantic prosody as a result of the intention to negatively frame their mandating. The repercussions of this are further explored in the *Discussion*.

Pre-Pandemic Collocates of *Przymusowy* and *Obowiązkowy*

To access a complementary vantage point, we also looked at a greater sample of collocates of *przymusowy* (coercive) and *obowiązkowy* (mandatory) before the Covid-19 pandemic, utilizing all 1,000 sources available in Monco PL (see Table 7.7).

Following the findings presented in Tables 7.3 and 7.4 and Table 7.5, the data presented in Table 7.7 shows that contexts in which the two terms are used also substantially differ before the Covid-19 pandemic. The adjective *przymusowy* is used in contexts supposedly involving a kind of imposition or deprivation of a person's will, whereas the contexts of *obowiązkowy* would suggest that the object in question is acceptable to the public, perhaps as stemming from legislation. Although Table 7.7 provides some contradictory examples, we can observe a trend which supports our explanatory hypothesis. The collocates of *przymusowy* include *sterylizacja* (position 8), *obóz* (13), *wywieźć* (17), *deportacja* (24). Contrariwise, the pre-pandemic collocates of *obowiązkowy* include some, even high-ranking ones, of arguably much less markedly negative affect: *ubezpieczenie* (2), *zapas* (7), *język* (17), and *mowa* (18). As remarked by Zhang (2010: 193), '[d]ue to its nature of subtleness, S(emantic) P(rosody) is often hidden from human intuition and so can only be explored by the powerful means of corpus linguistics'. In our case, the data provides evidence for our intuition about the lexemes. The underlying mechanism here, we propose, is that the need to oblige individuals to do something they might not be willing to undertake of their own accord, with the lexeme *przymusowy*, presupposes that the object (e.g. receiving a vaccine) is not positive.

This, moreover, reinforces our assumption that the adjective *przymusowy* and the noun *przymus* have negative connotations – as things which are *przymusowy* are prototypically imposed on an individual or a group against their will. Słownik Języka Polskiego (Dictionary of the Polish Language) PWN defines *przymusowy* as 'arising out of necessity, or otherwise imposed by the circumstances', providing collocate examples of *przymusowy robotnik* (forced labourer) and *przymusowe roboty* (forced labour).[17] These particularly negative collocations, relating to the occupation of Poland during the Second World War, can be observed in astounding numbers for the case of *przymusowy* before 2019 (markedly positions 2, 10, 13, 17, 22; potentially also 3, 8, 11, 12, 14, 19, 21, 23, 24) and close to none when it comes to *obowiązkowy* (potentially positions 3, 11, 13).

Discussion

When it comes to the identified affective mismatch, an explanatory hypothesis is to consider different motivations behind framing vaccines as *przymusowe* and the possible relationship between the perceived anti-vaccine sentiments, on the one hand, and negatively framing the governmental intervention, on the other hand. Our analysis uncovers cases of political discourse where the speaker can be pro-vaccination while simultaneously considering vaccine mandates as something undesirable (see e.g. position 782 in Table 7.6). A suggestion here is that there is an opposing viewpoint which considers the negative framing of vaccination mandates in discourse as equivalent to negatively framing vaccination.

Some relevant insight may come from the study by Klimiuk et al. (2021) who conducted a content and sentiment analysis on data collected from 'the most popular Facebook page advocating for the refusal of the mandatory vaccinations in Poland' from 2019 (Klimiuk et al. 2021: 2027). The researchers grouped the comments into argument categories, in order of prevalence (Klimiuk et al. 2021: 2027–8). Among those 'themes', there were arguments relating to vaccine mandates supposedly repressing 'civil rights' or 'civil liberties', as well as those relating to 'morality, religion or ideology' (Klimiuk et al. 2021: 2030). Notably, those were less prevalent (representing respectively 13.2 per cent and 8.5 per cent of the set) than content criteria categories relating to 'safety and effectiveness', 'misinformation and falsehoods' or 'conspiracy theories' (Klimiuk et al. 2021: 2028–30).[18]

Another study, by Wawrzuta et al. (2021: 7), suggested that a given group's vaccination beliefs may be influenced by the satisfaction of that group with a given country's government, whereby 'the most common arguments against COVID-19 vaccines are based on the lack of trust in the government, which is responsible for organizing the vaccination programs'. A similar observation was put forward by Lee et al. in the context of obtaining non-medical exemptions from childhood vaccinations, as parents 'who distrust the government also had increased odds of distrusting vaccine information acquired at their healthcare providers' offices' (2016: 1).

However, even more variables may be at play here, especially when it comes to explaining the right-left asymmetry illustrated in our findings. Keeping in mind that Poland scores low on '[c]onfidence in national government in 2020' and '[t]rust in government during the first wave of COVID-19' (Organisation for Economic Co-Operation and Development 2021: 207), the aforementioned observations by Wawrzuta et al. (2021: 7) and Lee et al. (2016: 1) might be thought-provoking, as the current ruling party in Poland, which runs the national vaccination programme, *Prawo i Sprawiedliwość* (*Law and Justice*), can be considered right-wing by many standards. This would perhaps contrast with the discussed negative view of vaccination (mandates) in the political discourse, particularly from the right-wing sources.

Table 7.7 General collocates of *Przymusowy* and *Obowiązkowy* before 31 December 2019 (Monco PL)

	Przymusowy (coercive)			**Obowiązkowy (mandatory)**		
#	Collocate	Freq.	Dice	Collocate	Freq.	Dice
1	wykup (squeeze out)	989	0.0407	rezerwa (the reserves)	648	0.0908
2	robotnik (labourer)	1113	0.0405	ubezpieczenie (insurance)	713	0.0853
3	relokacja (relocation)	530	0.0362	podlegać (be liable/subject)	567	0.0749
4	hipoteka (mortgage)	603	0.0337	szczepienie (*vaccination*)	256	0.0443
5	pauza (pause)	407	0.0277	przedmiot (course/subject)	387	0.0422
6	urlop (leave/vacation)	1067	0.0252	matematyka (mathematics)	220	0.035
7	postój (halt)	459	0.0234	zapas (supply)	210	0.0333
8	sterylizacja (sterilization)	301	0.0209	matura (secondary school exams)	226	0.0332
9	leczenie (treatment)	843	0.0173	lektura (reading)	184	0.0315
10	robota (labour)	977	0.0166	egzamin (test/exam)	260	0.0309
11	wysiedlić (displacement)	228	0.0164	wbrew (against)	203	0.0307
12	przesiedlenie (resettling)	219	0.0156	stopa (rate)	291	0.0307
13	obóz (camp)	847	0.0146	zajęcie (seizure)	281	0.0258
14	doprowadzenie (drive)	252	0.0129	składka (dues)	186	0.0248
15	szczepienie (*vaccination*)	283	0.0128	OC (insurance)	132	0.0238
16	lądowanie (landing)	326	0.0125	wprowadzić (launch)	305	0.0188
17	wywieźć (deport)	265	0.0122	język (language)	207	0.0185
18	zarządca (administrator)	285	0.0121	mowa (speech)	129	0.0154
19	emigracja (emigration)	252	0.012	wojskowy (military)	174	0.0154
20	restrukturyzacja (restructuring)	353	0.0117	wymiar (measuring/administration)	111	0.0143
21	migracja (migration)	208	0.0109	szkolenie (training)	128	0.014
22	rzesza (reich)	242	0.0106	służba (service)	194	0.0134
23	wysiedleń (displacements)	131	0.0098	ziemny (land/natural)	78	0.0129
24	deportacja (deportation)	146	0.0093	opłata (fee)	126	0.0121
25	przymusowy (*coercive*)	170	0.0089	obecność (attendance)	95	0.0118

Ultimately, it could be explained by the conventional nature of the popular binary political classification, adopted in this chapter based on how the sources utilizing the term *przymusowy* (coercive) in the context of vaccines view themselves politically (see Section *Classification of Sources*). The governing party's official website states that its 2014 Programme was as follows: 'We firmly reject the juxtaposition of security and freedom [. . .]. The state must be truly capable of combatting pathology.'[19] We hypothesize that the apparent schism in the Polish conservative discourse could be attributed to the political programme of the governing conservative party generally being interpreted by some of the supposedly conservative journalists with more radically liberal leanings as potentially incompatible with their ideas of civil liberty, case in question being the possibility of vaccine mandates. Practically speaking, the Polish political discourse shows shades within and across the categories of the dual 'conservative-liberal' axis. Above all, both *Do Rzeczy* and *Najwyższy Czas*, two of the sources classified in this chapter as right-wing, which have been shown to utilize the lexeme *przymusowy* functionally as a synonym of *obowiązkowy* (see Table 7.3), present themselves on their respective websites as liberal and conservative simultaneously: 'The weekly *Do Rzeczy* is a [. . .] liberal-conservative opinion magazine';[20] '*NAJWYŻSZY CZAS!* A liberal-conservative portal'.[21] We pose that this is one way to account for the resulting pre-emptive criticism of the notion of (mandating) Covid-19 vaccinations, which we find to be exemplified by our analysis of the use of the lexemes *przymusowy* and *obowiązkowy* as represented in the sources classified as 'right-leaning' in this chapter.

The account could be fine-tuned by considering the implications of studies like Hart et al. (2020) and Bright et al. (2020). The former concentrates on the politicization in health news, analysing early Covid-19 coverage. The latter, focusing on selected state-backed news outlets (China, Iran, Russia and Turkey) on social distribution networks, measured heightened engagement with sources which can 'politicise health news and information by criticizing democracies as corrupt and incompetent, praising their own global leadership' (Bright et al. 2020: 6). Despite not strictly adhering to our subject area, these papers are relevant in relation to our analysis of the 'ideologized' poll result coverage (see Table 7.1, Table 7.4). Namely, they may provide material to reflect on the idea of domestic news outlets being able to take advantage of information reportage to covertly convey a (positive or negative) stance towards certain leaderships and promote (or oppose) certain ideologies.

Design Limitations

Several limitations of our study arose from our source classification. First, the eight sources selected for analysis imposed some constraints in terms of collocation/concordance sampling. Incidentally, the openly right-wing outlets were more prolific in terms of their contributions to the corpus, so our sample size was restricted by the maximum size of available unique cases in the left-leaning group. Moreover, during the design stage, we found that the content from one of the relatively popular left-leaning sources initially selected for corpus data extraction, *Codziennik Feministyczny*, could not be parsed by Monco PL. Consequently, it had to be substituted with an arguably centre-left internet periodic, *Gazeta*.

Another important caveat of large-data computation in the context of affect, as pointed out by Mejova (2016), is the question of '*whose* sentiment it is that we are catching. It is possible that articles were simply quoting or attributing these words to other parties', also reminding us that 'framing the issue by the words of others' may be a conscious decision. Combining quantitative and qualitative accounts is a way to address such concerns, at least to a considerable extent.

Conclusions

Discursive construction of phenomena, events and people has the potential to significantly (re)shape our perception and reasoning, therefore, having tangible real-world implications. This is especially important when it comes to health-related decisions taken by individuals without a medical background, where media are a key source of input. In this vein, Rzymski et al. (2021: 11) suggested that '[i]dentifying specific groups with the lowest level of acceptance of further COVID-19 vaccination is essential for effective science communication'. With this in mind, relatively subtle axiological clues – such as the ones discussed in this chapter – can pass unnoticed by receptors while influencing their judgement.

While a follow-up experiment would be required to offer a falsifiable account of how the choice between the lexemes under scrutiny here shapes receptors' cognitive processes, in this chapter we have attempted to better understand the potential of such expressions to affectively frame messages, departing from the observation that in some cases *przymusowy* (coercive) replaces *obowiązkowy* (mandatory) when opinion polls are reported. Our corpus-based account shows that formulaicity and affect may converge, which is evidenced when *przymus(owy)* is employed to communicate a prefabricated negative stance towards vaccination, governmental interventions or the acceptance thereof.

Notes

1 'The vaccinations are *volitional* (dobrowolne), except for medical professions, pharmacists, medical students and employees of medical entities [. . .]. All others are encouraged to be vaccinated against COVID-19' – retrieved from https://www.gov.pl/web/szczepimysie/pytania-i-odpowiedzi (accessed 1 March 2022).
2 'Ponad 64 proc. emerytów chce wprowadzenia obowiązkowych szczepień' (*WNP* 2022). Retrieved from WNP.pl (captured 1 February 2022).
3 'Sondaż: Czy szczepienia powinny być obowiązkowe?' (Szaniawski 2019). Retrieved from RP.pl (captured 27 April 2019).
4 'Lewica chce obowiązkowych szczepień i kar dla niezaszczepionych' (Sowa 2021). Retrieved from WydarzeniaInteria.pl (captured 5 December 2021).
5 'Polacy nie chcą ani obowiązkowych szczepień, ani obostrzeń w całym kraju' (Ćwiek 2021). Retrieved from RP.pl (captured 7 November 2021).
6 The corpus search engine *Paralela* demonstrates that for queries *obowiązek/obowiązkowy* and *przymus/przymusowy*. Retrieved from: http://paralela.clarin-pl.eu (accessed 1 March 2022); cf. Pęzik (2016).
7 Retrieved from: https://source.opennews.org/articles/analysis-emotional-language/ (accessed 1 March 2022)
8 Retrieved from: https://www.who.int/news/item/29-06-2020-covidtimeline (accessed 14 March 2021).
9 'DoRzeczy.pl liderem wśród prawicowych portal' (*Do Rzeczy* 2018b). Retrieved: DoRzeczy.pl (accessed 1 March 2022).
10 'wPolityce.pl zdecydowanym liderem wśród informacyjnych serwisów konserwatywno-prawicowych' (*wPolityce.pl* 2015). Retrieved: wPolityce.pl (accessed 1 March 2022).
11 'Pierwsze prawicowe pismo w Polsce: publicystyka, wywiady, felietony' (*F.R.* 2019). Retrieved: nCzas.com (accessed 1 March 2022).
12 'Strona startowa polskiej lewicy'. Retrieved from: Facebook.com/portalstrajk/ (accessed 1 March 2022)
13 'Zorientowany na czytelników o poglądach lewicowych i centrowych'. Retrieved from: TygodnikPrzeglad.pl/o-przegladzie/ (accessed 1 March 2022).
14 'Świecki i lewicowy tygodnik *Przegląd*' (Tabiasz 2015). Retrieved: Racjonalista.tv (accessed 1 March 2022).
15 'gazeta prezentująca ścisłe, ukierunkowane poglądy o lewicowym charakterze'. Retrieved: Prenumerata.ruch.com.pl/prenumerata-dziennik-trybuna (accessed 1 March 2022).
16 $2|(X \cap Y)|/(|X|+|Y|)$, where $X \cap Y$ is the number of co-occurrences and X and Y are the frequencies of the adjectives and nouns, respectively.
17 Retrieved from: https://sjp.pwn.pl/szukaj/przymusowy.html (accessed 1 March 2022).

18 Although the latter criteria encompassed subcategories of themes e.g. based on the belief that 'vaccination policies (are) motivated by profit', 'vaccine information (is) withheld from the public', or from the 'encouragement to make educated decisions for oneself/one's children' (Klimiuk et al. 2021: 2028), which could be considered as largely related to an anti-governmental sentiment.
19 Retrieved: https://pis.org.pl/partia/law-and-justice (accessed 1 March 2022).
20 'liberalno-konserwatywny tygodnik opinii' (Liciski 2012). Retrieved: DoRzeczy.pl (accessed 1 March 2022).
21 'Portal konserwatywno-liberalny'. Retrieved: Nczas.com (accessed 1 March 2022).

References

A.A.P. (2021). 'Robią z ludzi idiotów. Więcej osób popiera obowiązek szczepień i segregację niż się zaszczepiło [SONDAŻ]'. nCzas.com/2021/09/04/robia-z-ludzi-idiotow-wiecej-osob-popiera-obowiazek-szczepien-niz-sie-zaszczepilo-sondaz

A.B. (2021). 'Przemysław Czarnek o szczepieniach w szkole'. NaszDziennik.pl/polska/24 2142,przemyslaw-czarnek-o-szczepieniach-w-szkole.html

Augustyn, R., and Prażmo, E. M. (2020). 'The spread of Chinese virus in the internet discourse: a cognitive semantic analysis'. *GEMA Online® Journal of Language Studies*, 20(4). Doi.org/10.17576/gema-2020-2004-12

Bartkiewicz, A. (2021). 'Koronawirus. Sondaż: Czy szczepienia na COVID powinny być obowiązkowe? Polacy podzieleni'. RP.pl/swiat/art18860061-koronawirus-sondaz-czy-szczepienia-na-covid-powinny-byc-obowiazkowe-polacy-podzieleni

Bright, J., Au, H., Bailey, H., Elswah, M., Schliebs, M., Marchal, N., Schwieter, C., Rebello, K., and Howard, P. N. (2020). 'Coronavirus coverage by state-backed english-language news sources understanding Chinese, Iranian, Russian and Turkish government media'. Oxford Internet Institute, University of Oxford, COVID-19 Series (COMPROP Data Memo 2020.2). Oxford, UK. https://comprop.oii.ox.ac.uk/wp-content/uploads/sites/93/2020/04/Coronavirus-Coverage-by-State-Backed-English-Language-News-Sources.pdf

Clarin-pl.eu (2014). 'Paralela'. The bilingual corpus search engine developed in the CLARIN-PL project for a large collection of annotated Polish-English parallel texts. Paralela.clarin-pl.eu. Consider visiting Clarin-pl.eu for further information.

Codziennik Feministyczny (2022). 'News portal'. Codziennikfeministyczny.pl

Ćwiek, J. (2021). 'Polacy nie chcą ani obowiązkowych szczepień, ani obostrzeń w całym kraju'. RP.pl/spoleczenstwo/art19083821-polacy-nie-chca-ani-obowiazkowych-szcz epien-ani-obostrzen-w-calym-kraju

Deckert, M., Pęzik, P., and Dróżdż, Ł. (2016). 'Formulaic sentiment markers in online political discourse'. In Lewandowska-Tomaszczyk, B., Kopytowska, M., Osborne, J., Schmied, J. and Yumlu, K. (eds), Languages, Cultures, Media (pp. 253–75).

Éditions de l'université de Savoie, Chambéry. Université de Savoie, UFR Lettres, langues, sciences humaines, Laboratoire Langages, Littératures, Sociétés, Etudes Transfrontalières et Internationales. ISBN: 978-2-919732-75-3

Do Rzeczy (2018a). 'Polacy chcą przymusowych szczepień [SONDAŻ]'. DoRzeczy.pl/kra j/56564/polacy-chca-przymusowych-szczepien-sondaz.html

Do Rzeczy (2018b). 'DoRzeczy.pl liderem wśród prawicowych portali'. DoRzeczy.pl/kraj /78737/dorzeczypl-liderem-wsrod-prawicowych-portali.html

Do Rzeczy (2018c). 'Sondaż DoRzeczy.pl w sprawie szczepień: Połowa elektoratu PiS i Kukiz'15 chce wolności'. DoRzeczy.pl/kraj/80842/zobacz-sondaz-o-szczepieniach .html

F.R. (2019). 'Pobierz świeży "Najwyższy Czas!". Pierwsze prawicowe pismo w Polsce: publicystyka, wywiady, felietony'. nCzas.com/2019/08/20/pobierz-swiezy-najwyzszy -czas-pierwsze-prawicowe-pismo-w-polsce-publicystyka-wywiady-felietony/

Hart, P. S., Chinn, S., and Soroka, S. (2020). *Politicization and Polarization in COVID-19 News Coverage*. SAGE; Science Communication. Doi.org/10.1177/1075547020950735

Jarynowski, A., Wójta-Kempa, M., and Belik V. (2020). 'Perception of "coronavirus" on the Polish Internet until arrival of SARS-CoV-2 in Poland'. Wrocław Medical University; ahead of Print: Pielęgniarstwo I Zdrowie Publiczne, ISSN 2082-9876 (print), ISSN 2451-1870 (online) Piel Zdr Publ. 2020;10(2). DOI:10.17219/ pzp/120054

K.M. (2021). 'Prawie co drugi Polak za ograniczeniami dla niezaszczepionych'. Wirtu alneMedia.pl/artykul/szczepienie-koronawirus-ograniczenia-dla-niezaszczepionych

Karwelis (2022). 'Kiedy hipokryta tropi hipokryzję'. DoRzeczy.pl/opinie/256297/kiedy -hipokryta-tropi-hipokryzje.html

Klimiuk, K., Czoska, A., Biernacka, K., and Balwicki, Ł. (2021). 'Vaccine misinformation on social media – topic-based content and sentiment analysis of Polish vaccine-deniers' comments on Facebook'. *Human Vaccines & Immunotherapeutics*, 1–10. Doi.org/10.1080/21645515.2020.1850072

Krupa, J. (2021). 'Rzeczywistości równoległe – wizerunek kandydatów na urząd Prezydenta Rzeczpospolitej Polskiej w 2020 roku w "Gazecie Wyborczej" i "Naszym Dzienniku"'. *Annales Universitatis Paedagogicae Cracoviensis. Studia Politologica*, 26(336), 54–63. Doi.org/10.24917/20813333.26.4

Lee, C., Whetten, K., Omer, S., Pan, W., and Salmon, D. (2016). 'Hurdles to herd immunity: distrust of government and vaccine refusal in the US, 2002–2003'. *Vaccine*, 34(34), 3972–3978. Doi.org/10.1016/j.vaccine.2016.06.048

Lin, W. H., Wilson, T., Wiebe, J., and Hauptmann, A. (2006). 'Which side are you on? identifying perspectives at the document and sentence levels'. Proceedings of the 10th Conference on Computational Natural Language Learning (CoNLL-X). New York City, June 2006. ©2006 Association for Computational Linguistics.

Lisicki, P. (2012). 'Tygodnik Do Rzeczy'. DoRzeczy.pl/obserwator-mediow/1/tygodnik -do-rzeczy.html

Liu, B. (2010). 'Sentiment analysis and subjectivity'. In Indurkhya, N., and Damerau, F. J. (eds), *Handbook of Natural Language Processing*, 2nd edn. Herbrich, R. & Graepel, R. – Chapman & Hall/CRC Press (Machine Learning & Pattern Recognition Series), New York, 2010.

Liu, B. (2020). *Sentiment Analysis: Mining Opinions, Sentiments, and Emotions*. Cambridge University Press. (Original work published 2015). Doi.org/10.1017/CBO9781139084789

Louw, B. (1993). 'Irony in the text or insincerity in the writer? The diagnostic potential of semantic prosodies'. In Baker, M., Francis, G., and Tognini-Bonelli, E. (eds), *Text and Technology: In Honour of John Sinclair* (pp. 157–75). Amsterdam, Netherlands: John Benjamins.

Macagno, F., and Walton, D. (2010). 'The argumentative uses of emotive language'. *Revista Iberoamericana de Argumentación* 1: 1–37.

Martin, J. R., and White, P. R. R. (2005). *The Language of Evaluation: Appraisal in English*. New York: Palgrave Macmillan.

Mejova, Y. (2016). *Analyzing Emotional Language in 21 Million News Articles*. Source .opennews.org.

Mesthrie, R. (2020). 'More eyes on COVID-19: Perspectives from Linguistics - Pay attention to how people are talking about the pandemic in different languages'. *South African Journal of Science*, 116(7–8), 1–1. Doi.org/10.17159/sajs.2020/8497

Mężyk, Ł. (2018). 'STAN GRY: GW: 47% Polek i Polaków uważa, że rodzic ma prawo nie szczepić dziecka, Szefernaker: Likwidacja wojewodów to 16 różnych polityk bezpieczeństwa, Stankiewicz/Gajcy: Nie każdego na prawicy martwią taśmy'. 300polityka.pl/stan-gry/2018/10/05/stan-gry-gw-47-polek-i-polakow-uwaza-ze-rodzic-ma-prawo-nie-szczepic-dziecka-szefernaker-likwidacja-wojewodow-to-16-roznych-polityk-bezpieczenstwa-stankiewicz-gajcy-nie-kazdego-na-prawicy-martw/

Monco PL (2019). 'Monitor corpus search engine for recent examples of real Polish usage'. Monco.frazeo.pl

Najwyższy Czas (2022). 'Homepage of 'NAJWYŻSZY CZAS!''. Nczas.com.

Organisation For Economic Co-Operation And Development. (2021). 'Government at a glance 2021'. ISBN: 9789264909694. OECD.org/gov/government-at-a-glance-22214399.htm

Pacewicz, K. (2018). '47 proc. Polek i Polaków uważa, że rodzic ma prawo nie szczepić dziecka [SONDAŻ]'. (Gazeta Wyborcza). WysokieObcasy.pl/wysokie-obcasy/7,163229,24004426,47-proc-polek-i-polakow-uwaza-ze-rodzic-ma-prawo-nie-szczepic.html?disableRedirects=true

Pęzik, P. (2016). 'Exploring phraseological equivalence with paralela'. In *Polish-Language Parallel Corpora*, edited by Ewa Gruszczyńska and Agnieszka Leńko-Szymańska, 67–81. Warsaw: Instytut Lingwistyki Stosowanej UW, 2016. Depot.ceon.pl/handle/123456789/13396

Pęzik, P. (2019). 'Korpusowe narzędzia weryfikacji frazeostylistycznej tłumaczeń' ['Corpus tools of phraseo-stylistic verification of translation'] *KSJ* 7(3), 317–339.

Konińskie Studia Językowe, Wydział Filologiczny, Państwowa Wyższa Szkoła Zawodowa w Koninie. Doi:10.30438/ksj.2019.7.3.4

Pęzik, P. (2020). 'Budowa i zastosowania korpusu monitorującego Monco PL'. *Forum Lingwistyczne* 7(7), 133–150. Doi.org/10.31261/FL.2020.07.11

Prawo i Sprawiedliwość (2014). 'Law and justice programme'. PiS.org.pl/partia/law-and-justice

Quintilian, M. (circa 95 C.E.). 'Institutio Oratoria'. Book 8, chapter 5. In Perseus Digital Library Project (1985–2021) Harold Edgeworth Butler (trans. eds.). www.Perseus .tufts.edu/hopper/text?doc=Quint.%20Inst.%208.5 (accessed 2021.03.14).

Ruch, S. A. (2014). 'Opis tytułu pod "Prenumerata - Dziennik Trybuna"'. Prenumerata .Ruch.com.pl/prenumerata-dziennik-trybuna

R.P. (2020). 'Masowe szczepienia na COVID-19. Polska przedstawi harmonogram w ciągu dwóch tygodni'. nCzas.com/2020/10/31/masowe-szczepienia-na-covid-19-pol ska-przedstawi-harmonogram-w-ciagu-dwoch-tygodni/

Rzymski, P., Poniedziałek, B., and Fal, A. (2021). 'Willingness to receive the booster COVID-19 vaccine dose in Poland'. *Vaccines*, 9(11), 1286. Doi.org/10.3390/ vaccines9111286

S.G. (2020). 'Andrzej Duda przeciwko przymusowi szczepień? Prezydent szybko się z tego wycofał'. nCzas.com/2020/07/07/andrzej-duda-przeciwko-przymusowi-szcze pien-prezydent-szybko-sie-z-tego-wycofal/

S.K. (2021). 'Sondaż: zwolennicy przymusu szczepień są w mniejszości'. ePoznan.pl/ news-news-120974-sondaz_zwolennicy_przymusu_szczepien_sa_w_mniejszosci

Service of the Republic of Poland (2022). 'Koronawirus: szczepienia i ważne informacje'. Gov.pl/szczepimysie

Sinclair, J. (1991/2001). 'Corpus, concordance, collocation'. 100. Oxford University Press.

Słownik Języka Polskiego PWN (Online Dictionary). 'Przymusowy'. Wydawnictwo Naukowe PWN SA.

Sowa, P. (2021). 'Lewica chce obowiązkowych szczepień i kar dla niezaszczepionych'. Wydarzenia.Interia.pl/raporty/raport-koronawirus-chiny/polska/news-lewica-chce -obowiazkowych-szczepien-i-kar-dla-niezaszczepion,nId,5688368#utm_source=past e&utm_medium=paste&utm_campaign=firefox

Strajk.eu (2022). 'Strajk.eu's fanpage on Facebook'. Facebook.com/portalstrajk/

Stubbs, M. (1995). 'Collocations and semantic profiles: on the cause of the trouble with quantitative studies'. *Functions of Language* 2(1), 1–33. Print.

Syder, F. H., and Pawley, A. (1983). 'Two puzzles for linguistic theory: nativelike selection and nativelike fluency'. In Richards, Jack C., and Schmidt, Richard W. (eds), *Language & Communication*. London and New York: Longman.

Szaniawski, P. (2018). 'Sondaż: Czy szczepienia powinny być obowiązkowe'. RP.pl/spol eczenstwo/art2112221-sondaz-czy-szczepienia-powinny-byc-obowiazkowe

Szaniawski, P. (2019). 'Sondaż: Czy szczepienia powinny być obowiązkowe'. RP.pl/spol eczenstwo/art1361241-sondaz-czy-szczepienia-powinny-byc-obowiazkowe

Szymański, L. (2021). 'NASZ SONDAŻ. Czy Polacy zaakceptowaliby przymusowe szczepienia przeciwko koronawirusowi? Bardzo CIEKAWE WYNIKI. Sprawdź!'.

wPolityce.pl/polityka/550916-sondaz-czy-polacy-zaakceptowaliby-przymusowe-s zczepienia

Tabiasz, J. (2015). 'Świecki i lewicowy tygodnik Przegląd. Jerzy Domański'. Racjonalista .tv/swiecki-i-lewicowy-tygodnik-przeglad-jerzy-domanski/

Tygodnik Przegląd (2022). 'O Przeglądzie'. TygodnikPrzeglad.pl/o-przegladzie/

Warzecha, Ł. (2021). 'Straszliwy Omikron nadciąga! Bójcie się!'. DoRzeczy.pl/opinie/2 32687/warzecha-straszliwy-omikron-nadciaga-bojcie-sie.html

Wawrzuta, D., Jaworski, M., Gotlib, J., and Panczyk, M. (2021). 'What arguments against COVID-19 vaccines run on facebook in Poland: content analysis of comments'. *Vaccines*, 9(5), 481. Doi.org/10.3390/vaccines9050481

WNP [PAP] (2022). 'Ponad 64 proc. emerytów chce wprowadzenia obowiązkowych szczepień'. WNP.pl/parlamentarny/wydarzenia/ponad-64-proc-emerytow-chce-wprowadzenia-obowiazkowych-szczepien,534504.html

World Health Organisation. (2020). 'Listings of WHO's response to COVID-19'. Who.int

wPolityce.pl (2015). 'wPolityce.pl zdecydowanym liderem wśród informacyjnych serwisów konserwatywno-prawicowych. Dziękujemy Czytelnikom!'. wPolityce.pl/me dia/257197-wpolitycepl-zdecydowanym-liderem-wsrod-informacyjnych-serwisow -konserwatywno-prawicowych-dziekujemy-czytelnikom

wPolityce.pl [PAP/EPA/SEAN/GALLUP/POOL] (2021). 'Merkel zapowiada, że nie będzie obowiązkowych szczepień. Grecja wprowadza obostrzenia w restauracjach, niepokój na Wyspach'. wPolityce.pl/swiat/558534-merkel-zapowiada-ze-nie-bedzie -obowiazkowych-szczepien

Zhang, C. (2010). 'An overview of corpus-based studies of semantic prosody'. *Asian Social Science*, 6(6). Doi.org/10.5539/ass.v6n6p190

Zhao, J., Liu, K., and Xu, L. (2016). 'Association for computational linguistics: computational linguistics'. Review of "Sentiment Analysis: Mining Opinions, Sentiments and Emotions" by B. Liu. *Computational Linguistics*, 42(3), 595–8. Doi .org/10.1162/coli_r_00259

Part III

Emotion in Multimodal Discourses

8

Arabic–English Code-Switching in Egyptian Rap Music and Social Networks

Lucia La Causa

Introduction

Speakers concretely communicate emotions through language (Dewaele 2006: 121), and the way they encode feelings, attitudes and beliefs permeates the linguistic system to the point that it is possible to claim that 'language has a heart as well as a mind of its own' (Ochs and Schieffelin 1989: 22; Bock 2008). Emotions are, thus, strongly linked with language (Dewaele 2004, 2006, 2008; Wilce 2009; Dewaele and Qaddourah 2015, among others) and this link is a very complicated one (Bakić and Škifić 2017: 35) especially because 'such relations between inner states and outward expression are culturally variable' (Ochs and Schieffelin 1989: 7; Dewaele 2010) and socially linked (Fiehler 2002: 79). Each emotion word owns a precise kind of meaning (BakićŠkifić 2017: 37) which is different from one language to another since 'the set of concepts by means of which the speakers of any given language make sense of their own and other people's feelings is specific to a particular language' (Wierzbicka 2004: 94). In other words, 'different languages have different ways of expressing what they feel' (Drobot 2017: 294) and as a consequence, two languages participating in code-switching utterances are inevitably not used in the same way (Al-Sayadi 2016: 4).

Many studies have been dedicated to this topic and researchers, such as Pavlenko (2002, 2005, 2008, 2012), Ożańska-Ponikwia (2013), Dewaele (2013), Dobrot (2017), El-Dackhs and Altarriba (2019) among others, have tried to examine the factors affecting the code choice in the expression of emotions in bi-/multilingual contexts (Bakić and Škifić 2017: 35). However, these previous studies have investigated the emotional dimension of the English language almost uniquely in contexts where English is the L2 and, where it is thus used as a native language. In the current chapter, which is part of a wider research project, the code choice in Egypt is investigated with Egypt being 'a foreign context', 'a country that does not speak it [English]' (El-Dacks and Altarriba 2019: 1064) natively, and where it holds no official status being formally categorized as a foreign LX almost exclusively but extensively spoken by the educated elite and the young generation.

In this chapter, the attention is focused on the youngest, in detail to rap singers and young Arabic–English bilingual rappers' fans, and on their diffuse habit of code-switching between their mother tongue, (Egyptian) Arabic, and English in the expression of emotions through rap songs lyrics and their writing practice on social network pages. The main questions are: which language(s), between the L1 and English, does this group of Egyptians prefer for the expression of emotions? Is English equally used by them as a language of intimacy although being an LX? In case of a positive answer, which kind of feelings do they prefer expressing in their LX?

This chapter aims at demonstrating that contrary to what studies on language and emotions have shown, even in contexts, such as the Egyptian, where English is a foreign language and then it is supposed to create a 'detachment effect' (Marcos 1976), it is instead used as a tool for expressing feelings, even the strongest, sometimes together with the L1 other times even at the expense of the L1, the 'language of the heart' (Dewaele 2013).

In order to reach this goal, a qualitative and quantitative analysis has been carried out through the examination of a video interview with Mr Kordy, one of the most famous Egyptian rappers, retrieved online (https://www.youtube.com/watch?v=xzI9SLHIT88), the analysis of some of his rap song lyrics and of users' comments on his social Facebook page (https://it-it.facebook.com/Mr.KordySandNikka/), and by means of a questionnaire to a sample of twenty Egyptian English speakers, in detail, Egyptian rappers' fans and Facebook users who frequently use English when commenting on rappers' Facebook pages.

Multilingualism, Code-Switching and Emotions

In expressing emotions, language choice plays a very important role and individuals may have preferences for specific languages (Dewaele 2006: 119). Usually, multilingual speakers rely better on their L1 (Dewaele 2004: 208), especially if it is the dominant language (Dewaele 2004: 220), which is perceived as more emotional (Bakić and Škifić 2017: 43) and more powerful (Dewaele 2011: 25) having the advantage to create multiple traces in memory (Altarriba 2003; Dewaele 2008) being experienced in many more contexts and applied in various ways (Altarriba 2003). There is no doubt that 'everything is a closer and more familiar experience in our mother-tongue. Emotions are no exception' (Drobot 2017: 294). With the L1, speakers feel more secure, comfortable, natural and spontaneous (Drobot 2017: 294), especially in expressing their deepest feelings. Indeed, 'the stronger the emotion, the more likely for it to be expressed in the L1' (Dewaele 2004: 220) because when dealing with strong emotions, speakers need to find words immediately to serve their cathartic function without thinking about appropriate emotion words in the LX (Dewaele 2010: 215).

This concept presupposes that 'languages other than the first are the languages of distance and detachment, or at least, languages that don't have an emotional resonance' (Dewaele 2004: 220; 2006: 119) and, consequently, languages that speakers unconsciously avoid when they express emotions. In fact, while the first language is learned spontaneously in informal contexts so that it acquires a richer emotional connotation (Dewaele 2011: 32), the L2/LX is often learned in a more rational and formal context and later than the L1 (Dewaele 2004: 208) with the consequence that it takes more time, maybe years, to be connected to the emotional system and to the autobiographical memory (Pavlenko 2008: 157).

However, even if expressing emotion is conceptually more difficult in the L2 or LX, this does not necessarily mean a preference for the L1 (Dewaele 2011: 25), especially in those cases where the dominant language does not automatically coincide with the first acquired language (Pavlenko 2005: 186). Indeed, reasonably, if speakers are bi-/multilinguals, it means that they are socialized into their L1 as well as into their L2 or LX and consequently that they can become dominant in their second or foreign language which could eventually be chosen and preferred for expressing emotions, even strong ones. Accordingly, many speakers, especially the educated L2 or LX learners and the youngest, who are mostly involved in the process of linguistic change and evolution, sometimes transfer emotional elements of the L1 to the L2/LX (Pavlenko 2008: 156) with the consequence that their 'strong emotional arousal' can lead them 'from monolingual into bilingual language mode with more CS [Code-Switching]' (Dewaele 2010: 219).

Multilingualism and Code-Switching in Egypt

The linguistic situation in Egypt, as well as in many Arab countries, is quite a complex (Ibrahim 2017: 49) and an intertwined one (Poese 2014: 8). Egypt has long been defined as a diglossic society (Ferguson 1959; Ibrahim 2017: 50), meaning that a 'High variety' and a 'Low variety' of the Arabic language coexist.

Studies of code-switching in the Egyptian community are mostly restricted to this diglossic switching between Modern Standard Arabic (MSA), and the Egyptian dialect (Kniaź and Zawrotna 2013: 599), also called Egyptian Colloquial Arabic (ECA). However, diglossia is not the unique linguistic phenomenon characterizing the Egyptian society. Contrarily, it is also possible to claim that Egypt has become a multilingual society, with English being an integral part of the Egyptians' linguistic system. Indeed, English is currently the main foreign language spoken in Egypt (Abdel Latif 2017: 33) and its use is even increasing in many social domains (Stadlbauer 2010: 3) and contexts. This is principally due to the more general globalization phenomenon with English as the main means for international communication that allowed it to penetrate other linguistic communities, even those in which it does not have an official status, acquiring important functions and becoming a fundamental language for people who want to participate in the world change and development. In 'Egypt [which is strongly involved in this global phenomenon]' (Diana 2010: 7), English is widely spread within its boundaries and has become the new prestigious language being the means for financial success (Mollin 2006: 21) and progress allowing Egyptians to enjoy a higher economic, more cultural and social opportunities which cannot be guaranteed by any of the Arabic varieties, not even by the national language, MSA (Stadlbauer 2010: 16). In such a linguistic context, bilingual (Egyptian) Arabic–English speakers, especially young people (Kniaź and Zawrotna 2013: 599), emerged in all social strata contributing to the 'shift from the traditional diglossia in Egypt to increased multilingualism, with both English (from "above") and Egyptian Arabic (from "below")' (Warschauer, Said and Zohry 2006: 31).

The fact of having more 'semiotic resources' belonging to different languages – in this specific case MSA, ECA and English – requires Egyptian speakers to have a certain capacity to use all these resources either separately or mixing them[1] (McArthur 1992), taking into consideration that each one of these codes is linked to different social meanings (Ochs 1992; Silverstein 1996) and carries a different symbolic charge (Warschauer, Said and Zohry 2006: 5). Code choice is thus regulated by sociolinguistic motivations and by a 'negotiation principle' meaning that speakers choose a language in accordance with 'a set of rights and obligations' (Kniaź and Zawrotna 2013: 603) imposed by the emotional culture of the society to which they belong. Starting from this assumption, one should expect all Egyptians to prefer the Arabic language because it is strongly associated with family values, Islamic religion (Othman 2006; Dewaele and

Qaddourah 2015: 96) and Arab cultural traditions. However, although their presupposed stronger emotional attachment towards Arabic, the practice of switching to English is widespread in Egypt and it does not necessarily occur in harmony with the Egyptian social rules of emotionality (Fiehler 2002: 79) but in a spontaneous and uncontrolled way. English is more commonly used, especially together with the Egyptian dialect, in informal interactions that take place in natural contexts (Zentella 1999; Kim 2006: 50), including the everyday conversations (Al-Sayadi 2016: 13) and interactions on social networks, even to express the most intimate thoughts and emotions. This phenomenon can be observed mainly in the young Egyptian generations (Kniaź and Zawrotna 2013: 599), for whom English is becoming the new mark of group belonging (Aboelezz 2018) and identity without this necessarily meaning an approximation to Western culture or abandonment of Egyptian identity (Warschauer, Said and Zohry 2006: 31).

(Egyptian) Arabic–English Code-Switching in Egyptian Rap Songs

The strong global influx of the English language has not spared the Egyptian popular culture. This definitely occurred with rap which, being a 'global phenomenon' (Chang 2007: 66) and a 'transnational artistic creation' (Baker 2012: 91), easily reached Egypt through Western satellite televisions and music channels such as MTV or VH1 or through the internet by the means of big video platforms such as YouTube which are accessible to the wider population (Schneider 2016: 255).

However, it was only during and after the 25 January 2011 revolution that a local form of rap developed in Egypt. Indeed, rap is historically the music of struggle (Cantrall 2013: 24), especially used in young generation protests and resistance (Mitchell 2001) and this 'lent it to embodying the monumental struggles of the Arab people' (Cantrall 2013: 24). The January revolution has been a significant event not only from a political and social point of view but also from an artistic and linguistic perspective. Indeed, the Egyptian demonstrations 'sent a shock wave through the nation's culture' (Billet 2012) with the composition of conspicuous songs dedicated to the riots which, being sung in Tahir Square during protests (Billet 2012), even became emblems of the revolution. It was in this context that several Egyptian rappers such as MC Amin, Mr Kordy, Y-Crew, Asphalt, Dawsha, Abyusif, Mekky, or crew like Arabian Knightz (a trio formed by Sphinx, Rush and E-Money) and MTM (a tree-member band which singers are Mahmoud, Taki and Mikey), started to emerge and became popular to the point that كل الناس دلوقتي عارفة راب مصر *All people now know Egypt rap* (from MC Amin's song *Rap mas*) and to the degree that while visiting Egypt today, one would be exposed to rap music (Bibar 2017).

Very good examples are Arabian Knightz' songs *Rebel* recorded during the first week of the Egyptian revolution, the night before the Friday of Anger, which invites people 'to rebel against oppression, to rebel against the divide and conquer of our [Egyptian] society, and to rebel against the dumbing of our [Egyptian] people' (Sphinx 2011 during an interview with the hip-hop blogger Hass Re-Volt), or *Prisoner*, the theme of which is totally centred on the Egyptian revolution (Figure 8.1).

As evident in the lyrics in Figure 8.1, from a linguistic point of view, a common habit of many rappers is employing different linguistic resources, including the association of different varieties and languages, especially MSA, ECA and English (Bassiouney 2012: 107). On the one hand, the use of English approximates the Egyptian rap songs to the global rap genre, allowing rappers and fans to feel part of this big world 'homie', on the other hand, continuing using their local language(s), they can communicate their ethnicity (Oreoluwa 2013: 10) and still identify themselves with their cultural background (Oreoluwa 2013: 9). The result is a 'glocal' (Williams 2009: 1) product characterized by a

[...]
Want to draw your own opinions bout the bombs we face?
What's your opinion if you're enslaved and your mom is raped?
It's too easy to speak when you're far from the heat
Through the White House I creep and yes I'm armed to the teeth
With a mic and a pen and a pad here's your evidence:
"Weapons of Mass Destruction," Mr President!

CHORUS:		TRANSLATION
	أنا عايز بلد حرة من الظلم	*I want a country free from injustice*
	عايز بلد حرة من القهر	*I want a country free from oppression*
	عايز بلد حرة من الشر	*I want a country free from evil*
	عايز أرضى وأرض العرب - بي	*I want the land and the land of Arabs – Yeah!*
	العرب - بي! العرب - بي! العرب - بي	*Arabs - Yeah! Arabs - Yeah! Arabs – Yeah!*

Figure 8.1 Lyrics taken from the first verse and from the chorus of the song 'Prisoner' by Arabian Knightz. Reproduced with permission of Arabian Knightz (full lyrics available on Genius.com https://genius.com/Arabian-knightz-prisoner-lyrics, accessed 23 November 2020).

'convergence between the "localness" of the identity and "globalness"' (Terkourafi 2012: 48; Alim 2009: 103, Taviano 2016: 183) with both an international taste and a 'national flavour' (Krims 2000 cited in Chang 2007: 66).

Since the introduction of English is absolutely new within the artistic landscape of Egyptian music, it is possible to claim that rappers' merit is 'exploiting local themes and language conventions, as well as creating new language practices' (Williams 2009: 3), and consequently, providing a new corpus for the study of code-switching (Baker 2012: 91) between (Egyptian) Arabic and English.

Empirical Analysis: Questionnaire to Egyptian Rappers' Fans

The questionnaire used for this chapter was designed on the basis of the Bilingualism and Emotion Questionnaire (BEQ) (Dewaele and Pavlenko 2001–3). It was, however, largely modified, and adapted to the analysis of the linguistic preferences of Egyptians in rap songs and social networks and their usage of English to express emotions. It consists of forty-one items, was created with Google Forms and conducted through Facebook, where participants were looked for and Messenger, through which communication occurred.

The questionnaire is made up of both close- and open-ended questions and is divided into four parts which will be dealt with systematically later: PART 1 is dedicated to the acquisition of the general information of participants including their age, their student or professional carrier, the language(s) knowledge, their proficiency in English and experiences they had in English-speaking countries in order to frame their answers in a specific sociolinguistic context; PART 2 is devoted to the analysis of the sociolinguistic reasons why Egyptian rappers use English in their songs lyrics and to the examination of the link between English and emotions in them.

In PART 3, the link between the English language in rappers' social network pages and emotions is investigated, more specifically it focuses on why and to what extent Egyptian participants prefer using English and why and to what extent they like mixing the two languages, (Egyptian) Arabic and English, on rappers' social network pages. In addition, the kind of emotions participants prefer expressing in English on social networks are highlighted.

In PART 4, more generally, the reasons for the use of English to express emotions by Egyptians are analysed. In detail, the focus is on understanding whether participants feel more emotionally involved, more comfortable and more powerful when they use English for expressing emotions, whether they use English for more functional reasons or whether switching to English in songs and internet is only a trendy and common habit without any emotional involvement.

The full questionnaire is available online on the following link: https://forms.gle/9eT2FK2tsxqg49fN9.

PART 1: Participants' General Information. Items 1–11

For this analysis, and specifically with questions 1–11, different sociolinguistic aspects including socio-biographical factors (Dewaele 2013: 6) and the speakers' personal language experience(s) (Dewaele 2013: 5), which could affect language choice in the expression of emotions, have been taken into consideration, gender, age, context of language use (Dewaele 2006: 126), religion, level of education (McArthur 1992; Pavlenko 2008; Dewaele 2008), speakers' linguistic and cultural background, speakers' proficiency and degree of socialization in English (Dewaele and Qaddourah 2015: 85), as well as duration of exposure to the LX language being a long-term contact to an LX culture a better and easier occasion for an 'emotional acculturation'; (Dewaele and Qaddourah 2015: 86; De Leersnyder, Mesquita and Kim 2011; Dewaele 2008).

The group examined in this chapter is composed by twenty Egyptian Facebook users and rappers' fans from Cairo, Alexandria and Giza. They are all male but one female participant, and all between fifteen and thirty-nine years old. Nineteen of them are Islamic and one participant preferred not to say their religious beliefs.

The participants belong to various social and cultural background: only one of them is a high school student while the others are workers in different professional fields: business management, marketing and communication management, export and general trading, project management, Math teaching, photography, singing, fashion, geology, engineering, electrical engineering, contracts engineering, renewable energy engineering, architecture, pharmacy, veterinary medicine, English literature, customer service and script writing.

All the participants' mother tongue is Arabic, but they all are Arabic–English bilinguals even if with different degree of proficiency. Sixty per cent of the participants is fairly well skilled in English, 20 per cent claims to be even close to English native speakers, while other 20 per cent is not very proficient in English even if communication is not affected. However, although this last group does not feel so well skilled in English, intense use of English in Facebook comments can be noticed. This might allow to think that English knowledge and code-switching practice does not depend only on linguistic factors and school education, but it is mostly acquired through socialization (Kniaź and Zawrotna 2013: 618): people tend to use a specific language depending on how much they are exposed to that language and its culture.

In this regard, eighteen participants claim they have always used English uniquely inside Egypt, a foreign context, having never experienced a stay in an English-speaking country. Only two of them have been exposed to English in a native context, one having lived in North Carolina (United States) for more than six months, and another having lived in a not-specified anglophone country for one year and a half.

PART 2: English in Rap Songs' Lyrics and Emotions. Items 12–18

This part of the questionnaire is devoted to the investigation of the relation between language and emotions in Egyptian rap songs. In order to analyse the speakers' attitude towards the use of English and towards the (Egyptian) Arabic–English code-switching practice, participants were asked to comment on the following questions:

- Question (henceforth Qu.) 12: What is your opinion about the use of English in Egyptian rap songs?
- Qu. 13: What do you think about the phenomenon of mixing (Egyptian) Arabic and English in Egyptian rap songs?

Answers suggest that the use of English in Egyptian rap songs, as well as code-switching into English, is welcomed by the majority of participants (60 per cent in total). The linguistic practice of switching from local language(s) to English is neither casual nor naïve. It is not casual because it seemingly depends on specific events, and it is not naïve because it occurs for different conscious or unconscious reasons. With the following question, the socio-historical and sociolinguistic reasons that led to the spread of English in the Egyptian popular rap music, and the participants' awareness of these factors are examined. The question is:

- Qu. 14: Which socio-historical event do you think led to the use of English in Egyptian rap songs?

Fifty per cent of choices fell on *Egyptian personal interest in English*, followed by 40 per cent on *Egyptian relationship with Europe and America*. The two responses altogether allow us to claim that Egyptian themselves are becoming aware of the extreme importance of English outside but also inside Egyptian boundaries giving rise to a proper 'English fever' (Ibrahim et al. 2017: 285), especially because English allows to maintain relationships with the Western world, which also means exposure to the advanced Western culture (Schneider 2011: 46) and connection with the 'prosperity' – both economic and cultural (Schaub 2000: 228) – of Europe and North America.

Twenty-five per cent of answers were for *The introduction of English at school* and 15 per cent for *British colonialism*. The two answers are somehow linked since English was introduced in the Egyptian educational system properly during British colonization. Indeed, British colonizers tried 'to introduce many Westernization policies in Egyptian society, including an anti-Arabic, pro-English language campaign' (Poese 2014: 3). This historical event has perhaps had two opposite consequences on the relationship between language and emotions: on the one hand, being emotions 'prototypical scripts that are formed as a result of repeated experiences [. . .] causal antecedents, appraisals, physiological reactions' (Pavlenko 2008: 150), a long-lasting period of British domination allowed English words to become rooted in the Egyptian context (Poese 2014: 3) and emotionally charged; on the other hand, being colonialism a negative experience and trauma, it may have caused the speakers' unconscious avoidance of those words in order to distance themselves from negative feelings (Pavlenko 2005: 185-6; Bakić and Škifić 2017: 42).

Strangely, all participants, but one, excluded *recent Egyptian revolutions* as one of the reasons for the widespread use of English in Egypt. This is strongly in contrast with a number of theories such as Bassiounney's (2014), Poese's (2014) or Abouelhassan and Meyer's (2016) that have noticed a stronger use of English by Egyptians during and after the 25 January 2011 revolution. Indeed, it has been noticed that it was during these uprisings that young Egyptians became more politically active not only in the Squares but also online (Khalil 2012: 12), developing widespread political and social discussions on Facebook and Twitter to such a degree that it was defined 'The Facebook Revolution' (Eprile 2017: 4), the 'Twitter revolutions' (Bruns, Highfield and Burgess 2013: 895) or the 'media war' (Bassiouney 2012: 107). Interestingly, these discussions took place mostly in ECA, which allows speakers to feel freer and more direct (Khalil 2012: 1), in English or in a mixed form (Bruns, Highfield and Burgess 2013: 872). Protesters deliberately chose to use English probably with the aim of promoting the mass appeal of their message to a wider audience (Poese 2014: 7), 'drawing more global attention to particular issues' (Bruns, Highfield and Burgess 2013: 875) and escaping censorship exercised by the Egyptian government (Choudhary et al. 2012: 75). Even more interestingly, they showed such a high fluency and sophistication on their written messages and banners (Abouelhassan and Meyer 2016: 147) that they were accused not to be 'real Egyptians' (Bassiouney 2012: 112). Hence, it is possible to assert that revolution with its 'online communications featured a new and unusual diglossia-between a foreign language, English, and a Romanized, predominantly colloquial form of Arabic' (Warschauer, Said and Zohry 2006: 14) and that it surely resulted in an increased use of English. However, this linguistic process has been so fast and so unconscious that speakers are not even aware of it.

With the next question, the issues that make Egyptian rappers prefer using English according to participants' opinion are investigated. The question asks:

- Qu. 15: Why do you think Egyptian rappers use English in their songs?

Sixty-five per cent of answers fell on *In order to create a better stylistic effect*, being it necessary for a more authentic rap rhythm, as added by one of the participants, soon after followed by the answer *In order to express stronger emotions* with a good 40 per cent of choices. This last reason is also extremely clear in Egyptian rap songs' lyrics. Evidence of this is the song *Gold* by Mr Kordy in which it seems obvious that the two languages convey a diverse emotional meaning and with a different emotional charge (Figure 8.2).

As can be clearly seen in Figure 8.2, the (Egyptian) Arabic lyrics are characterized by a smoother tone, by a simpler and almost childish and naïve meaning and by words which are generally positively connotated (underlined words in the text). However, when switching to English the tone drastically changes. The English lyrics are full of swearwords, bad language, vulgar expressions related to gangster lifestyle and sex (words in bold in the text) which reveal a major emotional force (Dewaele 2004). This is a fundamental datum in this chapter since it confirms the original claim and proves that English de facto serves Egyptians a more emotional channel for expressing strong emotions than (Egyptian) Arabic itself (Halim and Maros 2014: 131).

Equally significant is the percentage (30 per cent) related to the following statements: *To imitate American rappers and songs* and *Because using English rappers can became more famous in the world*. As for the former, the American lifestyle, including music, language and behaviours, is appreciated by many young Egyptians to such an extent that the reliance on Western models is causing a form of cultural 'schizophrenia' (*al-fisam*) (Cook 2000: 486). For such a reason, 'with the exception of religion, English has found a significant role

	TRANSLATION:
[Verse 2 Mr Kordy]	
مباخدش بالاسامي	Scratched in name
هديك خلفي وامامي	Your guide is behind me and in front of me
منطقتك كلها يا زميلي حافظين كلامي	Your whole area, my colleague, kept my words
اخدان الحق حرفة	Chugging the right craft
والمطوة عندي زفرة	And I have a sigh
قفلت من المجال فجاتلي فكرة	I locked out of the field, so get an idea
اسيبله ذكرى	[Asibla?] remembrance
احذر مني انا عندي جنود	Beware of me, I have soldiers
هنا في حدود	Here in limits
بري الرمية	Throwing throw
قبل مموت وبموت مبسوط	Before a death and a happy death
قد وقد وقد قدود	May be and may be and may be and may be
جوا الادغال عندنا اشبال	In the jungle we have cubs
اصوات احفادي بتهد جبال	The voices of my grandchildren soften mountains
طب مين اللي جاي سكة	Doctor who is coming
طبل عالدكة	Drum on the bench
حطلها قطرة	Drop it off
وسيبها فترة	And Sepha [British company serving the pharmaceutical industry] period
الشمس حامية	The sun is the protector
اشكالنا خطرة	Our shapes are dangerous
حطلها توم	Tom broke it
وسيبها يوم	And Sepha on
حطلها فوم	Dissolve it with foam
[...]	

> I'm **fuckin'** right
> Even when I'm wrong
> **Shit is strong**
> **I will smoke you all bitches**
> Hommie where is da **bong** [pipe for smoking drugs]
> Where is da bong esse
> Where is da bong hommie
> Where is da bong where is da bong hommie
> Da **shit is on**
> **I will smoke you all bitches**
> Hommie where is da **bong**

Figure 8.2 Lyrics taken from verse 2 of the song 'Gold' by Mr Kordy (full lyrics available on Genius.com. Reproduced with permission of Mr Kordy. https://genius.com/Mr-kordy-gold-lyrics, accessed 23 November 2020).

also in the popular culture of Egypt, as manifested in advertisement, television, clothing, and music' (Schaub 2000: 225). This would explain, for example, the reason why Egyptians produce rap songs imitating American rappers not only in rhythm, lyrics and topics but also in their way of behaving, including fashion like tattooing, street dance, graffiti, beatboxing or selling pit bull dogs (Bibars 2017). As for the latter answer, undoubtedly, rappers seek fame and fortune; they want to show their music and culture and wish to sell their products to many consumers (Pope 2005: 79) both in Egypt and in the world. Undoubtedly, the use of English, the 'Global language' (Crystal 2003), is the perfect tool for the singers to reach these goals (Oreoluwa 2013: 9). In the same way, English permits Egyptians *to let people know about their social problems internationally* (15 per cent of answers).

Another 15 per cent of choices fell on the answer *because English is more and more used in Egypt* which allows to assert that, generally, the use of English has become a common linguistic practice in Egypt while no one answered *because rappers singing in Egypt are American born* confirming the Egyptian origins of rappers even if they maybe *have lived for many years in America* as underlined by one participant.

Finally, with questions 17 and 18, participants' preference and emotional involvement towards the English parts of the songs were asked. The results show that participants equally express a preference for the (Egyptian) Arabic lyrics (40 per cent) and the parts in which rappers mix it with English (40 per cent). As for the emotional participation, with 25 per cent of choices they claim to feel much more emotionally involved when they listen to the English lyrics than when they listen to the (Egyptian) Arabic ones, even if, with a higher 55 per cent of choices, the majority assert to have *a neutral* attitude. However, this impartiality is due to the fact that for them, *both Egyptian (Arabic) and English are good means through which to express and perceive emotions*. In carrying out this function, English is compared to (Egyptian) Arabic.

PART 3: English on Egyptian Rappers' Facebook Pages and Emotions. Items 19–22

Code-switching not only occurs in Egyptian rappers' song's lyrics but also in their normal conversation and/or in their 'electronic discourses' (Halim and Maros 2014: 133). These include, for instance, videos in which rappers advertise their products and themselves and posts and comments on social networks.

As an example, the transcription of the first 1:53 minute of a 10-minute video with an interview with Mr Kordy is reported by his permission (Figure 8.3).

Significantly, in this video, not only does Mr Kordy continuously code-switch from English to (Egyptian) Arabic but he also mixes the two codes in the same utterance. This confirms that the introduction of English and the English code-switching and code-mixing practices have become normal linguistic phenomena among Egyptian rappers and their audience. Probably, as a consequence of that, on rappers' social network pages, such as Facebook, English is frequently employed also by Egyptian rappers' fans when writing their comments which

MR. KORDY	TRANSLATION
Like if you weak, nigga you die.	
أي حد يقولك أنا أول واحد أغنى **راب**	Anyone telling you that they are the first to rap
في مصر ده بيفسى عايك	in Egypt is bullshitting you
هو أنا كنت من أوائل الباس اللى كانت بتفنى راب في مصر	I was one of the first rappers in Egypt
زمان كان الوضوع صعب	Back in the day it was really hard
يعنى صعب إن أنت تسجل، صعب إن أنت تنثر **الموسيقى** دي أصلًا	hard to record and hard to publish this music
الإنترنت ده لسه ماكانش موجود	Internet hadn't yet permeated our lives
أن ولاد عمى كانوا بييجوا من كاليفورنيا زمان	My cousins would come from California
بييجوا معاهو *mix tapes* دي	and would bring with them this mix tapes.
فيها *Easy E, Dr Dre, Ice Cube Lord of Underground all of these rappers.*	They had Easy E, Dr Dre, Ice Cube
هو كان في رابرز كتير جدًا في الساحة	There were many rappers on the scene
كلهم كويسين	They are all good
بس أخوك كان بتاع نمر	but I was about pulling stunts
I was an O.G. since I was 19, 18 something like this	
اتوادت وعشت منا في الزيتون	I was born and raised here in Zeitoun
قضينا ال *childhood* طفولتنا هنا	We spent our childhood here.
I lived all of that motherfuking problems That you thinking or like you taking about	
فاهم؟	Know what I mean?
Problems with the police	
problems with the drug dealers, فاهم قصدي؟	problems with the drug dealers, *get it?*
كنا بنعمل مشاكل كتير	We caused a lot of troubles
فاهم قصدي؟	Know what I mean?
طبعا لا بتكبر في السن العهاية بتختاف	Of course, when you get older things change
I used to be a gangster rapper	
يعنى انا *started that shit in here*	Meaning I *started that shit in here*
And people believe you because they saw And they heard a lot of shit. The system watch that shit, your manager watch that shit	
They don't like that They need you part of the system So they let you go	

Figure 8.3 Transcription of the first 1:53 of a 10-minute video containing an interview with Mr Kordy. Reproduced with permission of Mr Kordy. (full video available on this link: https://www.youtube.com/watch?v=xzI9SLHIT88, accessed 24 November 2020).

would demonstrate that English is used by them to express the most spontaneous emotional responses and states.

In this part of the questionnaire, the relation between the use of English in rappers' social network pages and emotions is investigated with a special focus on the frequency of code-switching from (Egyptian) Arabic to English and the frequency of use of the only English language in writing comments by Egyptian participants. For this analysis, a five-point Likert-type scale is used. Questions are the following:

- Qu. 19: How often do you switch from Arabic to English and vice versa when you write on rappers' social network pages?
- Qu 20: How often do you write comments entirely in English?

Surprisingly, answers are almost equally subdivided into the different levels of frequency, with the 65 per cent of participants sometimes (20 per cent), usually (20 per cent) and always (25 per cent) code-switching between English and (Egyptian) Arabic on rappers' social network pages while the remaining 35 per cent never (20 per cent) or rarely (15 per cent) switch to English. Similarly, question 20 shows that a total of 70 per cent of participants always (15 per cent), usually (15 per cent) or sometimes (40 per cent) write comments entirely in English, while only the 30 per cent rarely (20 per cent) or never (10 per cent) use it. This would demonstrate that English is actually used in social networks even if not always and not everyone chooses it to write comments. In addition, as proved through question 20, it is possible to claim that English is slightly more preferred in its individual form instead of in a mixed form.

With the next question, the main reasons why Egyptian participants use English on social network pages are investigated. The question is:

- Qu 21: Which are the main reasons why you use English on these social network pages?

With a large 50 per cent of choices, participants state that they use English on social networks because *mixing the two languages is generally a common habit in various Egyptian sociolinguistic contexts* and that *they always introduce English words and sentences when they write on Facebook* (30 per cent of answers). This phenomenon, which is *more common among the youngest* (25 per cent of answers), demonstrates that English in Egypt has already permeated many Egyptian fields and that Egyptians deliberately make an extensive use of it, mixing it with their mother tongue.

Another statement that received attention at 25 per cent was *because all Egyptian fans of rappers use English in social networks comments*. So, *using the same language* they *feel part of the same 'familia' or 'homie'* which allows to claim that code-switching creates solidarity (Gumperz 1976). This also validates those studies according to which speakers could feel more comfortable using an LX in certain situations or with certain people (Dewaele 2011: 26).

Still, with a 15 per cent of choices, participants agree that since *rap music is an international artistic form, it is better and more natural to use English*, the international language, on social networks related to this musical genre.

With question 22, the kind of emotions participants prefer expressing in English on the specific context of social networks is investigated. The question is the following:

- Qu. 22: Which kind of emotions do you prefer expressing in English on social networks?

Love (55 per cent), friendship (35 per cent), trust (30 per cent) and anger (30 per cent) were the most-quoted answers, followed by revenge (25 per cent), confidence (20 per cent) and confusion (18.8 per cent), fear, sadness, joy, kindness, courage, suffering, anxiety, modesty, excitement, interest, and nostalgia (12.5 per cent), disgust, pity, sense of belonging, disappointment, calmness, despair, devotion, astonishment, admiration, amusement, satisfaction, relief, pride, cruelty and horror (6.3 per cent).

As evident, Egyptian participants link English with the strongest emotions (both negative and positive) and this contradicts previous studies according to which speakers prefer expressing strong emotions such as anger (Pavlenko 2002; Dewaele 2006) and love (Dewaele 2008) by using their mother tongue (Dewaele 2013: 2; Dewaele and Qaddourah 2015: 85).

PART 4: Reasons for the Use of English in the Expression of Emotions. Items 23–41

According to previous studies and in line with the concept of 'indexicality' (Ochs 1992; Silverstein 1996), speakers choose to use or mix different linguistic codes for diverse functions (Ferguson 1996; Bassiouney 2012: 108), intentions and motivations. PART 4 aims at investigating language preferences for the expression of emotions and the reasons leading to this preference to writing on Egyptian rappers' social network pages. For this analysis, a 5-point Likert scale is used.

One first reason why Egyptians switch to English is the association of the language *with the domains of rap music and social networks* (statements [henceforth st.] 32 and 33), as corroborated by 60 per cent and 75 per cent of participants agreeing with the claims. According to 75 per cent of them, English is mainly used for quotations and *to report words or sentences cited by rappers in their songs* (st. 28).

Statement 34 aims at verifying whether participants use English *only because it is cool and trendy*. Answers were almost negative with 55 per cent of participants disagreeing with this claim. This might imply the presence of much deeper motivations. Indeed, code-switching to English can occur for pragmatic socio-economic reasons (Coulmas 2005; Cenoz and Genesee 1998), especially because knowledge of English is 'a prerequisite for success' (Holmes 2001: 59), and/or for functional communicative tasks, for example, speakers may use English when they want to express objectivity and create a certain distance with the message conveyed thus hiding embarrassment and reducing speakers' anxiety (Dewaele 2011: 27) in cases in which their words could be disturbing in their L1 (Dewaele 2004: 207). In support of this claim, the majority of Egyptian participants agree that they use English because *it is sometimes difficult to express specific meanings and emotions in (Egyptian) Arabic* (st. 25) while, through English, they can more easily talk about taboo topics without being offensive (Ritchie and Bathia 2006: 342) and *communicate threat-related and sex-related explicit words and expressions* (Aquino and Arnell 2007: 430) *without feeling embarrassment* (st. 35), *still continuing feeling polite* (st. 38) and *without being judged* (st. 39). These data are also confirmed by item 30, in which 40 per cent of participants agree with the fact that *English allows Egyptians to express feelings and emotions that they cannot express in Arabic* (st. 30). Similarly, swearing in the foreign language allows Arabic speakers to 'circumvent the social prohibition of swearing in their L1, which carries strong social stigma' (Dewaele and Qaddourah 2015: 85) and which considers vulgar expressions as highly offensive (Dewaele 2011: 27). Consequently, English seems to allow them (50 per cent) to *feel more spontaneous when using English than when using (Egyptian) Arabic* (st. 26) and to *feel more comfortable with English for expressing strong emotions such as anger and revenge* (55 per cent) (st. 23) all this being in line with the original thesis.

The results also suggest that 45 per cent, 50 per cent and 55 per cent of participants tend to change their mother tongue to English *to be more accurate and clearer* (Abu Melhim 1991: 242) *in the expression of emotions* (st. 29) and because *with English they can convey the right meaning and feelings* (st. 31) considering *English* as *a more direct and powerful language* (st. 36). This is in contrast with those studies according to which L1 emotion words are felt as more powerful than in the L2 (Dewaele 2011: 25) or LX.

Generally speaking, a positive attitude towards the use of the English language on behalf of Egyptians, who have no trouble claiming *that it is not a problem to use English even at the expense of the Arabic language* (st. 41), can be highlighted. Consequently, this surely permits the development of a 'highly "mixed" [. . .] discourse' (Seargeant and Tagg 2011: 510) with more English–(Egyptian) Arabic code-switching (Hamdi 2017: 22), as it is already evident on Egyptian rappers' songs and social networks.

Conclusion

Although previous studies have demonstrated that multilingual speakers feel more comfortable with their L1 for expressing emotions, especially the strongest ones such as anger (Pavlenko 2002; Dewaele 2006) and love (Dewaele 2008), this study has proved, instead that in a bi-/multilingual community, even if the mother tongue is surely the language of intimacy, this does not automatically mean that it is the unique code used by speakers in the expression of emotions (Dewaele 2011: 25). Contrary to common belief, in such context, the mother tongue does not necessarily prevail on the foreign language.

Indeed, although the L2/LX has been defined as the language of detachment (Marcos 1976; Dewaele 2004) 'speakers may use these languages to index a variety of affective stances, and they may also mix two or more languages to convey emotional meanings' (Pavlenko 2005: 131) depending on many factors and for different reasons. This is what happens in Egypt which far from being a simple diglossic society is a multilingual one struggling 'with the concurrent use of three Arabic languages (CA, MSA, and EA) as well as parallel use of the English language' (Poese 2014: 5).

In this work, the specific domains of Egyptian rap music and social networks have been investigated through the examination of songs' lyrics, videos and comments on Facebook rappers' pages and through a questionnaire to Egyptian rappers' fans and Facebook users. The results show that English, which is extensively used in those contexts, strongly influence the way Egyptians use the language (Warschauer, Shetzer and Meloni 2000) and vary their linguistic practice and means through which they communicate emotions. Egyptians frequently seem to code-switch from their L1 to their LX, the English language, to express the most intimate thoughts and feelings and even prefer it for its major objectivity, accuracy, clarity and emotional power. English is thus perceived by many Egyptians as a parallel or even a better means than the L1 in communicating emotions.

Note

1   it is important to point out that in Egypt code-switching with foreign languages and even with the same Arabic dialects does not occur with Classical Arabic (CA) since it is the 'holy' language which, then, must be protected and preserved from alterations and foreign intrusions perceived as a menace to the purity of the language and to the religious and social values it carries. Foreign linguistic interferences, thus, 'are most easily integrated in the Arabic dialects' (Van Moll 2003).

References

Abdel Latif, M. M. M. (2017), 'English Education Policy at the Pre-University Stages in Egypt: Past, Present and Future', in R. Kirkpatrick (ed.), *English Language Education Policy in the Middle East and North Africa* (Language Policy 13), 33–46, Cham, Switzerland: Springer International Publishing AG.

Aboelezz, M. (2018), 'The Arabic Language and Political Ideology', in E. Benmamoum and R. Bassiouney, *The Routledge Handbook of Arabic Linguistics*, pp. 504–17, London: Routledge.

Abouelhassan, R. S. M., and Meyer, L. M. (2016), 'Economy, Modernity, Islam, and English in Egypt', *World Englishes*, 35 (1): 147–59.

Abu Melhim, A. R. (1991), 'Code Switching and Linguistic Accommodation in Arabic', *Perspectives on Arabic Linguistics*, V: 231–50.

Alim, H. S. (2009), 'Translocal Style Communities: Hip Hop Youth as Cultural Theorists of Style, Language, and Globalization', *Pragmatics*, 19 (1): 103–27.

Al-Sayadi, M. (2016), 'Traces of English in Arabic Dialects', *Lingwistyka Stosowana*, 16 (1): 1–17.

Altarriba, J. (2003), 'Does cariño equal 'liking'? A Theoretical Approach to Conceptual Nonequivalence Between Languages', *International Journal of Bilingualism*, 7: 305–22.

Aquino, J. M., and Arnell, K. M. (2007), 'Attention and the Processing of Emotional Words: Dissociating Effects of Arousal', *Psychonomic Bulletin & Review*, 14 (3): 430–5.

Baker, C. (2012), 'Languages of Global Hip Hop', *IASPM Journal*, 3 (1): 91–2.

Bakić, A., and Škifić, S. (2017), 'The Relationship between Bilingualism and Identity in Expressing Emotions and Thoughts', *Íkala: Revista de Lenguaje y Cultura. Medellín, Colombia*, 22 (1): 33–54.

Bassiouney, R. (2012), 'Politicizing Identity: Code Choice and Stance-Taking During the Egyptian Revolution', *Discourse & Society*, 23 (2): 107–26.

Bassiouney, R. (2014), *Language and Identity in Modern Egypt*, Edinburgh: Edinburgh University Press Ltd.

Bibars, S. (2017), 'Mic Drop: Mr Kordy Sand Nikka and The Cairo City Gangsters', *Scene Noise*, 28 November. Available online: https://scenenoise.com/Features/mic-drop-mr-kordy-sand-nikka-and-the-cairo-city-gangsters (accessed 16 October 2020).

Billet, A. (2012), 'Interview: Rapper Sphinx on Why Egypt Uprising Had a Hip-Hop Soundtrack', *The Electronic Intifada*, 24 January. Available online: https://electronicintifada.net/content/interview-rapper-sphinx-why-egypt-uprising-had-hiphop-soundtrack/10852 (accessed 18 October 2020).

Bock, Z. (2008), '"Language has a Heart": Linguistic Markers of Evaluation in Selected TRC Testimonies', *Journal of Multicultural Discourses*, 3 (3): 189–203.

Bruns, A., Highfield, T., and Burgess, J. (2013), 'The Arab Spring and Social Media Audiences: English and Arabic Twitter Users and Their Networks', *American Behavioral Scientist*, 57 (7): 871–98.

Cantrall, S. (2013), 'The Influence of Rap in the Arab Spring', *Augsburg Honors Review*, 6 (12): 21–32.

Cenoz, J., and Genesee, F. (1998), *Beyond Bilingualism: Multilingualism and Multilingual Education*, 110, Clevedon: Multilingual Matters.

Chang, J. (2007), *Can't Stop Won't Stop: A History of the Hip-Hop Generation*, New York: St. Martin's Press.

Choudhary, A., Hendrix, W., Lee, K., Palsetia, D., and Liao, W. (2012), 'Social Media Evolution of the Egyptian Revolution', *Communications of the ACM*, 55 (5): 74–81.

Cook, B. J. (2000), 'Egypt's National Education Debate', *Comparative Education*, 36 (4): 477–90.

Coulmas, F. (2005), *Sociolinguistics*, Cambridge: Cambridge University Press.

Crystal, D. (2003), *English as a Global Language*, 2nd edn, Cambridge: Cambridge University Press.

De Leersnyder, J., Mesquita, B., and Kim, H. (2011), 'Where Do My Emotions Belong? A Study on Immigrants' Emotional Acculturation', *Personality & Social Psychology Bulletin*, 37: 451–63.

Dewaele, J.-M. (2004), 'The Emotional Force of Swearwords and Taboo Words', *Journal of Multilingual and Multicultural Development*, 25 (2 and 3): 204–22.

Dewaele, J.-M. (2006), 'Expressing Anger in Multiple Languages', in A. Pavlenko (ed.), *Bilingual Minds. Emotional Experience, Expression and Representation*, 118–51, Clevedon, Buffalo, Toronto: Multilingual Matters Ltd.

Dewaele, J.-M. (2008), 'The Emotional Weight of I Love You in Multilinguals' Languages', *Journal of Pragmatics*, 40 (10): 1753–80.

Dewaele, J.-M. (2010), *Emotions in Multiple Languages*. Basingstoke, UK: Palgrave Macmillan.

Dewaele, J.-M. (2011), 'Self-Reported Use and Perception of the L1 and L2 Among Maximally Proficient Bi- and Multilinguals: A Quantitative and Qualitative Investigation', *International Journal of the Sociology of Language*, 208: 25–51.

Dewaele, J. -M. (2013), 'Multilingualism and Emotions', *The Encyclopedia of Applied Linguistics*, Oxford: Blackwell Publishing Ltd.

Dewaele, J.-M., and Pavlenko, A. (2001–2003), *Web Questionnaire Bilingualism and Emotions*, London: University of London.

Dewaele, J.-M., and Qaddourah, I. (2015), 'Language Choice in Expressing Anger Among Arab-English Londoners', *Russian Journal of Linguistics*, 19 (4): 82–100.

Diana, C. (2010), *Globalization Impact on Education in Egypt* (Working paper), Florence: European University Institute.

Drobot, I. (2017), 'The Influence of Foreign Languages on Emotions', *Journal of Romanian Literary Studies*, 12: 293–9.

El-Dakhs, D. A. S., and Altarriba, J. (2019), 'How do Emotion Word Type and Valence Influence Language Processing? The Case of Arabic–English Bilinguals', *Journal of Psycholinguistic Research*, 48: 1063–85.

Eprile, B. T. (2017), 'Songs of Change: How Music Helped Spark the Arab Spring Revolutions in Egypt and Tunisia', Honors Thesis, Oberlin College, Ohio.

Ferguson, C. A. (1959), 'Diglossia', *Word*, 15 (2): 325–40.

Ferguson, C. A. (1996), *Sociolinguistic Perspectives: Paper on Language in Society, 1959–1994*, New York: Oxford University Press.

Fiehler, R. (2002), 'How to Do Emotions with Words: Emotionality in Conversations', in S. R. Fussell (ed.), *The Verbal Communication of Emotions. Interdisciplinary Perspectives*, 79–106, Mahwah, NJ/London: Lawrence Erlbaum Associates.

Gumperz, J. (1976), 'Conversational Code-Switching', in J. Gumperz (ed.), *Discourse Strategies*, 59–99, Cambridge: Cambridge University Press.

Halim, N. S., and Maros, M. (2014), 'The Functions of Code-switching in Facebook Interactions', *Procedia – Social and Behavioral Sciences*, 118: 126–33.

Hamdi, S. (2017), 'Lexical Borrowing in Arabic and the Role of Orthography', *International Journal of Language and Linguistics*, 4 (2): 17–28.

Hass, Re-Volt. (2011), 'Rebel Through Hiphop: Talkin' About a Revolution', *Mashallah News*, 7 February. Available online: https://www.mashallahnews.com/rebel-through-hiphop/ (accessed 21 October 2020).

Holmes, J. (2001), *An Introduction to Sociolinguistics*, London, & New York: Routledge.

Ibrahim, M. K., and Ibrahim, Y. A. (2017), 'Communicative English Language Teaching in Egypt: Classroom Practice and Challenges', *Educational Research*, 27 (2): 285–313.

Ibrahim, Z. (2017), 'Language Variation, Identity and Planning', in H. Medhat-Lecocq (ed.), *Arabe standard et variations regionals. Quelle(s) politique(s) linguistique(s) ? Quelle(s) didactique(s) ?*, 49–58, Paris: éditions des archives contemporaines.

Khalil, S. (2012), *The Evolution of the Arabic Through Online Writing: The Explosion of 2011. British Society for Middle Eastern Studies* (BRISMES 2012 Annual Conference

(Graduate Section) Change and Continuity in the Middle East: Rethinking West Asia, North Africa and the Gulf after 2011), Faculty of Asian and Middle Eastern Studies. Cambridge: University of Cambridge.

Kim, E. (2006), 'Reasons and Motivations for Code-Mixing and Code-Switching', *English as a Foreign Language*, 4 (1): 43–61.

Kniaź, M., and Zawrotna, M. (2013), *Patterns of Arabic-English Code-Switching in Youth Communication in Cairo*, Poland: National Science Center, Jagiellonian University in Krakow, 599–621.

Marcos, L. R. (1976), 'Linguistic Dimensions in the Bilingual Patient', *American Journal of Psychoanalysis*, 36: 347–54.

McArthur, T. (1992), *The Oxford Companion to the English Language*, New York: Oxford University Press.

Mitchell, T. (2001), *Global Noise: Rap and Hip-Hop Outside the USA*, Connecticut: Wesleyan.

Mollin, S. (2006), *Euro-English: Assessing Varieties Status*, Tübingen: Gunter Narr Verlag Tübingen.

Ochs, E. (1992), 'Indexing Gender', in A. Duranti, and C. Goodwin (eds), *Rethinking Context: Language as an Interactive Phenomenon*, 335–58, Cambridge: Cambridge University Press.

Ochs, E., and Schieffelin, B. (1989), 'Language has a Heart', *Text*, 9 (1): 7–25.

Oreoluwa, K. A. (2013), 'Code-switching in Contemporary Nigerian Hip Hop Songs', MA diss., University of Ghana, Ghana.

Othman, M. F. A. (2006), 'Language Choice among Arabic-English Bilinguals in Manchester, Britain', MA diss., University of Manchester, Manchester.

Ożańska-Ponikwia, K. (2013), *Emotions from a Bilingual Point of View. Personality and Emotional Intelligence in Relation to Perception and Expression of Emotions in the L1 and L2*, Cambridge: Cambridge Scholars Publishing.

Pavlenko, A. (2002), 'Bilingualism and Emotions', *Multilingua*, 21: 45–78.

Pavlenko, A. (2005), *Emotions and Multilingualism*, Cambridge, MA: Cambridge University Press.

Pavlenko, A. (2008), 'Emotion and Emotion-Laden Words in the Bilingual Lexicon', *Bilingualism: Language and Cognition*, 11 (2): 147–64.

Pavlenko, A. (2012), 'Affective Processing in Bilingual Speakers: Disembodied Cognition?', *International Journal of Psychology*, 47 (6): 405–28.

Poese, M. (2014), 'The Expanding Circle of English Use in Egypt: English Use in Egypt', *TSOL*, 536: 1–12.

Pope, H. L. (2005), 'Protest into Pop: Hip-hop's Devolution into Mainstream Pop Music and the Underground's Resistance', *Lehigh Review*, 13 (5): 79–98.

Ritchie, W. C., and Bhatia, T. K. (2006), Social and Psychological Factors in Language Mixing, in W. C. Ritchie, and T. K. Bhatia (eds), *The Handbook of Bilingualism*, 336–52, Oxford: Blackwell Publishing.

Schaub, M. (2000), 'English in the Arab Republic of Egypt', *World Englishes*, 19 (2): 225–38.

Schneider, E. W. (2011), *English Around the World, An Introduction*, Cambridge: Cambridge University Press.

Schneider, E. W. (2016), 'World Englishes on Youtube: Treasure Trove or Nightmare?', in E. Seoane and C. Gómez, *World Englishes: New Theoretical and Methodological Considerations*, 253–82, Amsterdam: John Benjamin Publishing Company.

Seargeant, P., and Tagg, C. (2011), 'English on the Internet and a 'Post-Varieties' Approach to Language', *World Englishes*, 30 (4): 496–514.

Silverstein, M. (1996), 'Indexical Order and the Dialectics of Sociolinguistic Life', *SALSA*, 3: 266–95.

Stadlbauer, S. (2010), 'Language Ideologies in the Arabic Diglossia of Egypt', *Colorado Research in Linguistics*, 22: 1–19.

Taviano, S. (2016), 'The Global Imaginary of Arab Hip Hop: A Case Study', *Imago Journal*, 7: 183–99.

Terkourafi, M. (2012), *The Language of Global Hip Hop*, New York: Continuum Publishing Corporation.

Van Moll, M. (2003), *Variation in Modern Standard Arabic in Radio News Broadcasts: A Synchronic Descriptive Investigation into the Use of Complementary Particles*, Leuven: Peeters Publishers.

Warschauer, M., El Said, G. R., and Zohry, A. (2006), 'Language Choice Online: Globalization and Identity in Egypt', *Wiley Online Library*, 7 (4): 1–38.

Warschauer, M., Shetzer, H., and Meloni, C. (2000), *Internet for English Teaching. Teachers of English to Speakers of Other Languages*, Alexandria, Egypt.

Wierzbicka, A. (2004), 'Preface: Bilingual Lives, Bilingual Experience', *Journal of Multilingual and Multicultural Development*, 25: 94–104.

Wilce, J. (2009), *Language and Emotion*, Cambridge: Cambridge University Press.

Williams, A. S. (2009), 'We Ain't Terrorists, But We Droppin' Bombs: Language Use and Localization of Hip Hop in Egypt', Thesis, University of Illinois at Urbana-Champaign, Urbana.

Zentella, A. C. (1999), *Growing Up Bilingual*, Malden: Blackwell.

Innovation and Emotion in Teen Talk in TV Series

Silvia Bruti

Introduction

This chapter aims to further investigate the language spoken by teenagers as a source of change and innovation on the one hand and as a repository of heightened emotions on the other. Given its volatility and the desire of its users to be understood mainly by group members, it is quite difficult to pin down the ongoing changes and new forms that are constantly being adopted. In this regard, the few specialized corpora available, the COLT (http://korpus.uib.no/icame/colt/) being the most typical, are either too old to register contemporary uses, or rather limited in the kind of situations portrayed. For these reasons, talking media may represent an advantageous source, as they 'put standard and vernacular ways of speaking on display, contextualize them and imbue them with the socio-cultural values that we associate with standardness and vernacularity – very differently across different genres and contexts, and differently over time' (Mortensen, Coupland and Thøgersen 2017: 36). The influential role of media in moulding sociolinguistic change has by now been universally recognized: they may raise awareness, readjust attitudes, values and sociocultural norms, for example, promoting standardization or de-standardization (Bednarek 2018). The first decade of the twenty-first century in particular marked an incredible expansion of American TV series and has consequently been labelled 'the new "golden age of television"' (Bednarek 2018: 82).

This contribution relies on a corpus-assisted methodology (Partington, Duguid and Taylor 2013) and extends the research in Bruti (2021), by comparing and contrasting the data already obtained (from a self-compiled corpus of American contemporary teen drama) with fresh data from comparable texts, one featuring British English (*Skins* 2007–13) and the other offering a snapshot of a previous decade (*Dawson's Creek* 1998–2003). The purpose is, therefore, to ascertain whether the markers of teen language identified in a previous study, for example, *wanna/gonna*, *totally* and the lexical items *fuck*, *shit* and *dude*, can be considered characteristic elements of contemporary American teen talk as represented in drama series or if they also surface in British English and in previous decades.

Even though a discussion of these aspects exceeds the purposes of this contribution, the idea of investigating teen language in contemporary TV series also responds to the need to find suitable models of spoken discourse that display a wide array of recent or incipient linguistic trends to be effectively employed in teaching English as a foreign language. Exposure to these models could stimulate both reflection and learning of useful ways of interacting and communicating with peers (Dose 2013; Duff and Zappa-Hollamn 2013; Jones 2017). Lastly, as discussed in Bruti (2021), given the pervasiveness of pop culture in our lives, familiarity with one of its genres may also raise awareness 'of its commercial and materialistic aspects' (Trotta 2018: 41).

Teen Talk

The language used by teenagers has only recently become the focus of scholarly investigations, in particular, in the last decades of the twentieth century (Androutsopoulos 2005; Androutsopoulos and Georgakopoulou 2003; Catala Torres 2002; Herrero 2002; Ito and Tagliamonte 2003; Jørgensen 2010; Kotsinas 1992; Palacios Martínez 2011a, b; Romaine 1984; Rodríguez González 2002; Rodríguez González and Stenström 2011; Stenström 1997, 1998, 2014; Stenström and Jørgensen 2009; Tagliamonte 2016).

Each generation of youth tends to differentiate its way of speaking from the previous, so not all innovations are destined to remain, not even those in the vocabulary, which is where change is particularly prominent.

As William Labov pointed out when he started his studies on language variation (1969), people decide to use non-standard or deviant forms not because they are not educated or capable of using the standard, but because non-standard uses carry implications of covert prestige. As a consequence, language choice is often used to express identity and group membership, and in the case of teenagers it is an expression of their attempt at seeking separation from the adult world and finding an identity of their own. As Palacios Martínez contends, 'adolescence is a turning-point in life, as the individual matures both physically and cognitively, and thus has a direct influence on language acquisition and development' (Palacios Martínez 2011b: 5). The interplay of age and other factors is responsible for the language variety that is used and accounts for the fact that no two teenagers speak identically, although they share a set of common features.

The typical foci of interest when analyzing teen talk are some distinctive phenomena, such as slang, swearwords, discourse markers and dialectal features (Stenström, Andersen and Hasund 2002) because they are particularly noticeable in this register. The most frequently employed approach is mainly lexical, because vocabulary is the level where linguistic innovation is most clearly reflected. Most innovations occur in fact in the lexicon and in word-formation processes, although sometimes deviations can be observed in pronunciation and in textual organization. The main component of teen talk is provided by colloquial English, which is enriched with items drawn from slangs and jargons (e.g. that of drug dealers and their underworld), specialized languages and the language of mass-media, especially new (social) media, the internet, YouTube and the like. To quote Eckert (1997: 52), 'adolescents are the linguistic movers and shakers, at least in western industrialized societies, and as such, a prime source of information about linguistic change and the role of language in social practice.'

As hinted at before, researchers interested in taking a closer look at teen talk should concentrate on situations in which spontaneous spoken languages is used, that is peer-to-peer communication. Specialized materials of this type are not abundant, as corpora of spoken language are very time consuming to assemble. Today, however, even though the selection of corpora of spoken English is quite wide, the language of teenagers is still not well represented. The main resource is the already-mentioned COLT, a data set of samples of spoken English compiled in 1993 from tape recorded and transcribed conversations by teens between the ages of 13 and 17 in schools throughout London. This corpus, which also constitutes a part of the spoken component of the BNC, has offered material for several studies at the intersection of sociolinguistics and pragmatics (Stenström, Andersen and Hasund 2002; Stenström 2014; Palacios Martínez 2011a, b). The only other corpus of juvenile language mentioned in Tagliamonte's book-length study (2016) is the Toronto Teen Corpus, amounting to one million words collected in the period between 2002 and 2006 by a group of student researchers who acted as interviewers within their own social and familiar networks to elicit spoken conversation (Tagliamonte 2016: 12).[1] Tagliamonte also resorts to data from the Toronto Instant Messaging Corpus (2004–6) and the Toronto Internet Corpus (2009–10), the latter including different registers such as emails, instant messaging and SMS. The data from these two corpora are certainly colloquial but do not provide an example of conversation proper.

Research Agenda, Methodology and Data

On the basis of previous research into teen talk (Tagliamonte 2016) and in media language (Bednarek 2018) and the results in Bruti (2021), this contribution aims to further investigate the role and function of a selection of items – the phonological reductions *gonna* and *wanna*, the lexical items *fuck*, *shit* and *dude*, and the intensifier *totally* – that have been considered good markers of teen talk. These elements have been chosen on the basis of studies by Tagliamonte (2016), Tagliamonte and Roberts (2005) and Bednarek (2018, 2019), which indicated some typical markers of teen talk. The three items *fuck*, *shit* and *dude* were selected from a list of frequently employed emotional words in recent media language, as explained in Bruti (2021: 42–3).

More specifically, the following questions will be addressed:

1. Are the two phonological reductions *gonna* and *wanna*, which are mainly used in informal talk, significantly present in British English, as represented in the TV series *Skins*, and in *Dawson's Creek*, which was released slightly before the other TV series investigated so far? This survey might identify different stages of a long and often complex grammaticalization process (Traugott 1994);
2. Are the words that I selected as markers of teen talk in Bruti 2021, for example, *fuck*, *shit* and *dude*, especially frequent in American vis-à-vis British English? Have they spread considerably over the last two decades in teen dramas?
3. How does *totally*, an intensifier that has been described as polysemous and flexible for its syntactic mobility and collocational profile especially in the American variety (Aijmer 2011; Tagliamonte 2016), behave (in terms of frequency and collocational behaviour) in British English? In which stage of its evolutionary trajectory is this intensifier in the shows under investigation?

With these objectives in mind, I assembled another small corpus of teen talk, choosing other TV series that revolve around the life of adolescents but either feature British English (*Skins*) or were released before (*Dawson's Creek*). Data from these two shows could thus be compared with previous results for the Teen Corpus, which consists of 801,418 words from the first three seasons of *Pretty Little Liars* (2010–17), of *Riverdale* (2017–), and of *13 Reasons Why* (2017–).[2] All these shows are classified as teen drama and mystery,[3] so they share to large extent genre and topic. Although the plot revolves around the daily lives of a group of teenagers, they are rich in mysterious and dark elements. All in all they render a rather faithful portrayal of contemporary US society, by either hinting at or describing explicitly problems of ethnic and cultural integration, homosexuality and bullying. As the analysis highlights, the languages in *Pretty Little Liars* (from now on abbreviated as *Liars*) and *Riverdale* is similar, on account of the fact that a big part of their appeal resides in their unique vocabulary and playful and memorable one-liners. The plot of *Thirteen Reasons Why* (from now on abbreviated as *Reasons*), on the other hand, is dominated by crimes and transgressions, all of which are depicted graphically, both visually and verbally. As a result, the language employed often sounds coarse and violent.

The new component assembled for the purposes of extending the investigation includes the first season of *Skins* (2007–13) and the first of *Dawson's Creek* (1998–2003), respectively amounting to 29,701 and 64,467 words. I relied on orthographic fan transcriptions (from https://transcripts.foreverdreaming.org/) that I spot-checked for accuracy.[4] I availed myself of various software, that is, Wmatrix, a part of speech and a semantic tagger that displays key word and key semantic domains (Rayson 2003), and AntcConc (Anthony 2019), to obtain wordlists and concordances.

Corpus Data: From the Teen Corpus to the Teen Corpus Part II

As suggested previously, for the Teen Corpus part II, I chose another two shows centred on adolescents, but I specifically selected a British TV Series, *Skins*, and an American one, but released at least a decade before the ones in the Teen Corpus, that is, *Dawson's Creek*.

Skins is a British teen comedy drama which narrates the adventures of a group of teenagers living in Bristol, from sixth form to A levels. The plot delves into problems that adolescents normally face in their lives, such as dysfunctional families, mental problems, sexuality, drug abuse and bullying. *Skins* premiered on E4, a British free-to-air television channel owned by Channel Four, on 25 January 2007 and ended on 5 August 2013. A rather unconventional feature of *Skins* is that it cast amateur young actors and young writers, and the main characters are replaced in the show every two years. There are, however, some narrative hooks in the plot that make the transition smooth and plausible. Although *Skins* at least partially aired in the United States on BBC America, in a heavily censored way ('with nudity pixillated and swearing dipped' https://deadline.com/2011/01/uk-skins-not-as-controversial-as-in-u-s-99292/), MTV produced an American adaptation set in Baltimore. In 2011, after the airing of the first season, the show was cancelled due to the loss of advertising sponsors and an ever-shrinking audience (https://skins.fandom.com/wiki/Skins_(UK)).

Dawson's Creek is a teen drama devoted to the lives of a group of school friends beginning high school and then continuing into college. It is set in the fictional town of Capeside, Massachusetts. Being produced and aired in the United States at the end of the 1990s, the show was criticized by columnists and parents alike, for the emphasis on sex, the frequent references to pornography, condoms and the acceptance of homosexuality (cf. https://en.wikipedia.org/wiki/Dawson%27s_Creek). As will appear from the analysis, such an attitude is probably linked to the times when the product was released, as the treatment of sex-related issues is far from being disrespectful and offensive, similarly to the language employed. Its launch on Netflix at the beginning of 2021, almost twenty years after its last episode, has been welcomed by groups of fans.

An Overview of the Teen Corpus – Part II: Key Word – and Key Domain Clouds

To get a preliminary idea of the new corpus component, I created a .txt file with the dialogues of each of the two series to be processed by means of Wmatrix (Rayson 2003). Wmatrix is available online, and, among other functionalities, it automatically runs a part of speech and a semantic tagger on textual data. Thanks to this application, the key words and key semantic domains for both *Skins* and *Dawsons' Creek* could easily be visualized, by selecting a reference corpus against which it was possible to establish keyness. In this case, I preferred to contrast the two series with the Teen Corpus, which supposedly shares many features with them, to isolate only their distinctive elements. The 'keyness' of words (key word clouds) and semantic domains (key domain clouds) in Wmatrix is related to the fact that they surface as 'key' elements in the corpus under investigation in comparison with a reference corpus. In the case of key domain clouds, the most relevant groupings of semantically related words are brought to light. The logic behind the clouds is that the words with the bigger font size are those with the highest level of 'keyness' in the corpus. This result is obtained by comparing the words that occur in the corpus under analysis against a reference corpus (which can be chosen in a selection of proposed choices or added by the researcher).

This corpus-driven analysis is meant as a first step to ascertain if there are significant expressions and domains that are peculiar to these series in comparison with those in the Teen Corpus. For *Skins* keyness emerges in the names of the characters of the series, and, most of all, in familiar vocatives (e.g. *mum, mate, man*), a series of extremely colloquial expressions, many of which are forms of swearing (e.g. *fuck, fuck off, fucking, wanker, arse, bollocks*). The fact that they surface as key terms means that they are comparatively insignificant in the reference corpus. In fact, the term 'fuck' only appears in *Reasons*, but not in the other two series in the Teen Corpus (Bruti 2021: 42–3). As Bednarek argues (2019), the more or less limited use of swearing depends on whether shows are produced for public channels or cable and streaming services (Figure 9.1).

Let's have a look at the domain clouds, which assemble related words together in homogeneous semantic domains (Figure 9.2).

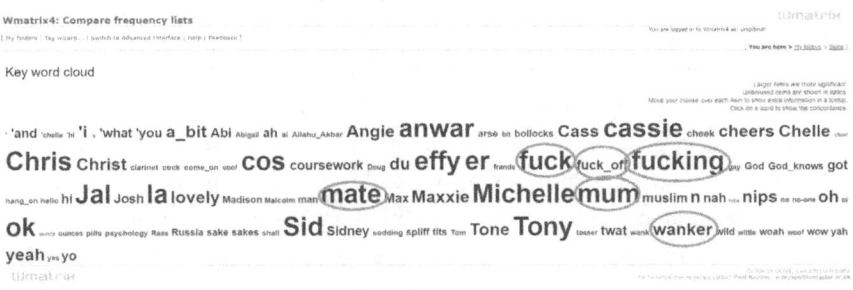

Figure 9.1 Key word cloud in *Skins* (vs. the Teen Corpus).

Figure 9.2 Key domain cloud in *Skins* (vs. the Teen Corpus).

As can be observed, among the domains represented with the biggest fonts, there are Anatomy_and_physiology, which refers to body parts and bodily secretions, and Relationship: Intimacy_and_sex, which again taps into physical relations.

If we take into account *Dawson's Creek* and carry out the same type of analysis, partially different features emerge. Names are obviously equally well represented, but there are also several routine formulae employed in peer talk and friendly conversations (e.g. *goodnight, alright, good-bye, guy*), some discourse markers (e.g. *you know, I mean*) and some particularly frequent lexical bundles (Biber et al. 1999; Cortes 2002; Biber and Barbieri 2007), for example, *going to, wait a minute*. No swearing emerges and references to the sexual sphere do not involve vulgar terms: there are in fact terms such as 'sex', 'kiss', 'virgin', and also 'romance and 'romantic'. As shall appear later on, the protagonists of this series are all emotionally involved and sex is obviously a frequent topic of discussion but the way they talk about it is sensitive and tactful. Interestingly, another dimension appears as characteristic of the series, which is tied to Dawson's passion for cinema, so terms such as 'film', 'cliffhanger', 'movies', 'Spielberg' (i.e. Dawson's favourite director) also qualify as key elements (Figure 9.3).

If we consider instead the key semantic domains, the ones that were mostly relevant in *Skins*, Anatomy_and_physiology and Relationship: Intimacy_and_sex are also present, the first one in a smaller font, that is, being less key. Relationships:_Intimacy_and_sex is instead quite crucial, but comprises a rather different assortment of terms (mainly *kiss, kissing, boyfriend, girlfriend*). Adverbs of degree modifying utterances seem to be quite often employed, either as boosters or diminishers. Equally significant are the domains Evaluation:_Good, accommodating positive responses and judgements (e.g. *okay, fine, well*),

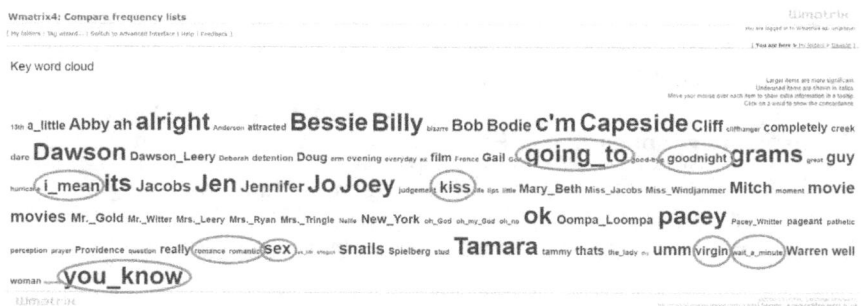

Figure 9.3 Key word cloud in *Dawson's Creek* (vs. the Teen Corpus).

People:_Female and People:_Male, The_Media:_TV,_Radio_and_Cinema, which depends on Dawson's passion for the cinema, and plenty of references to time, of which Time:_Momentary is the one which scores the highest in terms of keyness (Figure 9.4).

An Analysis of Some Markers of Teen Talk in the Teen Corpus – Part II

The next step in the analysis involved the investigation of the markers of teen talk that I selected for my previous study of 2021. A simple word count returns the results displayed in Figure 9.5.

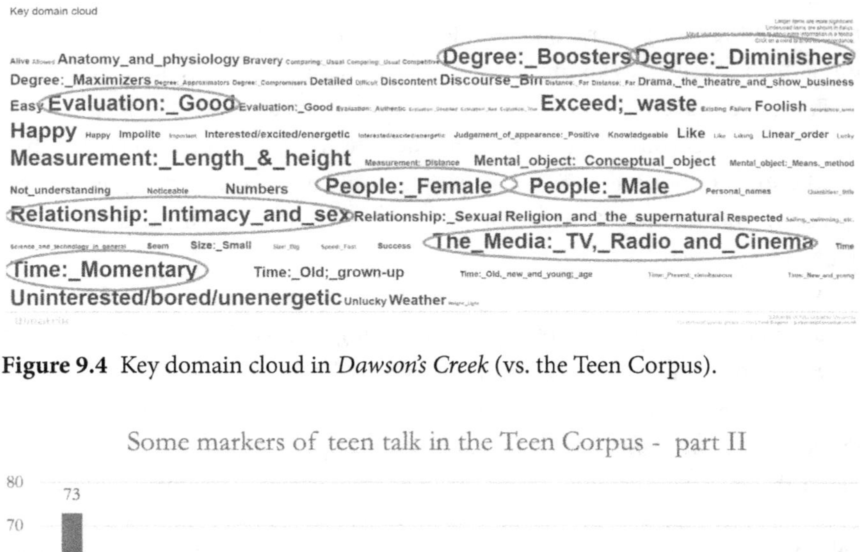

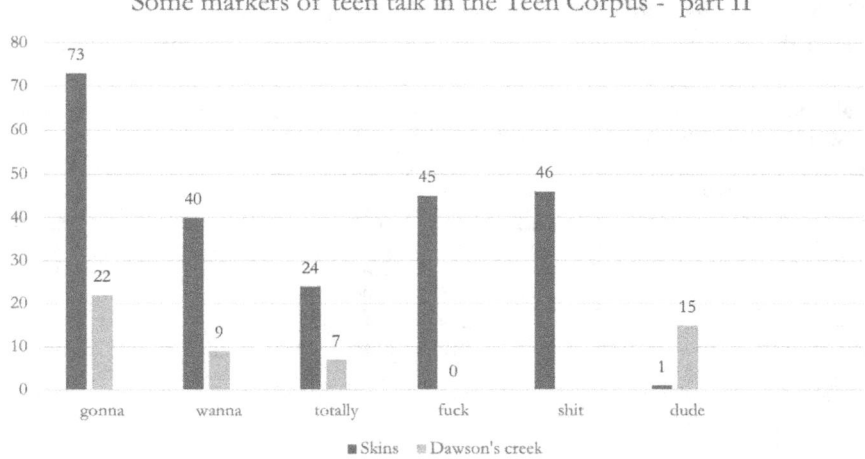

Figure 9.4 Key domain cloud in *Dawson's Creek* (vs. the Teen Corpus).

Figure 9.5 Some markers of teen talk in the Teen Corpus – part II.

A first observation on the two reduced forms *gonna* and *wanna* is in order: in line with the results for the Teen Corpus, *gonna* is more used than *wanna*, but a comparison with their more formal equivalents is necessary. Given the disproportion in word count between the two series, a more precise data description needs to take into account normalized data, which are displayed in Table 9.1. Both reduced forms are used substantially more in *Skins* than in *Dawson's Creek*, suggesting that frequency of use is probably linked to genre and style rather than to the language variety, that is, British versus American English.

The intensifier *totally*, in all its discursive functions, appears in both series, more frequently in *Skins* (cf. the normalized frequency in Table 9.1), also because it represents a turn of phrase employed, often idiosyncratically, by one of the characters.

As already hinted at earlier, forms of swearing do not feature in *Dawson's Creek*, but they are exceptionally frequent in *Skins*, where adolescents engage in unmediated exchanges among themselves in a rather graphic manner.

For a better evaluation of how frequent the selected markers of teen talk are in the various corpus components, old and new, I normalized results to 10,000 words, so as to be able to compare smaller and larger corpus components (cf. Table 9.1 and Figure 9.6, for a comparison between the Teen Corpus and the Teen Corpus – part II).

As for the two reduced forms *gonna* and *wanna* (compared to their non-reduced equivalents), the table highlights that *gonna* is more widespread than *wanna* throughout the corpus, so the trend probably began some decades ago on both sides of the Atlantic. What is interesting to notice is the ratio between the reduced forms and their non-reduced counterparts, that is, *going to* and *want to*. In this regard, *Dawson's Creek* seems to be a striking example, as the two

Table 9.1 Total and normalized frequencies of some markers of teen talk in the Teen Corpus and the Teen Corpus – Part II

	Skins		Dawson's Creek		Liars		Riverdale		Reasons	
	Total occurrences	Normalized to 10,000 words	Total occurrences	Normalized to 10,000 words	Total occurrences	Normalized to 10,000 words	Total occurrences	Normalized to 10,000 words	Total occurrences	Normalized to 10,000 words
wanna	40	13.46	9	1.39	333	10.44	199	7.57	161	7.32
want to	35	11.78	107	16.59	391	12.26	268	10.19	349	15.88
gonna	73	24.57	22	3.41	970	30.42	631	24.006	506	23.02
going to	37	12.45	192	29.78	230	7.21	280	10.65	201	9.14
fuck	45	15.15	0	0	0	0	0	0	473	21.52
shit	46	15.48	0	0	0	0	0	0	444	20.20
dude	1	0.33	15	2.32	15	0.68	41	1.55	149	4.67
totally	24	8.08	7	1.08	77	2.41	14	0.53	80	3.64

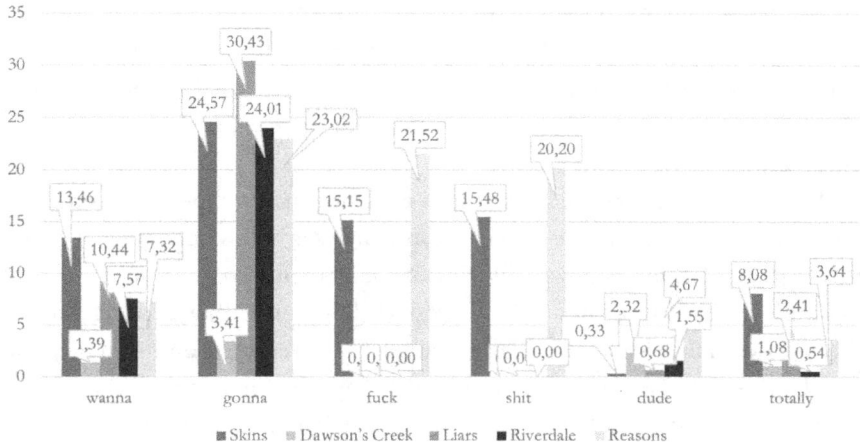

Figure 9.6 Some markers of teen talk in the Teen Corpus and the Teen Corpus – part II.

non-reduced forms are infinitely more frequent than the reduced ones. The only other exception is represented by *Reasons*, in which *want to* is more than twice as frequent as *wanna*. This latter case might be a trace of a grammaticalization process that is in a previous stage in comparison to that of *going to* > *gonna*. Both results in *Dawson's Creek* could instead be ascribed to a generally higher register: even though the show provides a rather realistic representation of the adolescent experience of lower to middle class living in the suburbs dealing with topics such as popularity, first love, divorce and financing college, the characters are adolescents that talk like older people, proving to be much more articulate than people their age usually are. This is particularly evident from the fact that they restrain from swearing or using vulgar words (cf. https://theconversation.com/why-dawsons-creek-in-all-its-cringey-glory-is-the-tv-show-90s-kids-need-right-now-148539). The scriptwriter himself admitted that 'even if their behavior [the characters'] is not that of an adult, they can sure talk like one' (Hills 2004: 60). The widespread adoption of the more formal variants *want to*/ *going to* could be a reflection of this mismatch between age and register, which is typical of this series.

The three lexemes chosen as representatives of heightened emotions and informality are well represented only in some of the TV products taken into account. Swearing, as also emerged from raw data, does not feature at all in *Liars*, *Riverdale*, nor does it in *Dawson's Creek*. *Skins*, instead, is almost as crude as *Reasons*, although they are respectively a British and an American product. The lexeme *dude* ranks first in *Reasons*, followed by *Dawson's Creek*, two series that do not have much in common apart from the American variety. There does not seem to be an objective explanation to account for this choice, and the only hypothesis that can be advanced is that *dude* might be used in the two series where it scores quite highly as a preferred address term, a kind of verbal tic, especially by boys.

As for *totally*, the normalized results evidence that it appears considerably more in TV series where the tone of the exchanges is highly colloquial. It scores the highest in *Skins*, followed by *Reasons* and then *Liars*. The fact that the intensifier is used most in a British product deserves further investigation, as the most complete study on *totally* (Aijmer 2011) reported on its vitality and variable use in American and not in British English. The temporal dimension, crucial as claimed by both Aijmer (2011) and Tagliamonte (2016) for the uptake of new functions, does not seem to be responsible for these results, as the TV series considered, apart from *Dawson's Creek*, are more or less contemporary, spanning the first and part of the second decade of the new Millennium. *Dawson's Creek* is indeed older than the other series, but, as we have seen, the fact that teenagers talk like they would like to be able to do in real life is a decision made by the authors. So it is difficult to isolate the true impact of the temporal dimension.

One further element to investigate is the colligation in which *totally* is found: as described in Bruti (2021: 44), the sequence *be + totally* is by and large more frequent than *totally + is*: however, data from the TV corpus, a huge resource of TV language,[5] highlight that the first combination nearly doubled from the 2000s to the 2010s, whereas *totally + is* grew more significantly (from 120 occurrences to 266). A detailed investigation follows in next Section.

From a Quantitative to a Qualitative Analysis: The Case of *Totally*

As a sample analysis, in what follows I will concentrate mainly on the intensifier *totally*. As findings from studies on other intensifiers have demonstrated (cf. Ito and Tagliamonte 2003), this class is very prone to changes and meaning shifts, because speakers want to be creative and impress their audience. In this case, normalized data are revealing, as *totally* proves to be most frequent in *Skins*, followed by *Reasons*, which has the highest number of raw occurrences. *Dawson's Creeks* ranks midway, but the pattern *totally + be* never surfaces. Three out of seven occurrences display in fact the pattern *be + totally + adjective* (exx. 1–3), three contain the combination *totally + lexical verb* (exx. 4–6), and one is an example of *totally* as an adverb of degree modifying an adjective (ex. 7):

(1) I'm totally okay with this question
(2) You guys were totally into it
(3) He was totally hung up on Jen
(4) After you totally busted up my nose
(5) I can totally picture you strolling
(6) We're totally gonna get caught
(7) Because guys are attracted to girls for totally superficial reasons

As Ajimer notices (2011), the main function identified for *totally* in British English is tied to its inclusion in the class of maximizers, that is, adverbs that are used with bounded or ungradable adjectives (Quirk et al. 1985, e.g. *totally dead, totally immoral*), whereas in American English it has begun to collocate with non-bounded adjectives and has developed a scalar use. This shift is explained by Traugott (2007) as triggered by cooperation in interactions (as approximation is found to be desirable in dialogic exchanges) and by a tendency towards hyperbolic expression. Finally, in British English, *totally* seems to elicit a rather negative semantic prosody (defined as 'the spreading of connotational colouring beyond single word boundaries' Partington 1998: 68; see also Partington 2004), which is not the case for American English, as claimed by Aijmer (2011: 160).

In the examples from *Dawson's Creek*, the adjectives and verbs used with *totally* are not all bounded or ungradable. The adjectives that appear in examples (1)–(3) are not 'negative' in meaning and express an emotional involvement or an evaluation of some kind: this confirms the widening of the pattern in American English, in which *totally* has gradually lost the meaning of totality and only specifies a high degree of a quality or property.

Totally sometimes collocates with unbounded verbs, such as *bust up* in (4), *picture* in (5) or *get caught* in (6), thus inducing a bounded interpretation, meaning that the action has been completely carried out or that it is very likely to happen. The latter function is evident in (6), which contains in fact a prediction for the future that the intensifier strengthens in the direction of more likelihood and emotional involvement.

The results for *Skins* are quite interesting and surprising, both because of the relatively high frequency of this intensifier and because the innovative uses which have been pinned down for American English (Aijmer 2011) seem to have spread to British English too. At the time of Aijmer's investigation, *totally* was in fact twice as frequent in American English as in British English (2011: 157). Likewise, Tagliamonte and Roberts (2005: 287) reported that among the intensifiers used in the popular TV series *Friends* (a Canadian production, in theory nearer to British than to American English) *totally* covered only 2.8 per cent of all intensifiers.

Skins's first season was aired in 2007 and the last one in 2013, so slightly after the aforementioned study by Aijmer was published. A viable hypothesis might be that media products sometimes promote innovative variants and novel uses, thus spreading trends that are employed in telecinematic texts to achieve effective characterization (see Mandala 2007). The same tenet is upheld by Tagliamonte and Roberts (2005), who underline how TV talk turns out to be 'a kind of preview of mainstream language', as the language that is employed is normally more innovative 'in the media than in the general population' (2005: 296).

In *Skins*, *totally* appears in four different patterns with different corresponding functions. The most frequent is *be + totally + adjective*, which occurs twelve times (only once with the verb *to be* implicit). Examples (8) and (9) belong to the first type, like (10) and (11), in which the discourse marker *like* precedes the intensifier (the combination of *like* and *totally* in the same utterance has been recognized as typical of informal teen talk, cf. Aijmer 2011: 155).

(8) I'm totally beside myself
(9) She is drunk, you know, totally mental and mistakes me for Tony
(10) It's like totally kind what you're doing
(11) You're like ... totally ...... totally ... fit

The adjectives modified by *totally*, as can be seen from the selection earlier, are pretty well balanced between positive and negative meanings, showing thus no marked preference in terms of semantic prosody.

The second most frequent pattern is that of *totally* as a response item (seven occurrences). Examples (12) to (14) show *totally* as a stand-alone item, accompanied by an interjection in (14). This responsive function, at least in previous studies, was found to be more typical of American English, 7 per cent versus 0.5 per cent for the British variety (Aijmer 2011: 161). In this corpus component, *totally* as a response form represents nearly 30 per cent of the total occurrences (seven out of twenty-four).

(12) You gonna eat this time, Cassie? Totally
(13) Do you know what you're doing? Oh, totally ...
(14) Have you been helping Michelle clear up? Oh, wow, totally

In (12) and (13), *totally* does not convey the idea of 'totality' but represents a subjective evaluation and clarifies the speaker's commitment, so it is a 'lexical resource for emotional highlighting and for strengthening or reinforcing the illocutionary force' (Aijmer 2011: 164). In (14) it is used in combination with the interjection *wow*, which is a typical turn of phrase in the speech of the character who is talking, Cassie. In English, *wow* expresses surprise or astonishment, both positive and negative, but in this utterance, as well as in other examples, it seems to have undergone desemanticization. As a result, its semantic meaning is 'bleached' and it takes on the function of a filler or a marker of uncertainty.

The other pattern is *totally* followed by a lexical verb (five occurrences, see exx. 15–17):

(15) it's too fucked up because she totally loves him
(16) these tablets will totally flush you out within 24 hours
(17) It's, like, you so totally will have to pay them

Here again, the patterns of combination of the intensifier are well assorted: some verbs are gradable, *flush out* and *love*, so in these cases *totally* acts as a booster, and in (17), where it is used in a modal context, it reinforces the deontic strength of the utterance.

Conclusions

My first analysis of the Teen Corpus, triggered by a genuine interest in the language of teenagers as a repository of new trends and uses, suggested several different lines of exploration worth pursuing, in itself and contrasted with comparable data. Although the comparability of telecinematic language with spontaneous language is a controversial issue, both sociolinguists and media scholars have recognized TV talk as a model of innovative and emotional language use, whose pedagogical assets in a language teaching context are manifold: it offers examples of emerging informal and non-standard uses that are in most cases not included in textbooks, and allows students to contextualize language in verisimilar situations, granting at the same time an enjoyable viewing experience (Dose 2013; Jones 2017; Jones and Horák 2014).

In particular, in this chapter, I meant to expand the results obtained in a previous study for a series of markers of teen talk, expressions that usually characterize the language of teenagers. My purpose was to ascertain whether the trends observed for these items in contemporary American TV dramas can be confirmed for

British English too and if they have only just started to appear in the last decade or if they showed incipient signs of development also fifteen to twenty years ago.

To this purpose, I collected the Teen Corpus – part II, containing the first season of *Skins*, a British TV dramedy set in Bristol that was broadcast across the first two decades of the twenty-first century, and the first season of *Dawson's Creek*, an American teen drama that first aired at the end of the 1990s.

Despite the fact that both TV shows focus on adolescents and their school and love lives, the style and registers used are quite dissimilar: rather raw but realistic in *Skins*, more polished and formal in *Dawson's Creek*, as appears from their key word and domain clouds.

Of the two reduced forms *gonna* and *wanna*, the former is more used than the latter, but, as the normalized data in Table 9.1 show, both reduced forms are considerably more frequent in *Skins* than in *Dawson's Creek*, suggesting that frequency is probably linked to genre and style rather than to the language variety, that is, British versus American English. In *Dawson's Creek*, the two non-reduced forms are infinitely more frequent than the reduced ones, a feature that is shared only by another series in the Teen Corpus, that is, *Reasons*, in which *want to* is more than twice as frequent as *wanna*. This trend might be the result of a grammaticalization process that is in a previous stage in comparison to that of *going to* > *gonna*. In *Dawsons' Creek*, instead, the extensive use of the more formal variants *want to/going to* is most likely a reflection of the register of adolescents who talk like thirty-year-olds.

As for the three lexemes chosen as markers of heightened emotions and informality, the new corpus shows different trends: neither *fuck* nor *shit* appear in *Dawson's Creek*, as in *Liars* and *Riverdale*, whereas *Skins* is almost as crude as *Reasons* and abounds in swearing. Taking the whole corpus into account, the address term 'dude' ranks first in *Reasons*, followed by *Dawson's Creek*, two series that do not have much in common apart from the American variety. Probably *dude* is chosen as a privileged vocative in some series, employed especially by boys, and seems to be quite stable, as it was already quite well spread in the 1990s (cf. *Dawson's Creek*) and still is in the 2010s.

The intensifier *totally* deserved a more in-depth analysis, as the category of intensifiers is particularly changeable both syntactically and semantically. Normalized data are illuminating, as *totally* proves to be most frequent in *Skins*, a British production, followed by *Reasons*, while *Dawson's Creeks* ranks midway. What emerged is that *Dawson's Creek* confirms the widening of the pattern of uses of the intensifiers in American English, for example, in the gradual loss of the meaning of totality, with the consequence that it specifies a high degree of a quality or property, and, more in general, emotional highlighting. The outcomes for *Skins* are remarkable, in that the intensifier is very frequent, but most of all because the innovative uses which have been recognized for American English (Aijmer 2011) seem to have broadened to British English too. These findings suggest several facts: first, the scripts were written by Bryan Elsley and Jamie Brittain, father and son (https://www.imdb.com/title/tt0840196/), the latter being obviously well acquainted with teen talk; second, *Skins* might have encapsulated the linguistics reality of British youth in that precise historic moment, which the TV show contributed to promote. Another possible alternative is that some of the innovative variants in *Skins* offered a preview of the language that would be spoken in a while in real life (Tagliamonte and Roberts 2005).

Rather than reaching conclusive findings, this contribution has shown that teen talk is extremely changeable and TV products help linguistic habits to settle. One more aspect that has emerged, however, which would deserve further investigation, is the idiosyncratic choice of giving adolescents the voice of adults in *Dawsons' Creek*. As a result, this show, chosen to account for another decade and previous trends in the language, proves to be quite unique in its type and the mismatch between age and register also casts some doubts on its faithful representation of the time period it portrays.

Notes

1 Tagliamonte (2016: 13) also mentions some corpora collected in the UK, in 1997, 2003 and 2004 in Glasgow, recording young people at different moments and totalling 150,000 words (2002–5) (cf. Stuart-Smith 1999).
2 The three corpus subcomponents contain the following number of words: *Pretty Little Liars*: 318,849; *Riverdale*: 262,843; *13 Reasons Why*: 219,726.
3 According to the *Internet Movie Database* (https://www.imdb.com), *Liars* is described with the labels 'drama', 'mystery', 'romance', *Riverdale* as 'crime', 'drama', 'mystery', and *Thirteen* as 'drama' and 'mystery'.
4 On the whole, they proved to be quite reliable, apart from occasional slips regarding features of orality, like hesitation markers, interjections, dysfluencies and the like. Apparently, this is not of concern for the present book.
5 The TV Corpus, one of the corpora of English available at https://www.english-corpora.org, contains 325 million words of data in 75,000 TV episodes from the 1950s to present. It is much larger than any other corpus of informal English, for example, thirty-three times as large as the spoken component of the BNC. It also allows researchers to investigate variation over time and between dialects.

Web references

http://korpus.uib.no/icame/colt/
https://deadline.com/2011/01/uk-skins-not-as-controversial-as-in-u-s-99292/
https://en.wikipedia.org/wiki/Dawson%27sCreek
https://skins.fandom.com/wiki/Skins_(UK)
https://theconversation.com/why-dawsons-creek-in-all-its-cringey-glory-is-the-tv-show-90s-kids-need-right-now-148539
https://transcripts.foreverdreaming.org/
https://www.imdb.com/title/tt0840196/

References

Aijmer, K. (2011), '"Are You Totally Spy?" A New Intensifier in Present-Day American English', in S. Hancil (ed.), *Marqueurs discursifs et subjectivité (Discursive Markers and Subjectivity)*, 155–72, Rouen: Université de Rouen & Havre.

Androutsopoulos, J. K. (2005), 'Research on Youth Language', in U. Ammon, N. Dittmar, K. J. Mattheier, and P. Trudgill (eds), *Sociolinguistics. An International Handbook of the Science of Language and Society*, Vol. 2, 1496–505, Berlin: de Gruyter.

Androutsopoulos, J. K., and A. Georgakopoulou (2003), 'Discourse Constructions of Youth Identities: Introduction', in J. K. Androutsopoulos, and A. Georgakopoulou (eds), *Discourse Constructions of Youth Identities*, 1–24, Amsterdam: John Benjamins.

Anthony, L. (2019), *AntConc* (Version 3.5.8), Tokyo: Waseda University. Available online: laurenceanthony.net/software/antconc (accessed 25 January 2022).

Bednarek, M. (2018), *Language and Television Series. A Linguistic Approach to TV Dialogue*, Cambridge: Cambridge University Press.

Bednarek, M. (2019), *Creating Dialogue for TV: Screenwriters Talk Television*, London: Routledge.

Biber, D., and F. Barbieri (2007), 'Lexical Bundles in University Spoken and Written Registers', *English for Specific Purposes*, 26: 263–86.

Biber, D., S. Johansson, G. Leech, S. Conrad, and E. Finegan (1999), *Longman Grammar of Spoken and Written English*, Harlow: Pearson Education Limited.

Bruti, S. (2021), 'Teen Talk in TV Series as a Model of Linguistic Innovation and Emotional Language', in V. Werner, and F. Tegge (eds), *Pop Culture in Language Education. Theory, Research, Practice*, 33–49, Abingdon: Routledge.

Catalá Torres, N. (2002), 'Consideraciones acerca de la pobreza expresiva de los jóvenes (Considerations about the Expressive Poverty of Young People)', in F. Rodríguez (ed.), *El lenguaje de los jóvenes (The Language of Adolescents)*, 124–35, Barcelona: Ariel.

Cortes, V. (2002), 'Lexical Bundles in Freshman Composition', in R. Reppen, S. M. Fitzmaurice, and D. Biber (eds), *Using Corpora to Explore Linguistic Variation*, 131–46, Amsterdam and Philadelphia: John Benjamins.

Dose, S. (2013), 'Flipping the Script: A Corpus of American Television Series (CATS) for Corpus-based Language Learning and Teaching', in M. Huber, and J. Mukherjee (eds), *Corpus Linguistics and Variation in English: Focus on Non-native Englishes*, Helsinki: VARIENG. Available online: http://www.helsinki.fi/varieng/series/volumes /13/dose/ (accessed 25 January 2022).

Duff, P. A., and S. Zappa-Hollman (2013), 'Using Popular Culture in Language Teaching', in C. Chapelle (ed.), *The Encyclopedia of Applied Linguistics*, 5997–6002, Malden: Wiley-Blackwell.

Eckert, P. (1997), 'Why Ethnography', in U.-B. Kotsinas, A.-B. Stenström, and A.-M. Karlsson (eds), *Ungdomssprak i Norden: foredrag fran ett forskarsymposium (Youth Language in the Nordic Region: a Lecture from a Research Symposium)*, 52–62, Stockholm: Stockholms Universitet.

Herrero, G. (2002), 'Aspectos sintácticos del lenguaje juvenil (Syntactic Aspects of Youth Language)', in F. Rodríguez (ed.), *El lenguaje de los jóvenes (The Language of Adolescents)*, 67–95, Barcelona: Ariel.

Hills, M. (2004), '*Dawson's Creek*: Quality Teen TV and Mainstream Cult?', in G. Davis, and K. Dickinson (eds), *Teen TV: Genre, Consumption and Identity*, 54–70, London: British Film Institute.

Ito, R., and S. Tagliamonte (2003), 'Well Weird, Right Dodgy, Very Strange, Really Cool: Layering and Recycling in English Intensifiers', *Language in Society*, 32 (02): 257–79.

Jones, C. (2017), 'Soap Operas as Models of Authentic Conversations: Implications for Materials Design', in A. Maley, and B. Tomlinson (eds), *Authenticity in Materials Development for Language Learning*, 158–75, Newcastle: Cambridge Scholars.

Jones, C. and T. Horák (2014), "Leave It Out!' The Use of Soap Operas as Models of Spoken Discourse in the ELT Classroom', *Journal of Language Teaching and Learning*, 4 (1): 1–14.

Jørgensen, A. M. (2010), 'Uso de expresiones vocativas de saludo y despedida en el lenguaje juvenil de Madrid y de Oslo (Use of Vocative Expressions of Greeting and Farewell in Youth Language in Madrid and Oslo)', in M. Penas Ibañez, and R. Martín (eds), *Traducción e interculturalidad: Aspectos teóricos y prácticos (Translation and Interculturality. Theoretical and Practical Aspects)*, 187–9, Bergen: Editorial Cantarabia.

Kotsinas, U.-B. (1992), 'Immigrant Adolescents' Swedish in Multicultural Areas', in C. Palmgren, K. Löfgren, and G. Bolin (eds), *Ethnicity in Youth Culture*, 43–62, Stockholm: Stockholm University.

Labov, W. (1969), *The Study of Nonstandard English*, Washington, DC: Center for Applied Linguistics.

Mandala, S. (2007), 'Solidarity and the Scoobies: An Analysis of the −*y* Suffix in the Television Series *Buffy the Vampire Slayer*', *Language and Literature*, 16 (1): 53–73.

Mortensen J., N. Coupland and J. Thøgersen (2017), 'Introduction: Conceptualizing Style, Mediation, and Change', in J. Mortensen, N. Coupland, and J. Thøgersen (eds), *Style, Mediation, and Change: Sociolinguistic Perspectives on Talking Media*, 1–24, Oxford: Oxford University Press.

Palacios Martínez, I. M. (2011a), 'The Language of British Teenagers: A Preliminary Study of its Main Grammatical Features', *ATLANTIS: Journal of the Spanish Association of Anglo-American Studies*, 33 (1): 105–26.

Palacios Martínez, I. M. (2011b), 'The Expression of Negation in British Teenagers' Language. A Preliminary Study', *Journal of English Linguistics*, 39 (1): 4–35.

Partington, A. S. (1998), *Patterns and Meanings. Using Corpora for English Language Research and Teaching*. Amsterdam: John Benjamins.

Partington, A. S. (2004), 'Utterly Content in Each Other's Company. Semantic Prosody and Semantic Preference', *International Journal of Corpus Linguistics*, 9 (1): 131–56.

Partington, A. S., A. Duguid, and C. Taylor (2013), *Patterns and Meanings in Discourse. Theory and Practice in Corpus-assisted Discourse Studies (CADS)*, Amsterdam: John Benjamins.

Quirk, R., S. Greenbaum, G. Leech, and I. Svartvik (1985), *A Comprehensive Grammar of English*, London: Longman.

Rayson, P. (2003), 'Matrix: A Statistical Method and Software Tool for Linguistic Analysis Through Corpus Comparison', PhD thesis, University of Lancaster.

Rodríguez González, F. (2002), 'Lenguaje y contracultura juvenil: Anatomía de una generación (Language and Youth Counterculture: Anatomy of a Generation)', in F. Rodríguez González (ed.), *El lenguaje de los jóvenes (The Language of Adolescents)*, 29–55, Barcelona: Ariel.

Rodríguez González, F., and A.-B. Stenström (2011), 'Expressive Devices in the Language of English and Spanish-speaking Youth', *Revista Alicantina de Estudios Ingleses*, 24: 235–56.

Romaine, S. (1984), *The Language of Children and Adolescents: The Acquisition of Communicative Competence*, Malden: Blackwell.

Stenström, A.-B. (1997), '"Can I Have a Chips Please? – Just Tell Me What One You Want": Nonstandard Grammatical Features in London Teenage Talk', in J. Aarts, I. De Mönnink, and H. Wekker (eds), *Studies in English Language and Teaching*, 141–51, Amsterdam: Rodopi.

Stenström, A.-B. (1998), 'From Sentence to Discourse: *Cos (because)* in Teenage Talk', in A. H. Jucker, and Y. Ziv (eds), *Discourse Markers: Description and Theory*, 127–46, Amsterdam: John Benjamins.

Stenström, A.-B. (2014), *Teenage Talk: From General Characteristics to the Use of Pragmatic Markers in a Contrastive Perspective*, Basingstoke: Palgrave Macmillan.

Stenström, A.-B., G. Andersen, and I. K. Hasund (2002), *Trends in Teenage Talk: Corpus Compilation. Analysis and Findings*, Amsterdam: John Benjamins.

Stenström, A.-B., and A. M. Jørgensen (2009), *Youngspeak in a Multilingual Perspective*, Amsterdam: John Benjamins.

Stuart-Smith, J. (1999), 'Glottals Past and Present: A Study of T-glottaling in Glaswegian', *Leeds Studies in English*, 30: 181–204.

Tagliamonte, S. (2016), *Teen Talk: The Language of Adolescents*, Cambridge: Cambridge University Press.

Tagliamonte, S., and C. Roberts (2005), 'So Weird; So Cool; So Innovative: The Use of Intensifiers in the Television Series *Friends*', *American Speech*, 80 (3): 280–300.

Traugott, E. (1994), 'Grammaticalization and Lexicalization', in E. Ronald, and J. M. Y. Simpson (eds), *The Encyclopedia of Language and Linguistics*, 1481–6, Oxford: Pergamon Press.

Traugott, E. (2007), 'The Concept of Constructional Mismatch and Type Shifting from the Perspective of Grammaticalization', *Cognitive Linguistics*, 18 (4): 523–57.

Trotta, J. (2018), 'Pop Culture and Linguistics – Is That, like, a Thing Now?', in V. Werner (ed.), *The Language of Pop Culture*, 27–45, New York: Routledge.

10

An Appraisal Approach to Emotion, Culture and Discourse in Audio Description

Exploring Audio Description Quality in Turkey

Hilal Erkazanci Durmuş and Şirin Okyayuz

Introduction

This chapter seeks to explore Turkish audio describers' perception of quality in audio description (AD) and pinpoint how the Turkish tradition of audio description approaches the emotional and cultural information inscribed in the visual images of audiovisual products. Underlining that the intersemiotic transfer of visual messages into the verbal modality necessitates the evaluative investment of audio describers, the study suggests that the appraisal system provides fruitful framework for the analysis of lexical realizations of evaluation. AD is based on a complex process of decision making regarding the use of mostly silent intervals in the audiovisual products ranging from films to theatre performances in order to compose a verbal description of the scenery, actions, body language and other details pertinent to the audiovisual content. The study argues that the appraisal system provides valuable insight into the exploration of how quality can be achieved in AD.

Appraisal can be described as a set of linguistic resources which are used to express judgements, emotions and valuations. Since audio describers' emotions are based on their evaluations (i.e. appraisals or assumptions) of the verbal utterances and visual elements, their appraisal of the audiovisual product results in an emotional or affective response that influences both the meaning-making process involved in AD (i.e. how the AD narrative is produced) and its reception (e.g. blind and partially sighted people's comprehension of the audio-described content). In this context, concentrating on a range of examples provided by SEBEDER, an institution in Turkey that delivers audio-described products, subtitling and sign-language interpreting services in various genres ranging from films to advertisements, this chapter sets out to explore the application of James Martin and Peter White's (2005) appraisal system to the exploration of quality in AD.

AD is written as a form of interaction between the audiovisual product and the audience, which also leads to an interaction between the audio describer and the audience, since it carries a message that would both guide the visually impaired end users' thoughts and emotions and motivate them to internalize the product being audio described. It is also significant to note that AD is also at the service of other audiences such as the cognitively challenged, the elderly who have trouble accessing the visual track, any individual (such as long-distance drivers) who do not have access to the visual track or housewives who wish to follow shows while doing housework.

At this point, it is worth noting that, in addition to conveying ideational and textual meanings, the wording of the AD narrative encodes interpersonal meaning which is based on the expression of the audio describer's attitude. In this context, an appraisal framework can help us explain how speakers (in the present study, audio describers) express emotions, whether they amplify or blur the emotional signifiers, and how they integrate visual messages into the verbal discourse (Martin and White 2005). Furthermore, given that the same appraisal resource might lead to variance in emotions across cultures, the appraisal system can help us analyse the potential motivations underlying audio describers' choices and preferences.

The appraisal system presents a framework for the evaluative language used in the communication of emotions and judgements. It differentiates between different types of attitude (personal affect, judgement of people and perception of culture-specific visual objects) and can help describe how audio describers use language to convey the meaning potential of the visual elements (e.g. visual cues which are necessary to interpret some sound effects). The appraisal system is based on lexical rather than grammatical resources through which speakers and writers express and negotiate meaning; therefore, this study is concerned with the words and semantic categories of words which audio describers use to express the non-verbal content of the audiovisual products they are working on.

Audio describers are responsible for analysing the original product and all its layers (the audial and visual channels and the product as a whole, etc.) and for identifying what is to be audio described (what is central information, what can also be inferred from the audial channel, what the intended sense/meaning of the visual channel and the whole of the product is, etc.). The fundamental starting point for audio description is the identification of what to describe, such as information about who is in the scene, who is speaking, the setting and the scene, entries and exits, the ambiance, the lighting, dominant colour themes, costumes, physical attributes of the characters, facial expressions, movement, fights, dances, the origins of sounds, written information displayed in the visual channel, and the like and how this is to be done (what are the silent intervals that can be used for audio description in the product, how long these are, what other sounds besides dialogues that can be voiced over those which cannot, etc.) (Okyayuz 2017; Beneke 2004: 1). The audio describer then prepares a text which is composed with due consideration of the aim, scope and intended message of the original product and if this professional is working in the most widespread type of AD and not extended AD the limitations of the audial track. This text is edited by a visually impaired editor working with the audio description text writer and then the audio describer (this may be the same person writing the text or someone else) adds this text to the product.

In the process described earlier, there are two intertwined points which the appraisal system can illuminate: (i) the way audio describers use language to perform speech functions unfolding in the original material such as questioning, forecasting and so on and (ii) the way their AD generates specific emotions and responses on the part of the audience. These two points are also significant for the consideration of how quality can be achieved in the AD practice because some cases in which audio description is implemented only at face value (i.e. the recitation of selective features of the visual channel as an audial channel) usually ends up with products that purport to be audio described but are not accessible. Therefore, the evaluative judgements of audio describers play a key role in the service of the quality of the AD product, since their personal, evaluative involvement in the AD narrative is revealed as they take stances towards the visual objects, happenings and situations being construed by the AD narrative.

Against the backdrop of these points, this chapter will shed light on how the quality of AD may be influenced by audio describers' delivery of emotions and non-verbal culture-specific elements and by the discourse-specific characteristics of their AD. As a case in point, the study will focus on SEBEDER, the oldest and most experienced group of audio describers in Turkey that was initially established by the end user's community itself in 2006. Working with industry stakeholders, end users and regulators, the association has vast experience in terms of end user's desires in the Turkish setting. Thus, the association has been able to develop a quality assessment management system, a guideline for practices, and to form an AD community of audio describers, technical experts and editors/evaluators in addition to a feedback network from end users.

The chapter presents an account of a focus-group research based on a semi-structured interview with SEBEDER to answer the following question which in turn help identify the benchmarks of quality in AD in Turkey: what features lead an end user to label an AD as inaccessible or of low quality? SEBEDER responds to this question by answering two relevant sub-questions: What should be audio described and how should it be described? SEBEDER's answers to the sub-questions are based on the specific examples that would illustrate its decisions on the content of AD and on the strategies its members use for AD. SEBEDER's examples which respond to this chapter's 'what' and 'how' questions are to be analysed considering the appraisal system. The answers given by the members of SEBEDER will further elucidate the institution's identification of the main pillars of audio description in Turkey.

In line with these points, this chapter is organized in five sections. The following section presents the study's analytical framework based on appraisal theory. The third section concentrates on an overview of audio description in Turkey to contextualize SEBEDER's framing of quality in audio-described products. The fourth section dwells on the aim, method and composition of our focus-group study to identify SEBEDER's stance towards quality in AD. The fourth section largely draws on appraisal theory to describe how the members of SEBEDER approach the intermodal reconstruction (visual to verbal) of the audiovisual product and the way they verbalize the visual message to create accessible or high-quality AD products. The conclusion section summarizes the key findings and makes recommendations for further studies.

Analytical Framework

The appraisal system is based on three semantic resources, namely attitude, graduation and engagement, which ensure an exploration of 'the semantic resources used to negotiate emotions, judgments and valuation, alongside resources for amplifying and engaging with these evaluation' (Martin 2000: 145). Attitude deals with speakers' and writers' 'feelings, judgements of behaviour and evaluations of things' and is categorized into effect, judgement and appreciation (Martin and White 2005). Affect is utilized to convey emotions about a person's reactions (e.g. happiness, sorrow); judgement foregrounds evaluations of a person's character in accordance with social norms (e.g. moral, deceitful) or evaluations of attitudes towards human behaviour (e.g. compliment, condemn); and appreciation foregrounds evaluations of the aesthetic qualities of semiotic phenomena (e.g. beautiful, disgusting).

Attitude is complemented by the subsystem of graduation, which is concerned with how the value of attitudes can be increased or toned down in the discourse. Graduation deals both with force through which speakers or writers can intensify or mitigate meaning (e.g. totally joyful, slightly anxious) and with focus through which they can sharpen or soften meaning (e.g. genuinely confident, kind of happy). Finally, engagement 'is concerned with the ways in which resources [. . .] position the speaker/writer with respect to the value position being advanced and with respect to potential responses to that value position' (Martin and White 2005: 36). In this context, engagement deals with the choices of monogloss (using categorical statements to create common values with the audience by presenting something as being common sense) and heterogloss (opening alternative ideas or supressing potential responses). Some of the examples of engagement are the use of 'possibly' (e.g. he possibly thinks that it is not true), 'there is no doubt' (e.g. there is no doubt that she feels better now), 'allege' (e.g. he tried to protect himself against alleged threats) and so on.

As such, appraisal resources can be used in the analysis of how visual meaning is conveyed to the audience with a view to exploring an evaluative stance in visual-verbal texts (e.g. Economou 2009). Appraisal resources can also be used to investigate the intermodal construction (visual-verbal) of discourse (Oteiza and Pinuer 2016). Appraisal semantics is further applied to the analysis of lyrics through which composers convey their emotions to their audience (e.g. Yuningsih 2018). At this point, it is worth noting that appraisal theory facilitates the analysis of translations; hence, it is used to see how translatorial choices may influence the reception of translations (Munday 2015). It is emphasized that appraisal theory helps the researcher 'study the expression of feelings, emotions, viewpoints, and intersubjective positioning in translation' (Tajvidi and Arjani 2017). The appraisal system is also applied to the subtitles of movies with a view to assessing the quality in translation (e.g. Khosravani 2019). Along similar lines, this study underlines that appraisal resources would be used to analyse how emotion-based cues are used by audio describers to facilitate the target audience's access to affective markers in audiovisual narratives, and by extension, to investigate how the quality would be attained by audio describers.

AD in Turkey

Though audio description existed in Turkey, just like in any other country, as an unprofessional practice in daily life for the visually impaired, the initiation of audio description in media products at the professional level starts with the founders of SEBEDER (the Audio Description Association). The journey of the association is written up on their website and provides the following information (SEBEDER, Hakkımızda 2021).

The association describes audio description as the depiction of the visual and the emotions through a description of the space, time, characters, and visually relayed events among other things through an added voice-over to silent intervals in products for the stage, theatre and other mediums to provide access for the visually impaired. Initial audio description efforts of the founders of the association started in 2006 at the Mithat Alam Film Center at Boğaziçi University; in 2010, the practice gained an institutional structure with the establishment of SEBEDER (the Audio Description Association).

SEBEDER is the first institution established in Turkey for the specific purpose of providing audio description and media accessibility. The association lists several short-, mid- and long-term aims as their goals that all concentrate on accessibility for all on all platforms. The association has several impressive achievements up to date: the provision of audio-described audiovisual material to many channels, platforms and film festivals; the establishment of an online audio-described film repository for the visually impaired of different interests and age groups; audio-described versions of ballet and opera performances by state institutions and municipalities; audio description for resources for disaster management; work with international institutions such as the UN in the provision of audio-described material; and so many others. The association currently has two other departments providing similar services in intra-lingual SDH and signed language interpreting. The association also has completed several important multi-partner projects with universities, other NGOs and government offices. With its impressive track record and by virtue of being the first in the field, the association also houses the most experienced audio describers in Turkey. It provides a several month-long training programme for those individuals who would like to join their group of audio describers. The experience of the association serves as a foundation to discover the culture of audio description and the discourse of audio description in the Turkish setting.

Focus-group Study

Method

The chapter aimed to identify and professionally analyse the reasons behind the 'low-quality products' that end users have been complaining about in Turkey recently through insight provided by the experienced audio describers group at SEBEDER to improve audio description quality.

The focus group specifically concentrated on highlighting issues such as the pillars of the audio description culture in Turkey (and in the world), the style and discourse of audio description with an added emphasis on objectivity and the relaying of intent and emotion in audio-described products.

The focus group consisted of five profiles of participants:

a. the audio description text writer;
b. the professional that writes the texts and verbalizes the textsl
c. audio description trainers with experience in audio description practice;
d. researchers of audio description; and
e. professionals coordinating audio description services.

Some participants fit more than one of the profiles stated previously, allowing them to contribute from multiple perspectives.

A series of questions and a template were used to conduct a semi-structured interview with the focus group.

Each participant was given the opportunity to speak, and the answers, comments, examples and the like were recorded and written up in a report delivered to SEBEDER and published online by the association (see: Sesli Betimlemelerde İyi Uygulamalar Nasıl olmalı?SEBEDER- 20.03.2021 /11:30-13:00/ZOOM.http://sebeder.org/Sesli_Betimlemelerde_Iyi_Uygulamalar_Nasil_olmali_-1827.html).

The focus-group work was undertaken at the suggestion of and for the association and included their own employees from which they had received consent to run the focus group. The academics in the process were also participants but were not the initiators of the process; the experts were asked to observe and draft the final report.

It is important to note that most of what the audio describers discussed has already been discussed extensively in the literature of the field. Some of the points they raised, especially in the details of strategies, or the views of the

Turkish end users, may be 'new information', but in many cases the information they provided, as can be verified with the references provided to highlight points throughout the analysis section of the chapter, is not new. But what makes their focus group output enlightening and important may be explained as follows:

a) They verify that what has been deemed as good practice in other settings is also good practice in Turkey, thus supporting the notion of certain universal standards.
b) They underline the importance of end user cooperation and input basing their discussions constantly on input they received from blind editors, end users thus serving as a voice of quality through their work.
c) They refer to specific examples of what happens when an unprofessional self-proclaimed audio describer undertakes the task.
d) In referring to specific strategies and examples, they provide a more concrete outline of what to do and what not to do than the generalist guidelines usually given by media providers.

Analysis

The participants in the focus-group research initially wished to identify the main pillars of AD before dwelling on the present study's central research question regarding what features lead an end user to label an AD as inaccessible or of low quality. To begin with, the tradition of audio description employed by the families of the visually impaired is seen as an initial pillar for the practice of audio describing the emotional and cultural content of the visual scenes. Neither in Turkey nor anywhere else in the world is audio description a type of translation that has been concocted by practitioners. Pujol and Orero (2007) are among a group of scholars who relay that this type of accessibility is not new and has existed for many centuries. As opposed to other translation types for accessibility audio description has been used to access the world by the visually impaired since they could grasp language. But, until 1985 it is not possible to refer to a set of guidelines that have been embraced and implemented widely for audio description (Udo, Acevedo and Fels 2010). Snyder (2007) details how this type of access was provided by the relatives and friends of the visually impaired as a recitation of what they deemed to be important in the visual of products. The families of the visually impaired used audio description as a tool to acquaint the blind individual with the world and allow them to watch television and cinema and so on. In this way the families of the blind are themselves audio describers.

These amateur audio describers, in accordance with their relation to the blind individual (e.g. as a mother, a younger sibling, an older sibling), learning from each other and the blind individual through observation, develop a style and manner of audio describing. This is not a professional process; it develops based on experience, observation and interaction and is a natural process. The purpose of the act is to facilitate the access of the blind individual to the world.

In turn, these traditions become important departure points on which to base professional audio description practice. The blind themselves have the most know-how about these endeavours and have internalized these styles. Thus, it falls to audio describers who have no visual impairment to work with blind editors and advisors to understand this 'blind culture and tradition'. Working together with the community and designing the process inclusively is integral to bringing in this experience that is the first pillar of audio description in a culture.

According to the group, the second pillar of audio description are the products and the services that have been provided and deemed to serve their purposes by the end users. An evaluation on the quality of audio description can at times be subjective. A product deemed to be of quality for some may not be considered so by others. Also, ages, experience with products with audio description and their habits will also be extremely relevant to their judgement of a products' quality (Szymanska and Zabrocka 2015: 117). But if the researcher or the audio describer digs deep enough, they will find that there are some common criteria. For example, everyone will agree that a subtitle that appears on the screen for a single second and even if it conveys the exact same message as the original is too long to read in that duration, it is of low quality. In the same vein, every descriptive recitation added to the silent slots of a product is not an audio description since it may not provide access to the product if not designed in a certain manner.

Even though there are other criteria for assessing quality, one of the most important benchmarks is previous examples that have been tested and approved by the users. If a certain style and approach to audio description has been developed and furthermore has evolved through time and feedback from end users stating that it provided access or should be tweaked in a certain manner to provide access, this is the style and practice of audio description embraced by the end users and it needs to be considered as a second pillar of the audio description tradition in a setting.

Of course, in no way is this cumulative practice absolute; it is always upon to development and change. But, audio describers firmly state that through time end users develop an 'ear for a certain style of audio description' (i.e. a hearing-access-habit for a better description). Thus, it becomes important for the audio describer to internalize the products and practices that have been embraced. If not, a new approach or practice that is implemented for the sake of innovation may not serve the purpose of accessibility. The addition of an AD track may give the impression that access has been provided to the product, when in reality, if it does not reflect the pillars and traditions the end users will deem this to be of poor quality and furthermore will be under the impression that they have not been afforded a service that hinges on their sensitivities and desires. This type of an endeavour points to a venture undertaken by a seeing group that dictates how audio description should be to the end users and is a direct violation of the principle of 'nothing about us without us'.

Thus, the second pillar of high-quality AD is embracing previous practices and learning from these. It also needs to be underlined that AD is not a static practice and will develop over time in all cultures through new technologies, training and so on. But the change should be guided by the correct teams and the best perspectives.

The third pillar of AD, according to the focus group, is the joint decisions of the AD team. The AD team is composed of the AD text writer, the person who verbalizes the text (may be the same person) and the blind editor. In this scenario, there is a collaboration between the professional producing the AD and the end user editing it. In order for AD to develop through time, for it to reflect what is deemed as good practice by the end users, for the practice to be able to deal with (come up with strategies to overcome) the challenges culminating from the constraints of the type and the expectations and aims, in short for the translation to serve its purpose of providing accessibility, it is vital for the end users to be included in the process as editors.

The fourth pillar of audio description according to the team of experts is the appropriation of good practices and examples from other languages, cultures and platforms when necessary. AD is practised in many countries. There are professionals and media providers with vast experience in the practice. Furthermore, there is extensive research on the subject. There are also particular good practices appreciated by the end users. This is something that needs to be weighed in when striving to produce high-quality products. In consideration of the traditions and previous examples, in a language and culture appropriating 'good examples' from another, this needs to mean that other practices not yet approved by that specific end user group be brought in as 'best practices'. The important point is to move from the current accumulation in each culture (learning from good examples and learning what to avoid from bad examples) and designing a modelling, training that embraces a solid foundation.

The different forms of description and oral recitation traditions in different countries is also an added challenge in audio description. Storytelling and description techniques that evolve differently in countries effect audio description (Orero 2008: 180). Even though description of a visual is viewed as a universal experience, there are different approaches in countries. Thus, it is important to investigate the traditions in each country. Only when the product is fashioned in line with the style choices of previously acknowledged high-quality products does the product achieve cohesion and coherence for the users. In short, according to the focus group, any AD designed without due attention to the AD traditions in a given country, that does not take into account the repertoire composed thus far, that is not vetted by the lenses of the blind editors and users and is not open to development is going to be considered as poor-quality work by the end users in the Turkish culture.

It is vital that the effect, the message and the sense of the original visual track be relayed in a complete manner. For example, the directions in a script may guide the director in providing the visual track, but these directions cannot serve as the basis of an AD text. Unfortunately, there have been examples in Turkey where these have been used as the basis of an AD text. The importance of a feature in a certain scene (whether this will be included in the AD or not) will change from one product to another and the meaning units in the original and the way that these are utilized.

Having identified the four points summarized previously as the main pillars of AD, the participants moved on to discussing the sub-questions as to 'what should be described in AD' and 'how it should be described' (e.g. concerns about using plain, clear and communicative language; the use of complete sentences unless otherwise necessary or explaining references when using concise language; a discourse befitting the discourse of the original product; not using terminology intense language; the use of a politically correct discourse; non-repetitive structures and words). Their discussion is informed by a focus on emotional and cultural accessibility in AD.

Emotional Accessibility in AD

The audio description of emotions, along with the emotion relayed through audio description (the first is produced intentionally by the product, the actors, music setting, the second in implied through one of these and produced by the audio describer), occupied a significant place in the focus-group discussions. The participants place heavy emphasis on the manner and extent to which emotions should be integrated into the AD narrative. The discussions reveal that certain appraisal resources which audio describers use facilitate the accessibility of emotions. Therefore, the audio describers accentuate that the denseness (i.e. the wordiness and the information load) of an AD text needs to be guided by the original product. For example, where the description of the full sexy lips of a female character may be important in a romantic comedy, the same may not be important in the depiction of a female character in a short documentary about women's rights. In the first instance, the portrayal of the female character's full lips is considered within the appraisal category of appreciation (i.e. assessment of the woman's physical appearance) that becomes an indispensable part of reaping the full comedy effect, whereas the depiction of full lips may be considered redundant information which needs to be omitted in the second instance. Another relevant example is the audio description of red lipstick. Whereas the visual details of a character's sexy red lipstick do not facilitate the target audience's enjoyment of comedic elements in a scene, the wearing of red lipstick may be evaluated in line with the appraisal category of judgement (i.e. assessment of behaviour with regard to social events or norms) in a film with feminist overtones in that red lipstick has become a symbol of female emancipation after red lipsticks were handed out to the suffragettes to enhance female empowerment in the suffrage movement. Therefore, the audio describer's delivery of red lipstick would invoke in the target audience a judgement of protest in the relevant scene.

The statements of the audio describers in the focus-group study further reveal that the appraisal category of judgement (i.e. attitudes towards behaviours) highly influences the word choices of the audio describers who seek to communicate the evaluative content of the audiovisual product. A case in point is *Mr. Bean*. Since the visual characterization of the protagonist departs from the conventional hegemonic image of masculinity on television, the audio describer's production of judgemental meaning, which is inscribed in the visual material, is of utmost importance. For instance, certain appraisal epithets of judgement (e.g. clumsy, fumbling, awkwardly, inaptly, botch, bungle, screw up) meticulously chosen by the audio describer would invoke in the target audience the impression that the image of an unsophisticated man ironically represents the 'other' that contrasts with the male body which represents both physical strength and heterosexual appeal. Along similar lines, the degree of negative appreciation which is expressed in relation to the concept of masculinity would also play a significant role in the AD. That is, the appraisal resource of appreciation (i.e. evaluation of natural phenomena and things) used to audio describe Mr Bean's body as slender and androgynous would, for instance, signal that the representation of masculinity in the comedy programme goes against the grain of the conventional media image of the strong and healthy male body.

Another example that reveals the significance of appraisal resources in the audio describer's delivery of the visualized emotional message is an episode where it is implied that Mr Bean has a girlfriend. Even though the episode neither visually nor verbally indicates any sort of sexual attraction, physical intimacy or exchange of emotional affection between the two protagonists, the only visual clue regarding their relationship would be the audio describer's focus on the feeling of envy on the part of Mr Bean. That is, the visual message which demonstrates that a suitor at a disco aroused Mr Bean's envy would imply to the target audience that they are more than ordinary friends. This point reveals that audio describers' verbalization of visual messages as an indicator of affect is essential for the construal of the emotive dimension of meaning.

Another point that concerns the audio describers in our focus group is related to the intensity value by which they graduate (i.e. increase or lower), the interpersonal impact of their descriptions and by which they blur or sharpen emotional meaning. Therefore, in the case of subtly or highly nuanced emotional content in an audiovisual product, they act in line with a scalar system with which appraisal semantics is largely concerned. The audio describers first identify the mental and emotional states of the protagonists and then they decide, for instance, whether a protagonist is contented, happy, joyous or ecstatic. Given that the intensity value of these adjectives ranges from a continuous scale extending from low to high, the appraisal category of focus plays a fundamental role in the narrative meaning-making. The same point also holds for the use of verbs in AD. For instance, the verbs that denote emotions are graded by the audio describers between the lower and higher-valued ends of a scale of intensity, as is the case in the lexicalizations that grade along dislike, hate and detest.

The audio describers are also aware of the fact that a meticulous 'reading' of facial expressions, body gestures and/or instances of emotive prosody helps them decide upon whether a protagonist feels, for instance, kind of upset or genuinely upset. At this point, the appraisal resources of force play a significant role. In cases where audio describers inadvertently raise or lower the force of their descriptions, they would in turn run the risk of increasing or decreasing the target audience's personal investment in other meanings circulated by the narrative of the audiovisual product. In this context, it is necessary to note that the audio describers stated that the use of adjectival and adverbials served as a major tool in relaying the intended emotion of the original. The too frequent and intense use of these tools may decrease the quality of the text, but a text devoid of adverbials or adjectivals is also deemed to be a dry rendition of what is essentially emotive (fictional) content. The selection of what is to be relayed is also a major marker for the emotion to be depicted.

Sometimes reiterations and repetitions may be used to highlight an important emotion. The length of sentences is also associated with emotion as well as the pauses between phrases in a sentence and in between sentences. The professionals state that coma and full stop are used to create emotive effect, just as the length of a sentence is influential in relaying emotional impact (e.g. 'her eyes closed, her hand went limp as she gave her last breath and died' versus 'She stopped breathing. . . . She died.'). At some points in the verbalization, it is important to allow for the sound effects to be fitted into the AD text. For example, to stop mid-sentence and continue after the effect sound (e.g. She ran to the stairs. . . . (falling sound) she fell two flights). The above-listed are some of the major strategies used to relay the intended emotion in a source text.

On the other hand, it is also worth noting that sometimes emotion is already relayed through the soundtrack and the music of the original. For example, the music used in the Turkish film *Babam ve Oğlum* harps on people's emotions and is central to the melodrama in the product. The product itself relays emotion through the soundtrack, and the extra layer of the depiction of the details of a mimic may at this point become redundant and invasive in terms of detracting from the coherence of the original.

When trying to chart where emotion comes into play in AD, the audio describers tried to outline instances. Whereas the professionals were adamant that their feelings need not enter the picture stating that as individuals they inevitably feel something (positive or negative) for the original they should follow the direction of the camera and storyline. Perspective and the order are imperative in audio description. Furthermore this should not be a recitation but it should be a description thus the story needs to be prioritized in terms of the individual scenes. At this interval, the professionals underlined the centrality of analysing the product from an objective perspective and spotting the intended emotion and relaying this in the AD. The emotion intended by the original holds the key to the emotional load and emotional message to be relayed in the AD.

In referring to feeling empathy with source AV products, all professionals said that in their experience this is partially always true. For example, there were those professionals who chose not to provide AD for a genre such as horror films or films with pornographic content. Once the audio describer sits to provide AD for a source, it is inevitable through the deconstruction of the visual that they feel a sense of empathy even when they do not necessarily like or agree with the message of the source.

The audio describers in the focus-group study further state that in the Turkish case the frequency and the density of AD can sometimes be a slippery slope. In some cases, in the Turkish tradition, the end users will report that they had the feeling that something was not being relayed if the silent interval is long (even a few seconds); thus, Turkish audio describers tend to refrain from leaving too many silent intervals without AD. But on the other hand, they must balance this with making sure that they are not producing verbal garbage that does not facilitate access or repetition of the information that is already provided by the audial track (e.g. the sounds of a storm) or repeating themselves. In such cases, the end users also comment on this extensive AD as a negative feature.

For example, in a scene where the AD has already provided information about a character crying and the scene continues for a certain duration, the audio describer will not choose to insert AD texts such as 'a tear drop is dripping down her right cheek, another drops down her left'. The professional will allow the audience to wallow in the feeling of the scene they have already described and can be further accessed through the crying sound on the audial track. But in the case, where in the audial the character is heard to be crying uncontrollably whereas in the visual no tears are seen this becomes vital information and the AD text reads 'she is not shedding tears' as this may point to other things such as the characters' inability to feel and reflect emotion, the character faking crying and so on.

In other cases, it is vital that the audio describer remains silent. If a character is walking down a lonely village road to the backdrop of melancholic music, the professionals have experienced that it is best to allow the end users to feel this loneliness (to hear the desperation of the loneliness) through silence and the music. At this juncture, the number of apples on the branch of a tree on the side of the road is redundant information, and not useful for processing the message. Allowing the end users the experience of living the intended sense and feeling of an AV product is an important feature; this needs to be balanced with concerns about how long the silent interval needs to continue.

The audio describers state that frequently the urge is to move with the motto 'we should ensure that if we access this our end users can too' and the idea that 'there should not be anything missing'. Thus, at first the text they produce tends to be quite long and dense even though it does fit into the designated time slots. In such cases, when self-editing the text, they tend to delete some portions and make it more concise in line with the idea of not formulating a text that will impair cognition. In such a demanding process, the resources of appraisal help serve audio describers' intention of fully engaging the target audience with the emotions and displays of socio-affective communication in the audiovisual product.

Cultural Accessibility in AD

The analysis of our discussion with the focus group reveals that the same appraisal resource might give rise to a range of variance in emotions across cultures. Therefore, the same culture-specific visual elements may be rendered into differing audio descriptions in different cultures. As Raquel Sans-Moreno (2017: 538) suggests, audio describers serve as 'mediator[s] between cultures; that is why the greater the cultural distance, the higher their presence and involvement'. Diaz Cintas (2007: 49–58) outlines a long list of competences an audio describer needs to have, one of which is the ability to serve as an expert mediator in multicultural settings. In this context, the task of an audio describer who is responsible for composing an intersemiotic rendition of cultural images into words is comparable to that of a translator who is responsible for carrying out intercultural mediation, given that not all cultures interpret cultural and emotional markers in the same way.

To start with, the first example given by the audio describers in our focus group is concerned with the dialectal phrases and words which convey different emotional messages to the target audience. To illustrate, the audio describers note that the Turkish style *gevrek* that resembles a bagel is more than food in western Turkey, since it is part and parcel of the local gastronomic identity of those living in the Aegean region of the country. Given that food carries cultural connotations in some audiovisual products, audio describers' assessment of foods in terms of how they are assigned social value (in appraisal terms, appreciation) gains significance in the audio description of the crispy and crunchy *gevrek* with due regard to the emotions (e.g. solidarity between rich and poor, sense of sharing, nostalgia) it invokes in Turkish society. By the same token, it is necessary to note that even in Turkish society there exists a dialectal and hence cultural difference between the Turkish *gevrek* and *simit* both of which refer to the same food yet have different emotional connotations.

Another example worth noting is the taboo elements. The verbalization of sex scenes may be toned down in various cultures where political correctness largely prevails. There always exists a possibility that audio describers avoid certain appraisal resources, such as adjectives and, in certain cases, even the visual scenes themselves (e.g. licking beautiful fake boobs) in order not to offend the religious and/or moral sensibilities of the target audience. In such cases, the audio descriptions produced by the audio describers tend to be less descriptive and more narrative, omitting the visual details of the tabooed acts. The audio describers in the focus group resort to the appraisal resource of graduation in such cases where they need to mitigate the sexual appeal (e.g. the use of 'intimate relationship' to render 'harsh blowjob') or entirely blur sexuality.

At this juncture, it is significant to point out that audio describers may have to work with source texts they do not like or empathize with; or texts that voice views they are opposed to. In such instances, it becomes even more important for the audio describer to take care to be impartial and objective and not to paint the text with their brush of emotion and thought. Researchers stress the importance of describing what appears in the scene (i.e. objects and people) and what is happening in the story (i.e. the flow of the storyline) in addition to how this is relayed (i.e. the camera angles, the distance, the perspective) and the effect created through these features (i.e. the intended effect) (Kruger 2010: 233–4). The widespread, accepted criteria are the verbalization of the visual to the extent that the movement and flow and interaction is relayed without subjective verbalization.

If there are cases where this sensitive balance is not achieved and objectivity is jeopardized or unrealistically implemented, this may result in an unrealistic product (Finbow 2010: 215). Objectivity in audio description has been researched extensively and the extent this is to be implemented is also being questioned. Ramos Caro (2016) underlines the imperative that cinema offers a strong emotional experience and the intent of audio description needs to entail a similar objective; thus, emotion needs to be a feature of audio description. Since like every translation it is in the end a man-made product it is impossible to talk about full objectivity.

Along similar lines, cultural symbols which are based on patriarchal values in certain societies carry a heavy emotional baggage that would create a challenge in the AD. For instance, many Turkish films are laden with patriarchal symbols, such as the red ribbon tied over the bride's wedding dress to represent virginity and virtue. The bridegroom's hanging of bloodied sheets also has similar connotations. In the case of such sensitive images, where one audio describer resorts to the appraisal resource of judgement (i.e. evaluating human behaviour in line with social norms) in order to foreground social esteem (e.g. by verbalizing female purity, morality, and decency in the AD) associated with the red ribbon and the bloodied sheet, an activist audio describer would wish to avoid describing those ideological–patriarchal messages, considering that the verbalization of such scenes would exacerbate social intrusion into the female body. In such instances, it is necessary to bear in mind that the message of the whole of an AV product is a construct derived from the individual scenes that compose it. So, there are two levels of analysis that are central: one is the analysis of the overall message and then the analysis of the importance and the intention of each visual within this framework.

A concept that all audio describers in the focus group highlighted as being essential was the concept of objectivity in AD composition. They stated that providing an objective text is essentially an ideal to be embraced but also explained that every audio describer will approach the text through their own accumulation and world knowledge and analyse the original to the best of their individual abilities. Thus, objectivity cannot be absolute but measured in terms of degrees.

Only describing what is seen is a must for objectivity. But it is not a definition of objectivity in AD in and of itself. Objectivity is a matter of achieving a balance; the professionals make decisions along the way in the act, and objectivity should guide them through the process. At this juncture, it is also worth noting that even though the codes of good practice emphasize that the wording of AD needs be as objective as possible, recent research reveals that the visually impaired audience welcomes alternative AD versions that rely on creative descriptions of emotional and cultural information (Walczkak and Fryer 2017: 7). If the existing guidelines on AD production is subject to future revision, it is inevitable that Turkish audio describers' utilization of appraisal resources will change. That is, any shift from impartiality to creativity in AD would cause extensive variation in audio describers' use of the appraisal resources, which would in turn display a strong sign of intervention.

Another challenging feature involved in audio description is the scarcity of intervals into which audio describers struggle to fit the descriptions. Audio description is a constrained type of translation in that it must be designed within the limitations of the silent slots, the importance of what needs to be relayed and also the reception abilities of the receivers; the text needs to be clear and concise. A striking case in point is *My Big Fat Greek Wedding*, a romantic comedy laden with cultural features that bear ethnic traces which would exoticize the Greek 'other' in the eyes of a non-Greek audience. One of the striking scenes focuses on the opening of the wedding ceremony, where the Greek guests spit upon the Greek–American bride as a traditional performance of averting the evil eye and making use of an apotropaic charm. Some of the non-Greek guests give the Greek fellows the stink eye, a kind of gesture which serves to reconstruct the southeastern European immigrant's image from the hegemonic Western point of view. It is worth noting that facial expressions and bodily gestures laden with cultural overtones might lead to an information overload which is closely related to identity politics. In such a case, on one hand, the audio describer needs to be economical with his/her description to fill the available intervals. On the other hand, he/she needs to audio describe not only the Greek cultural rituals but also the non-Greek people's marginalizing gaze at the 'other'. In such cases, an appraisal analysis of the context is a helping hand to describe the 'other' in an objective way, given that the audio describer's meticulous choices from the appraisal category of affect (i.e. positive or negative assessment presented as an emotional response) and judgement (i.e. positive or negative assessment of behaviour in terms of conventionalized norms) may trigger evaluative stances and position the target audience within a particular cultural context.

The participants of the focus-group study further noted that the message of the visual track needs to be identified. The AD text must serve to relay this message. For example, in a documentary about the feminist movement of an institution, the women appearing in the visual will not be characters selected for the role. They will be real-life feminists. In a fictional product, the characters will be specifically selected for the role. In this example, the visuals chosen to relay a message are joined with the audial message. The AD needs to capture this same essence. To identify the message and to make the correct decisions as regards this is central. For example, in the movie *Forrest Gump*, many references are made to the American culture which many blind end users may not be familiar with. How far to integrate these into the text and how far to present an explicit text without violating the tenet of objectivity becomes a challenge for the audio describers.

The participants of our focus-group study also underlined that not leading the end users is another important concern. As an individual every audio describer will have certain thoughts and emotions as regards a text, but needs to keep these separate from the text to be produced. At this juncture, it is the message of the original that takes precedence, and the source text guides the audio describer to the acceptable AD text. Another feature that needs to be considered is the fact that the AD text needs to be fashioned in a manner that is not difficult to process by the end users – it should not be too loaded to impede cognition. Users access the audial track of the original simultaneously with the AD. Even though, save some exceptions, the AD text is inserted into the silent intervals of the original, it is imperative that the professionals understand that every such slot need not be filled in with an AD text.

Even though not inserting the emotion intended by the original product in the AD may be seen as a lack of quality in most circumstances, the audio describers underline that the insertion of personal emotions into the AD text (an unobjective perspective of emotion) is a sign of poor quality in all instances. It is important to describe what the camera leads one to describe. Thus, it is important that these are considered in the design of audio description and the text produced (the relaying of information and emotion from the visual) is designed in a manner that interacts with the music, the dialogues and sound effects. Thus, though the audio description is a replacement of the visual track, it needs to be designed in alignment with the audial track. The dominant channel of the audiovisual product, the visual channel, is going to be relegated to the role of a subtrack of the audial channel. From this perspective, the importance of sound is also to be investigated; Fryer (2010: 206–7) refers to sound (soundscape) and its effects under six headings, including the use of sound as a realistic affirming effect to sounds used to create effect.

End users, according to the feedback the audio describers received, have varying opinions about the role, nature and reflection of emotion in an AD text. For example, one group wishing to access a completely neutral text opt for an AD, such as 'she is looking out the window'. In this example the audio describers underline that there are multiple interpretations of the reason and the way a character looks out a window. A character may be looking out a window to vent their frustration, may be daydreaming and so forth; the director has provided the visual information to understand the why and the how. Thus, analysing this information and using this in the AD text will be an objective process, not a subjective one. In the same example, another group of end users want to be described how the audio describer has reached this decision; what specific action or mimic of the character allowed the professional to draw this conclusion (e.g. did she purse her lips, did she raise her eyebrows, did her eyes glaze over).

Last but not least, the audio describers stated that describing only mimics and gestures may lead to misunderstanding. For example, one may crinkle their forehead when squinting in the sun, or when one is unable to understand something. The gesture, mimic, is not the sole source from which the analysis is drawn; it is the whole of the visual and in such cases describing the mimic or gesture may lead to confusion; thus, not only the mimic and gesture but what it implies also needs to be stated in the text.

Conclusion

This chapter has set out to investigate Turkish audio describers' perception of quality in AD, considering a focus-group research designed to reveal how emotional and cultural information which is inscribed in the visual images of audiovisual products can be transferred to the visually impaired. The research is based on the data obtained from the focus-group discussions of SEBEDER, a Turkish non-governmental organization founded to produce accessible audiovisuals for the visually impaired. For the purposes of the study, the participants of the research group were asked to identify what should be described in AD and how it should be relayed to provide the visually impaired audience with a similar experience to that offered by audiovisual products.

Acknowledging that the effective use of discourse to verbalize the visual modality (e.g. setting, lighting, objects, costumes, movements) plays a central role in providing the target audience with full audiovisual stimuli, the Turkish audiodescribers have underlined that they place central focus on evaluation which is based on addressing not only the verbal content of the audiovisual product but also the visual messages which more indirectly or covertly trigger evaluative stances and position the audience to provide their own assessments. In this context, the study has sought to apply elements of the appraisal system to audio description in which the visual content delivered by the original product is mediated through the expressions of a third party, the audio describer.

As for the first question of the study (i.e. what should be audio described), the participants have suggested that the central component of quality is based on compensation for the absence of culture-specific visual information and the emotional content of the audiovisual product to confront the visually impaired audience with the same stimuli experienced by the sighted audience. The study has also found that the Turkish audio describers aim at objectivity and impartiality to achieve quality in their descriptions. On the other hand, it is significant to note that the visual mode delivers information in an impressionistic manner (Braun 2008). Hence, the study has observed that however much the audio describers may endeavour to be objective, the reality is much more complex and blurred. Inevitably, the audio describer's emotions, background, beliefs and cultural baggage can sometimes be felt intensely in the AD, and the cultural context of the original product also plays a significant role in what to select for the AD.

As for the second question (i.e. how the visual content should be described), the study has observed that the Turkish audio describers studiously resort to the central pillars of appraisal, which are attitude (i.e. affect, judgement, appreciation), graduation (i.e. up-scaling or down-scaling the expression of attitude) and engagement (i.e. opening up or closing down potential responses of the audience) to recreate the emotional impact and cultural resonance of the original product. The most striking finding obtained from the discussions is that to make up for the emotions inscribed in images, the audio describers frequently resort to graduation (e.g. extremely, somewhat more) as a strategy to convey the intensity of attitudinal evaluation (e.g. brave, confident). Another finding worth mentioning is that the audio describers effectively use dialogic contraction and dialogic expansion, which are the appraisal resources that fall into the category of engagement. The study has found that in case the audio describers have to describe a visual message in a way that involves some kind of individual subjectivity, they resort to dialogic expansion to signal that the proposition conveyed through the AD is but one among a number of others in the immediate communicative context (e.g. it is likely that . . ., it is as if she feels . . .). Furthermore, when the audio describers strive to restrict the potential audience responses in line with the development of the plot, they resort to dialogic contraction (e.g. she is certainly sad, it is nearly like . . .).

The focus-group discussions have further displayed that lexical realizations of evaluation that fall into the appraisal category of attitude (i.e. affect (e.g. happy, sad), judgement (e.g. robust, brave, resolute) and appreciation (e.g. splendid, harmonious, beautiful)) display little variation in the perceptions and hence respective word choices of different audio describers. However, the participants have stated that the attitudinal meaning which is scaled may vary according to how audio describers 'graduate' their perceptions (e.g. slightly upset or very upset). Along similar lines, the degree to which an audio-described utterance allows for alternative responses and interpretations on the part of the audience (i.e. dialogic expansion) or limits the scope of such interpretations (i.e. dialogic contraction) also varies from one audio describer to another.

In light of the findings based on the discussions of the focus-group research, the study concludes that since audio description is a constrained type of translation that must be designed within the limitations of the silent intervals, audio describers' decision regarding what needs to be conveyed and how it is to be transferred requires the effective and economical use of appraisal resources, 'the most prototypical to convey evaluative meaning' to use Munday's (2012: 103) words. Given that 'evaluation is central to communication and central to translation' (Munday 2012: 11), the appraisal system can help audio describers render visual images into verbal descriptions through a 'systematic, detailed and elaborate framework of evaluative language' (Bednarek 2006: 32).

References

Audio Description International (2005), *Guidelines of Audio Description*. Available online: http://www.adinternational.org/ADIguidelines.html (accessed 30 August 2018).

Bednarek, M. (2006), *Evaluation in Media Discourse: Analysis of a Newspaper Corpus*, New York: London.

Benecke, B. (2004), 'Audio description', *Meta*, 49 (1): 78–80.

Braun, S. (2008), 'Audio description research: state of the art and beyond', *Surrey Scholarship*. Available online: http://epubs.surrey.ac.uk/translation/13.

Díaz Cintas, J. (2007), 'Por una preparación de calidad en accesibilidad audiovisual', *Trans. Revista de Traductología*, 11 (11): 45–59.

Economou, D. (2009), 'Photos in the news: appraisal analysis of visual semiosis and verbal-visual intersemiosis', PhD diss., Sydney University, Sydney.

Engellilerin Haklarına İlişkin Sözleşme (2009), Available online: http://www.ttb.org.tr/mevzuat/index.php?option=com_content&view=article&id=686:engeller-haklarina-k-slee&Itemid=36 (accessed 30 July 2020).

Fryer, L. (2010), 'Audio description as audio drama – a practitioner's point of view', *Perspectives*, 18 (3): 205–13. doi: 10.1080/0907676X.2010.485681

Khosravani, Y. (2019), *Translation Quality Assessment (TQA) of Subtitles*, Berlin, Germany: Peter Lang Verlag.

Kruger, J.-L. (2010), 'Audio narration: re-narrativising film', *Perspectives*, 18 (3): 231–49. doi: 10.1080/0907676X.2010.485686

Martin, J. R., and White, P. R. R. (2005), *The Language of Evaluation: Appraisal in English*, London: Palgrave.

Martin, J. R. (2000), 'Beyond exchange: appraisal systems in English', in S. Hunston, and G. Thompson (eds), *Evaluation in Text*, 142–75, Oxford: Oxford University Press.

Munday, J. (2012), *Evaluation in Translation: Critical Points of Translator Decision-Making*, Abingdon: Routledge.

Munday, J. (2015), 'Engagement and graduation resources as markers of translator/interpreter positioning', *Target. International Journal of Translation Studies*, 27 (3): 406–21.

Okyayuz, A. Ş. (2017), 'Sesli Betimlemenin Çeviribilim Sınıflarında Tanıtımı İçin Bir Eğitim Bileşeni Önerisi', *Turkish Studies*, 22 (12): 559–86.

Orero, P. (2008), 'Three different receptions of the same film', *European Journal of English Studies*, 12 (2): 179–93.

Oteiza, T., and Pinuer, C. (2016), 'Appraisal framework and critical discourse studies: a joint approach to the study of historical memories from an intermodal perspective', *International Journal of Language Studies*, 10 (2): 5–32.

Pujol, J., and Orero, P. (2007), 'Audio description precursors: Ekphrasis, film narrators and radio journalists', *Translation Watch Quarterly*, 3 (2): 49–60.

Radyo ve Televizyonların Kuruluş ve Yayın Hizmetleri Hakkında Kanun. Kanun Numarası: 6112, Kabul Tarihi: 15/2/2011, Yayımlandığı R.Gazete : Tarih : 3/3/2011 Sayı : 27863 https://www.mevzuat.gov.tr/MevzuatMetin/1.5.6112.pdf.

Sanz-Moreno, R. (2017), 'The audio describer as a cultural mediator', *Revista Española de Lingüística Aplicada*, 30 (2): 538–58.

SEBEDER (2021), 'Hakkımızda'. Available online: http://sebeder.org/Hakkimizda-3.html (accessed 12 March 2020).

Snyder, J. (2007), 'Audio description: the visual made verbal', *International Journal of the Arts in Society: Annual Review*, 2 (2): 99–104.

Szymańska, B., and Zabrocka, M. (2015), 'Audio description as a verbal and audio technique of capturing films', in Ł. Bogucki, and M. Deckert (eds), *Accessing Audiovisual Translation*, 117–36, Frankfurt: Peter Lang Edition.

Tajvidi, G. R., and Arjani, H. S. (2017), 'Appraisal theory in translation studies: an introduction and review of studies of evaluation in translation', *Research in Applied Linguistics*, 8 (2): 3–30.

Udo, J. P., Acevedo, B., and Fels, D. I. (2010), 'Horation audio describes Shakespeare's Hamlet: blind and low-vision theatregoers evaluate an unconventional audio description strategy', *British Journal of Visual Impairment*, 28 (2): 139–56.

Walczak, A., and Fryer, L. (2017), 'Creative description: the impact of audio description style on presence in visually impaired audiences', *British Journal of Visual Impairment*, 35 (1): 6–17. https://doi.org/10.1177/0264619616661603

Yayın Hizmeti Usul ve Esasları Hakkında Yönetmelik (2011), *Resmî Gazete Sayısı: 28103 Mevzuat Bilgi Sistemi*. Available online: http://www.mevzuat.gov.tr/mevzuat?MevzuatNo=15508&MevzuatTur=7&MevzuatTertip=5 (accessed 2 February 2019).

Yuningsih, Y. (2018), 'An appraisal analysis: the interpersonal meanings in the discourse of a lyric', *Getsempena English Education Journal (GEEJ)*, 5 (2): 74–81.

Conclusion

Raffaele Zago

As unanimously acknowledged in previous literature, expressivity is a radically complex phenomenon having an interdisciplinary nature and reach. Even when one looks at it from the perspective of one specific disciplinary field, it maintains a multifaceted nature, which, in the case of linguistics, is due – among other things – to the multiplicity of manifestations the expressive function has at all linguistic levels, as pointed out in Chapter 1.

The complex phenomenology of the expressive function demands selectivity: any study on expressivity presents a necessarily selective picture, one in which some aspects or dimensions have to be given priority, whereas others inevitably remain in the background or have to be excluded. This volume is no exception. Relying on the diverse expertise of its contributors and capitalizing on the description-by-diversification logic of the edited-book format, the volume has taken over from previous literature the task of adding tesserae to the expressivity mosaic, in the firm conviction that the present, articulated in emotional cultures, is a moment in which, offline and particularly online, expressivity has reached its peak, even at the expense of referentiality. It is, therefore, a moment in which reflecting on expressivity – on its many facets and forms – is especially necessary.

Most of the chapters collected in the book, each from its own particular empirical and methodological point of view, have originated precisely from the necessity of contributing to the observation of contemporary emotional cultures or, in other words, of exploring the present-day habit of expressivity in discourse. In doing that, the chapters have pointed to local differences (e.g. in English versus Polish online conflictual exchanges in Chapter 6; in the way audio describers verbalize taboo elements across cultures in Chapter 10) as well as to general similarities and patterns of convergence. As regards the latter, one of the most pronounced is the affinity between the findings reported by Di Silvestro (Chapter 5) and those obtained by Coschignano and Zanchi (Chapter 4), which highlights a convergence of newspaper prose and political discourse, in English and Italian, towards expressively resonant formulations. The expressivity of such formulations is in some cases a deliberate, calculated ploy, as in the far-right, populist discourses investigated by Di Silvestro, while in other cases seems a by-product – for example, the often expressive REFUGEES ARE NUMBERS metaphor in press discourse can be viewed, at least in some of its instances, as a by-product of the institutionalized, professional imperative of factual news reporting, as pondered by Coschignano and Zanchi. The analyses carried out in the chapters, and the affinities emerging from their juxtaposition, provide fresh evidence of the prominence of the expressive function of language in today's cultures. At the same time, the differences spotted by the contributors in the marking of expressivity serve as a reminder of the constant need of adopting a cross-linguistic and cross-cultural stance in research on emotionology, given the non-monolithic, locally inflected nature of emotions.

A common thread in Chapters 2 to 5 is metaphor. As these chapters have illustrated – continuing the cognitive line of research within emotionology mentioned in Chapter 1 – not only is metaphor routinely used to linguistically refer to, and to conceptually systematize, emotions (cf. Chapter 2) and emotion processes (cf. Chapter 3), but is also an analytical tool that is required for an in-depth analysis of expressively resonant discourses. The latter issue is evident in Chapters 4 and 5: the expressivity-via-dehumanization trend discussed in these chapters often operates metaphorically, and hence cannot be described thoroughly without employing the cognitive analytical tool of conceptual metaphor. In this sense, on a methodological plane, the book has documented the dialectic between the cognitive angle and the register-/discourse-analytic angle in research on emotionology.

Given the methodological frameworks it adopts, the range of languages it covers and the diverse discourses it explores, the book is primarily intended for researchers from a broad array of subfields within linguistics, including – but not limited to – applied linguistics, cognitive linguistics (particularly conceptual metaphor theory and its developments), corpus linguistics, (critical) discourse analysis, register analysis, sociolinguistics and appraisal theory. Also, the book targets scholars working in the field of media/communication studies (e.g. scholars interested in telecinematic communication, in technology-mediated communication). More in general, due to the inherently interdisciplinary and markedly multidimensional nature of expressivity, the contributions gathered in the volume may be of relevance to scholars from research areas such as sociology, psychology and political studies.

Index

affect 212
affrontare la paura 'to face, to confront fear' 45
Aijmer, K. 199, 200
Alba-Juez, L. 4
al-fisam 'schizophrenia' 173
allontanare i pensieri 'to take away thoughts' 43
allontanare la paura 'to take away fear' 43
allontanare la tristezza 'to take away sadness' 43
#Americafirst 95
anger 120
animal metaphors 56
AntcConc 191
anxiety cluster emotions 119, 120
appraisal, defined 209
appraisal resources 213
  of force 221
appraisal semantics 213
appraisal system 209, 210, 230
  analytical framework 212–13
appraisal theory 212, 213
Arabic-English code-switching practice
  in Egyptian rap songs 167–9
  multilingualism and code-switching, Egypt 165–7
  multilingual speakers, L1 functions 164–5
  questionnaire to Egyptian rappers' fans 169–70
    English in rap songs' lyrics and emotions 171–5
    English on Egyptian rappers' facebook pages and emotions 175–8
    participants' general information 170–1
    use of English in expression of emotions 178–80
Arabic lyrics 173

Aranea 40
arrestare i pensieri 'to block thoughts' 44
Arrival scenario 72
attitude 212, 213
audio describers 210–11, 221
  evaluative judgements of 211
audio description (AD) 209, 210
  appraisal (*see* appraisal system)
  Audio Description Association (*see* SEBEDER)
  cultural accessibility 224–8
  emotional accessibility 219–24
  objectivity of 225–6
  pillars of AD culture
    appropriation of good practices 218
    families of visually impaired 216–17
    joint decisions of AD team 218
    products and services 217
    translation types for accessibility 216
  in Turkey 214
audiovisual products 209, 210
Augustyn, R. 141

Baker, P. 67
barcone 'immigrants' boat' 100
Bednarek, M. 193
békai 'heart and lungs' 19
benevolence 29
bernde 'heart' 20
Bilingualism and Emotion Questionnaire (BEQ) 169
'Black Monday Protest' 130
bloccare la rabbia 'to stop, block anger' 44
Bright, J. 153
British National Corpus (BNC) 40, 112
Bruschi, C. J. 120
#BuildtheWall 94, 95

'calm heart' 26, 30

cardiocentric model 18
carico 'load' 96
    occurrences and co-occurrences of 97
Cartesian dualism 18, 31
Cartesian-type paradigm 4
clandestino 'illegal immigrant' 100
Clinton, H. 99
#closedharbours 94, 95
code choice 166
Codziennik Feministyczny 154
cognitive inhibition 38
cognitive model of mental activity 40
cognitive processes 40
Cole, P. M. 120
collective group identity 111, 113
    driving forces 114–16
    individualism *vs.* collectivism 116–17
    leadership function 114
    linguistic exponents of identity 112–14
COLT 187, 189
combattere la paura 'to fight fear' 45
companionate leadership model 114
compositional constructions (syntagms) 142
Computer-Mediated Communication (CMC) 114
conceptual domains 58
conceptualization of events 57
conceptual metaphor theory 21, 31
    cognitive processes 40
    culturally specific metaphors 40
    emotion-specific metaphors 39
    inhibiting unwanted emotions and thoughts 41–2, 46
        chasing and running away 44–5
        pushing away and moving away 42–3
        stopping movement 43–4
    metaphorical images and differences 45–6
    metaphorical linguistic expressions 39
    regulating emotions and thoughts 38
concrete-to-abstract metaphorization 39
confinare la rabbia 'to intern, retain anger within limits' 42
conflict devirtualization 129–30

contemporary discourses
    emotional regime of 2
    expressive markers in 4
    expressivity in 3 (*see also* expressivity)
contemporary linguistics 39
content-related warrants 88
continuum 18
cooperation 115, 116, 121
    English cooperative scenarios 122–3
    Polish cooperative scenarios 121–2
corpus-assisted methodology 187
corpus-based cognitive linguistics 40
Corpus di Italiano Scritto (CORIS) 40
corpus linguistics 95
    approach 88
Covid-19 vaccination, Poland
    adjectival collocates 144–7
    classification of sources 143–4
    design limitations 154
    and language 141–2
    noun collocates 147–9
    in Polish news websites 143
    polling public about vaccine mandates 137–40
    pre-pandemic collocates, *przymusowy* and *obowiązkowy* 149–50
Crime scenario 69
critical discourse analysis (CDA) 55, 56
cultura/culturale 'culture/cultural' 103
cultural embodiment 17
cultural symbols 225

Damasio, A. 31
Data Miner 87
Dawson's Creek 191, 192, 194, 196, 199
    key domain cloud 195
    key word cloud 194
Death scenario 70
detachment effect 164
Diaz Cintas, J. 224
diglossia 166
dil 'heart' 19
discourse-analytic instruments 112
Discourse Historical Approach 88
discourse scenarios, refugees 60–1
    automatic and manually detected scenarios 64

automatic scenario detection, Iramuteq 64
   manually identified scenarios 62–3
discursive strategies 85
dude 198

echo chambers 2
Eckert, P. 189
Egyptian Colloquial Arabic (ECA) 166
Egyptians' linguistic system 166
emotional culture 3
   establishment of 4
emotional turn 4
emotionology 4
emotion regulation 38
emotions 117
   in bi-/multilingual contexts 163
   conceptual organisation of 118
   profiles in English and Polish 117–21
engagement 213
English lyrics 173
expressivity 1, 4
   in contemporary discourses 3
   in non-fictional TV programmes 1–2
   psychologization of experience 3
   traditional territory of 1

'The Facebook Revolution' 172
far-right politicians 85, 86
filter bubbles 2
Flamarique, L. 3
flussi della morte (flows of the death) 96
flussi migratori (migratory flows) 96
Foolen, A. 18
Forbes, G. 120
framing 57, 58
'fuck' 193

Gazeta 144, 154
Geeraerts, D. 18
Gevaert, C. 18
going to 196
gonna 196
González, A. M. 2, 3
graduation 213, 230

Hale, S. C. 5
Handbook of Natural Language Processing 140
Hart, P. S. 153

hati 'liver' 19
heart, metaphoric meanings of 17
Hofstede, G. 111, 114, 117
human thinking 31
Humoral doctrine 20
Hungarian National Corpus (HNC) 21

Ikegami, Y. 19
illegal refugees 59
immigrants and refugees, representation of
   hashtags 94–5
   occurrences and co-occurrences
      of criminal 99
      of immigrant 104
      of Islamic 103
      of load in Salvini's corpora 97
      of [number] 100
      of pay 102
      of terrorism 98
      of terrorist 98
      of victim 103
   qualitative analysis
      metaphors 88–90
      representational strategies 88, 91–3
      topoi 88, 90–1
   quantitative analysis
      source domains 96–7
      specification, genericization and suppression 105
      topos of burden 101–2
      topos of danger, threat and fear 97–100
      topos of invasion and aggregation strategy 100–1
      topos of victim and opposition strategy 102–4
immigration discourse 58
immigrato 'immigrant' 59, 105
impotencia 'impotence'/'powerlessness' 120
Inclusion scenario 71–2
indexicality 178
infotainment genre 2
initiative scenario 69
innocente 'innocent' 102
interactional conflict scenarios 125–9
interconnectivity values 113
Iramuteq 61
ISIS 91
Islam/Islamico 'Islam/Islamic' 103

Issue/administrative scenario 70, 72
Issue/deceit scenario 70, 75
Issue/economic scenario 70
Issue/public health scenario 70
Italiani 'Italians' 104
#Italiansfirst 95, 100

jai 'heart' 19
Jäkel, O. 40
January revolution 167
Jarynowski, A. 142
júrek 'heart' 19

kaal 'ear' 19
kambét 'ear' 19
'keyness' of words (key word clouds) 192
Key Word in Context (KWIC)
    analysis 41
KhosraviNik, M. 3
Kitayama, S. 118, 119
Klimiuk, K. 151
Kövecses, Z. 39
koyu 'ear' 19

Labov, W. 188
Lakoff, G. 75
language
    choice 188
    corpora 40
    head-heart dichotomy 18–20
    variation 188
League's xenophobic tendencies 99
left-leaning group 143, 154
Lehr, C. 120
lexical proximity 112
Likert-type scale 177–8
Lindquist, K. A. 5
linguistics 4
    exponents of identity 112–14
loose balloons communication 113

Macagno, F. 139–40
Mackenzie, J. L. 4
manually identified discourse
    scenarios 62–3
media discursive representation 55
'media war' 172
Mejova, Y. 141, 154
Mesthrie, R. 141

metaphor 58
metaphorical identification
    procedure 41
mettere a tacere i pensieri 'to make
    thoughts silent, quiet' 45–6
migrante (migrant) 57, 65
    arrival *vs.* broadcast news coverage of
        migrations 66
    semantic space of 65
Modern Standard Arabic (MSA) 166
Monco PL corpus 137, 142, 143
moyo 'heart' 20

Najwyższy Czas 144
Nasz Dziennik 144
National Corpus of Polish (NKJP) 40
negative cooperation 123–5
negotiation principle 166
Newsom, V. A. 129
nie dopuszczać myśli 'not to let thoughts
    in' 44
non farsi prendere dalla tristezza 'not
    to let yourself be taken by
    sadness' 45
Norasakkunkit, V. 119
number-game strategy 56, 61, 70
nyugodt szívvel 'with a calm heart' 28

obowiązek 'mandate' 137
obowiązkowy 'mandatory' 138, 150
Obsessive Compulsive Disorder
    (OCD) 122
odganiać myśli 'to chase thoughts away
    from' 44
odrzucić obawy 'to throw away fears' 43
odsuwać myśli 'to put thoughts away' 43
Ogarkova, A. 120
ondata (wave) 65, 74
online discourse activity 112
online interconnectivity value/index 112
open-coding fashion 60
'open heart' 27
#openhearts 94, 95
Orero, P. 216
orientation 60

Paisà and Aranea for Italian 40
Palacios Martínez, I. M. 188
Pawley, A. 142

Index 239

peer-to-peer communication 189
PELCRA corpus tools 112
personification 45
   mappings 46
Pflug, J. 118
ping-pong communication 113
Polish online comments 115
populism 85
populist politicians 85
populist strategies
   corpora building 87
   data collection 86–7
   immigrants and refugees (*see* immigrants and refugees, representation of)
pozbyć się myśli 'to get rid of thoughts' 43
pozbyć się strachu 'to get rid of fear' 43
Prawo i Sprawiedliwość 'Law and Justice' 151
Prażmo, E. M. 141
prefabricated phraseological units (phrasemes) 142
Pretty Little Liars 191
profugo 57, 67
przełamać strach 'to break through fear' 39
przepędzić myśli 'to chase thoughts off' 44
przezwyciężać strach 'to vanquish fear' 45
przymusowy 'coercive' 138, 143, 146, 147, 150, 153
psychological constructionist approach 5
Pujol, J. 216

Quantity scenario 72
Quintilian's *Institutio Oratoria* 140

racism 55
radicalization *in absentia* 2
razdrazhenie 'irritation' 120
Rebel 168
#red 99
refugee crisis 79 n.8
refugees. *See also migrante* (migrant); *profugo*; *richiedente asilo* (asylum seeker); *rifugiato*
   corpus and study design 59
   dehumanized representation of 58
   discursive means of dehumanization
     active and passive scenarios with orientation 70
     active and passive scenarios with proportion of reference type 71
     discourse scenarios, orientation and reference type 69–73
     metaphors and orientation 73–6
     reference type and orientation 67–9
   in Italian press, quantitative analysis 65–7
   manual annotation parameters
     conceptual metaphors 65
     discourse scenarios 60–3
     orientation 60
     referent types 60
   metaphorical conception of
     immigrants are parasites 75
     inanimate physical objects 74
     refugees are bees 75
     refugees are fluids 74
     refugees are means/weapons 75
     refugees are numbers 73–4
     refugees are preys 75
     refugees are rats 75
     refugees are trash 75
     refugees are wild animals 75
     refugees-enemies' victims 76
   theoretical assumptions 57–8
regulation of fear 45
religione/religioso 'religion/religious' 102
Representation scenario 72
Rheingold, H. 116, 121, 130
richiedente asilo 'asylum seeker' 57, 67, 68, 105
rifugiato 56, 66, 67
right-leaning group 143
rimpatrio 'repatriation' 105
Riverdale 191
Roberts, C. 199–200
Romania 99

salvare 'save' 102
Salvini, Matteo 87–106
Salvini Traditional Corpus 87

Salvini Tweet Corpus   95, 97, 99, 100
Sans-Moreno, R.   224
sbarco 'disembarkation'   105
scacciare via i pensieri 'to chase away thoughts'   39, 44
scappare 'escape/runaway'   102
scappa 'runs away'   61
scaricare 'discharged'   96
scaricare 'unload'   96
SEBEDER   209, 211, 212, 214. *See also* audio description (AD)
  focus-group study   215–16
    audio describers in   220, 223–6
    pillars of AD culture   216–19
    profiles of participants   215
self-determination theory   115, 118–20
semantic domains (key domain clouds)   192
semantic satiation   5
sentiment analysis   141
sfuggire dalla tristezza 'to escape from sadness'   45
Sinclair, J.   141
Sketch Engine   88
Skins   191, 192, 196–200, 202, 203
  key domain cloud   193
  key word cloud   193
  totally   196
snowball communication   113
Snyder, J.   216
social actors' representational strategies   88
  aggregation strategy   93
  corpora   91–2
  crime and terrorism   93
  opposition strategy   93
  suppression strategy   93
social media   86
sofferenza 'suffering'   104
soffrire 'suffer'   102
Somali refugees   92
sondaż 'poll'   137
sopprimere i pensieri 'to suppress thoughts'   42
Soriano, C.   120
source domain vocabulary search   41
spazzare i pensieri 'to sweep thoughts away'   43
speaking 'form the heart'   27

state of well-being   114, 115
stłumić myśli 'to suppress thoughts'   42
#Stopinvasion   94
stuprare 'to rape'   100
swearing   197
Syder, F. H.   142
szczepienie 'vaccination'   137
szczepionka 'vaccine'   137
Szív 'Heart'
  conceptualizations   22–4
  head as seat of intellect   21
  honesty and conscience   24–5
  intellectual domains
    advice   27
    decision   28
    memories   25
    opinion   27
    thinking process   26
    understanding process   26
  metaphoric meanings
    as emotions   29–30
    as moral conscience   30
    for whole person   30–1
  thought and thinking metaphors   21–2

Tagliamonte, S.   189, 190, 199, 200
Tamang, B. L.   120
Teen Corpus   191–3
teen talk, TV series
  COLT   189
  component of   189
  corpora of spoken English   189
  emotional words, media language   190
  language used by teenagers   188
  language variation   188
  Teen Corpus Part II   192–5
    markers of teen talk   195–9
  typical markers of   190
tenere lontano i pensieri 'to keep thoughts away'   44
theory of objectification   39
Thirteen Reasons Why   191
tłumić gniew 'to suppress anger'   42
topoi   88, 90–1
Toronto Instant Messaging Corpus   190
Toronto Internet Corpus   190
Toronto Teen Corpus   189

totally 196, 198, 199
   unbounded verbs 199
   wow 201
Traditional and Tweet Corpora 99
Traugott, E. 199
#travelban 94
Triandis, H. C. 111
Trump, Donald J. 85–106
Trump Traditional Corpus 96, 99
Trump Tweet Corpus 96
Twitter 86
'Twitter revolutions' 172

UAM Corpus Tool 87, 88
Uchida, Y. 118, 119
uciec od smutku 'to run away from sadness' 45
uciszyć myśli 'to make thoughts quiet' 46

van Dijk, T. A. 88
van Leeuwen, T. 88
verbal thinking 46
Victim Support (VS) 123
vincere la paura 'to win, to defeat fear' 45
visual messages, verbalization of 221
vittima 'victim' 102

Walton, D. 139–40
wanna 196, 202
want to 197, 203
war leadership model 114
water source domain 96
Wawrzuta, D. 151
Welcome scenario 71
well-being 118
white bear problem 38
Wmatrix 191, 192
Wodak, R. 88
wyciszyć myśli 'to hush up thoughts' 46
wyprzeć myśli 'to displace, to crowd out ideas' 42
wyrzucić myśli 'to throw away thoughts' 43

xin 'heart' 19

zagłuszyć myśli 'to make thoughts inaudible, to deafen, stifle them' 46
zahamować gniew 'to stop anger' 44
zahamować myśli 'to stop thoughts' 44
Zhang, C. 150
zürxen 'heart' 19

www.ingramcontent.com/pod-product-compliance
Lightning Source LLC
Chambersburg PA
CBHW062136300426
44115CB00012BA/1944